P9-BZV-670

Preparing Early Childhood Professionals

NAEYC's Standards for Programs

Marilou Hyson, Editor

NAEYC's Standards for Initial Licensure, Advanced, and Associate Degree Programs

Also includes standards material from:

Council for Exceptional Children/
Division for Early Childhood (CEC/DEC)

National Board for Professional
Teaching Standards (NBPTS)

National Association for the Education of Young Children
Washington, DC

Preparing Early Childhood Professionals: NAEYC's Standards for Programs was provided as an NAEYC Comprehensive Member benefit in November 2003. Besides having all the benefits of Regular NAEYC membership, Comprehensive Members receive free 6 new books a year, sent to them automatically as the books are released. For more about Comprehensive membership, see www.naeyc.org/membership/benefits.htm or call 800-424-2460 or 202-232-8777 for member services.

The section "NBPTS Early Childhood/Generalist Standards, 2d ed." (pp. 147–158) is reprinted with permission from the National Board for Professional Teaching Standards, *Early Childhood/Generalist Standards, 2d ed.*, www.nbpts.org. All rights reserved.

Front cover photos (left to right): Bill Geiger; © BmPorter/DonFranklin; © Jean-Claude LeJeune. Back cover photos (left to right): © Jean-Claude LeJeune; © Michael Siluk

Copyright © 2003 by the National Association for the Education of Young Children. All rights reserved. Second printing 2004. Third printing 2006. Printed in the United States of America.

National Association for the Education of Young Children
1313 L Street NW, Suite 500
Washington, DC 20005-4101
202-232-8777 or 800-424-2460
www.naeyc.org

Through its publications program the National Association for the Education of Young Children (NAEYC) provides a forum for discussion of major issues and ideas in the early childhood field, with the hope of provoking thought and promoting professional growth. The views expressed or implied are not necessarily those of the Association.

Library of Congress Control Number: 2003112293
ISBN 10: 1-928896-14-6
ISBN 13: 978-1-928896-14-2
NAEYC #256

Suggested citation (volume): Hyson, M., ed. 2003. *Preparing early childhood professionals: NAEYC's standards for programs.* Washington, DC: NAEYC.
Suggested citation (individual standard, using Advanced as the example):
NAEYC. 2003. NAEYC standards for early childhood professional preparation: Advanced programs. In *Preparing early childhood professionals: NAEYC's standards for programs,* ed. M. Hyson. Washington, DC: Author.

Contents

About this Volume   v

Introduction   1

National Association for the Education of Young Children (NAEYC)   15

      Initial Licensure Program Standards   17
      Advanced Program Standards   65
      Associate Degree Program Standards   93

Council for Exceptional Children/Division for Early Childhood (CEC/DEC)   125

      CEC Special Education Content Standards   129
      DEC Recommended Practices in Personnel Preparation   139

National Board for Professional Teaching Standards (NBPTS)   143

      Early Childhood/Generalist Standards   147

ASSOCICTE DEGREE STANDARDS—

About This Volume

NAEYC first collected its "guidelines" to early childhood professional preparation in book form in 1996. This 2003 edition of our standards "red book" contains completely revised and updated standards documents from NAEYC, the Council for Exceptional Children (CEC) and Division for Early Childhood (DEC), and the National Board for Professional Teaching Standards (NBPTS).

Moreover, it contains three entirely new elements intended to add both value and greater readability. An informed and informative Introduction by Marilou Hyson sets out NAEYC's vision for a seamless system of professional preparation. Commentaries from persons and programs make real the many ways standards can improve practice. In statements written for this volume, CEC, DEC, and NBPTS describe the context of their respective standards work.

Adding the enlivening vignettes, quotes, program examples, and other commentary wouldn't have been possible without the help of the volume's "field editors"—Alison Lutton (associate programs), Debra Thatcher (initial licensure programs), John Johnston (advanced programs), Joan Isenberg (NBPTS), and Vicki Stayton (CEC/DEC). Aided by staffers Parker Anderson and Mary Duru, the group contributed their time and energy to helping NAEYC identify elements of the standards worthy of commentary, solicit material, and sort through the submissions. Thanks go also to the many people who submitted material, both bylined and not, about their own and their program's experiences with standards, as well as to Margie Crutchfield (CEC), Laurie Dinnebeil (DEC), and Pat Wheeler (NBPTS).

Finally, NAEYC's standards are consensus documents that rely for their credibility on the Association's members and other constituents within and beyond the field of early childhood education. The various Standards Work Groups over the years have devoted countless hours to researching, discussing, drafting, circulating, revising, and refining the standards documents, drawing on their own knowledge and experience as well as expert feedback from the field. The continued support from NAEYC's Governing Board for our work with NCATE in teacher education has also been critical.

Introduction

by Marilou Hyson
NAEYC's associate executive director for professional development

> *What the best and wisest parent wants for his own child,*
> *that must the community want for all its children.*
>
> —John Dewey, *School and Society*

Looking into young children's eyes, we wish them limitless joy, limitless opportunities, and limitless achievements. In our complex world, it takes a system—not just a village—to develop every child's full potential. Many institutions, policies, resources, and family and community services must work together to create conditions that support early learning and development.

Teachers and other early childhood professionals have a unique place in this system. As researchers describe how early childhood education can best effect positive outcomes for children from birth through age 8 (Peisner-Feinberg et al. 2000; National Research Council 2001), one finding stands out: *Teachers are the key.* Curriculum, teaching strategies, assessment, comprehensive services, public policies—all are important. But it is through caring, committed, and competent early childhood professionals that young children and their families experience the excellent curriculum, the appropriate teaching strategies, the thoughtful assessment practices, the supportive services, and the effective public policies.

Early childhood professionals at work

Not all early childhood professionals start at the same place or arrive at the same destination in their careers. Early childhood professionals work in many settings and many professional roles—family child care provider, public school kindergarten or primary grade teacher, home visitor, program director, media specialist, trainer, education coordinator, and many others. In visiting just one early childhood program (let's say a full-day child care center for infants through 4-year-olds), you might meet . . .

• A lead teacher with a bachelor's degree in early childhood education from a program accredited by the National Council for Accreditation of Teacher Education (NCATE) and the National Association for the Education of Young Children (NAEYC). She holds initial licensure in birth–kindergarten education and has been employed by the program for four years. This teacher is currently working toward certification

National Recognition and Accreditation— NAEYC and NCATE

The National Council for Accreditation of Teacher Education (NCATE) is an organization that accredits colleges, schools, or departments of education in higher education programs at the baccalaureate and advanced degree levels in the United States. Today 550 institutions are NCATE accredited, and another 100 are getting ready for accreditation. The number of institutional candidates for accreditation has almost tripled in the past five years.

As of fall 2003, NCATE is a coalition of 35 specialty professional associations (SPAs), of which 19—including NAEYC—have NCATE-approved standards. In 2001 and 2002, respectively, NCATE reviewed and approved NAEYC's standards for initial licensure and advanced (master's and doctoral) preparation in early childhood education. NCATE's standards for all professional education "units" (colleges, schools, departments of education) require that "candidates" (future education professionals) demonstrate competence in their identified content areas. NCATE uses its SPAs to provide feedback and quality control in each of those areas.

How does NAEYC play a part? Higher education institutions that aim for NCATE accreditation voluntarily undergo a rigorous review process. One part of the process is for the institution to prepare reports on each of its specialty programs and submit the "Program Reports" to NCATE for review by the pertinent specialty professional associations. As one of these associations, NAEYC reviews the Program Reports from institutions that have early childhood education programs. Using a report template that is completed and submitted online, each Program Report includes a brief description of the program's context and conceptual framework, information about 6–8 key assessments intended to document students' competence in relation to the NAEYC standards, data tables summarizing evidence from each assessment, and the program's interpretation and use of the evidence for program improvement. (A detailed outline of what NAEYC requires in an early childhood Program Report may be found at www.naeyc.org/profdev.)

Members of NAEYC's Professional Education Panel (selected through an application process and appointed by NAEYC's Governing Board) receive the reports electronically. Team members review the reports and assess the programs' compliance with NAEYC standards. After reaching consensus on the basis of the evidence, each team sends its findings to NCATE, which forwards the findings to each institution. Following this phase and the submission of an overall institutional report to NCATE, a team from the NCATE Board of Examiners visits the institution and submits its own findings to NCATE's Unit Accreditation Board. At each phase of the process, programs and institutions have opportunities to rejoin (write responses to) the findings of NAEYC, other specialty professional associations, and NCATE.

Quality assurance

Program standards that define the core components for teachers are critical to quality assurance in the teaching profession. The NAEYC standards support the preparation of early childhood teachers who can provide the educational base for learning throughout a child's schooling.

In addition, program standards provide the benchmarks for teaching that are necessary for building quality systems of teacher education in our colleges and universities.

—*Donna M. Gollnick,* NCATE

from the National Board for Professional Teaching Standards (NBPTS), with an emphasis on bilingual and multicultural programs and family involvement.

• A teacher with an associate degree in early childhood education who is taking courses toward a bachelor's degree to receive initial licensure from her state. She would like eventually to mentor and supervise new teachers.

• An assistant teacher with a CDA (Child Development Associate credential). Having grown up in the community, she started working in the program as a teacher aide. She is now taking courses for an associate degree at a local community college.

• A director who combines an early childhood education background with a recent master's degree in program administration and leadership. Her master's project included an assessment of child care staffs' professional development needs.

• A new teacher aide who is still unsure of her long-term goals. She is talking with other staff, searching the Internet, and evaluating her own interests, strengths, and needs as she considers applying for a scholarship that would allow her to take an early childhood education course at a local college.

• A faculty member from the local university who has a doctorate in child development and early education. She supervises student teachers placed in several of the program's classrooms. Using information from a summer institute she attended, she teams up with several experienced teachers to teach a weekly on-site course on children's challenging behaviors for staff from this and other programs.

• An early childhood special educator who serves this and several other local programs. He meets with staff, observes, coordinates assessments of children about whom staff have concerns, and works with staff and families to develop IEPs (Individualized Education Programs) for children with disabilities. He is just beginning work toward a master's degree focusing on infants and toddlers with developmental disabilities.

These early childhood professionals differ in their responsibilities, but all have set themselves on a continuous path of formal education, specialized training, and ongoing professional development.

New research finds strong relationships between teachers' educational qualifications and young children's development and learning. Of course there are individual exceptions; but in general, if early childhood practitioners have higher levels of formal education and specialized training, they are much more likely in their work with young children and families to use the evidence-based practices and possess the ongoing professional commitment we know are necessary to make a positive difference in children's lives (National Research Council 2001; Barnett 2003).

Professionals make connections

The value added by high-quality education and training goes far beyond specific skills or techniques. As early childhood professionals move forward in their own learning, they become better able to make connections—

• between research and daily practice

• between challenging content standards and children's positive outcomes

• between a curriculum and an individual child

• between homes and schools

• between prior knowledge/experience and new information

• between national and state policies and their effects on children's lives

• between the program and diverse cultures and communities

• between program staff and other professionals who can serve as sources of expertise and resources.

Professional preparation and ongoing professional development are really about *making meaning,* connecting diverse areas of knowledge and experience in ways that make sense. These connections—built on a sound base of general education and professional and pedagogical knowledge and skills—give greater power and coherence to professionals' work, multiplying the benefits for children and their families.

Standards for high-quality professional preparation

The kind of professional development that provides that sound base is not accomplished cheaply or quickly. Brief training in a narrow set of technical skills does little to create the connections teachers need in order to see their work in a wider context and to develop the deep commitment that keeps talented educators in the profession. Nor is the key just getting a degree. Degrees matter, but a degree alone—whether associate, baccalaureate, master's, or doctoral—is not a guarantee of professional competence. Courses in specified subjects, credit hours, and grade point averages mean little in the absence of an overall concept of the desired outcomes of early childhood professional preparation.

What does matter is what early childhood professionals know, what they are able to do, and the dispositions or "habits of mind" they possess to nurture and promote children's development and learning as a result of their preparation and continuing development. How can we encourage and recognize those competencies?

An answer is in the five sets of standards found in this book: NAEYC's standards for (1) associate degree, (2) initial licensure, and (3) advanced master's and doctoral programs; (4) the early childhood special education standards of the Council for Exceptional Children and its Division for Early Childhood (CEC/DEC); and (5) the Early Childhood/Generalist standards of the National Board for Professional Teaching Standards.

The very word *standards* makes some people nervous, and with good reason. If poorly developed and inappropriately implemented, standards can be rigid and incompatible with innovative practices. But at their best, standards—whether for children, for programs, or for practitioners—reflect a shared vision based on evidence and professional consensus.

The standards movement has been described as a very recent development, with early childhood education trailing behind other parts of the education field. However, the 75-year history of NAEYC is that of a major professional association building evidence- and values-based consensus around expectations for high-quality programs. The 1929 publication *Minimum Essentials for Nursery School Education* (National Association for Nursery Education 1929) began that history. A series of later publications and position statements outline early childhood program accreditation criteria (NAEYC 1998) and provide guidelines for developmentally appropriate practice (Bredekamp & Copple 1997) and expectations for early childhood curriculum and assessment (NAEYC & NAECS/SDE 2003). This volume presents new standards for professional preparation.

Many standards, unifying themes

The professional preparation standards of NAEYC and related organizations represent a comprehensive vision for what early childhood professionals should know and be able to do at various points along the continuing path of professional development—including associate degree, baccalaureate or initial master's degree, and advanced master's and doctoral degrees—as well as in the specialized preparation for becoming an early childhood special educator or an accomplished teacher certified by NBPTS. As the standards in this book emphasize, each of these has distinctive features, missions, and roles, and so the specific learning opportunities needed and the ways in which professional growth should be assessed vary considerably in each.

At the same time, these standards, which address diverse programs, levels of preparation, and professional roles, are unified by common themes:

• **Shared professional values.** Woven through each set of standards are a strong commitment to diversity and inclusion; responsibility for ethical behavior on behalf of children; respect for family, community, and cultural contexts; respect for evidence as a guide to professional decisions; and reliance on guiding principles of child development and learning.

• **A shared emphasis on the broad range of ages and settings included in early childhood professional preparation.** NAEYC defines early childhood as the years from birth through age 8. Linked by common developmental issues and learning needs, children in this age group require teachers and other professionals with specialized preparation and professional development. All standards for early childhood professional preparation give attention to kindergarten/primary-age children as well as younger children; this is especially important as

Meaningful, participatory program reviews

With the change in focus from input to outcomes, program reviews now serve a more meaningful function and require ongoing participation of all faculty. How can such a shift in responsibility occur? I think it begins with the consideration of faculty dispositions. What faculty attitudes and actions lead to program quality and improvement? What are faculty's responsibilities to the overall program as opposed to their own courses and scholarship? What relationships with university colleagues, school staff, community members, candidates, and students need to be fostered to improve candidate competence and children's lives? I welcome the challenge to create opportunities for faculty to dialogue about such issues and to develop trust in the program review as a meaningful process that enhances program integrity.

—*Debra Thatcher*,
Northern Michigan University

NAEYC's Standards

*What should tomorrow's teachers know
and be able to do?*

1. Promoting child development and learning

Well-prepared early childhood professionals

• understand what young children are like;

• understand what influences their development; and

• use this understanding to create great environments where all children can thrive.

2. Building family and community relationships

Well-prepared early childhood professionals

• understand and value children's families and communities;

• create respectful, reciprocal relationships; and

• involve all families in their children's development and learning.

3. Observing, documenting, and assessing

Well-prepared early childhood professionals

• understand the purposes of assessment;

• use effective assessment strategies; and

• use assessment responsibly, to positively influence children's development and learning.

4. Teaching and learning

Well-prepared early childhood professionals

• build close relationships with children and families;

• use developmentally effective teaching and learning strategies;

• have sound knowledge of academic disciplines or content areas; and

• combine all of these to give children experiences that promote development and learning.

5. Becoming a professional

Well-prepared early childhood professionals

• identify themselves with the early childhood profession;

• are guided by ethical and other professional standards;

• are continuous, collaborative learners;

• think reflectively and critically; and

• advocate for children, families, and the profession.

---

trends toward narrower curriculum and assessment in K–3 programs become accelerated. NAEYC and CEC/DEC address infant/toddler programs in their standards; although the standards of NBPTS apply only to teachers of children ages 3–8, they too consider the wider scope of early development and learning.

Similarly, descriptions of standards for early childhood professional preparation are based on the knowledge that practitioners work in diverse settings, including group programs for children ranging from infants and toddlers through the primary grades, family child care, specialized early intervention programs, and programs focused on children with disabilities; government and private agencies; higher education institutions; and organizations that advocate on behalf of young children and their families. The roles that professionals assume in these and other settings are equally varied, including classroom teacher, faculty member, trainer, home visitor, administrator, and resource specialist.

• **A shared set of desired outcomes for early childhood professional preparation at every level.** The three NAEYC standards documents (Associate, Initial Licensure, and Advanced) share a core of five standards:

> 1. Promoting Child Development and Learning
>
> 2. Building Family and Community Relationships
>
> 3. Observing, Documenting, and Assessing to Support Young Children and Families
>
> 4. Teaching and Learning
>
> 5. Becoming a Professional

These core standards outline a set of common expectations for professional knowledge, skills, and dispositions that are critical at every level and in every setting (see "NAEYC's Standards—What Should Tomorrow's Teachers Know and Be Able to Do?").

• **A multidisciplinary emphasis.** All five standards documents reflect a common recognition that early childhood education, more than other areas of education, is truly a multidisciplinary field. Each organization's standards, at each level, echo expectations that early professional preparation must draw from and connect multiple disciplines.

• **Emphasis on outcomes.** In every case early childhood professional preparation standards focus on outcomes or results: What should future professionals in associate degree programs, initial licensure programs, advanced programs, and early childhood special education programs know and be able to do for young children and families as a result of their preparation? What should experienced and accomplished National Board Certified Teachers know and be able to do? The details of how higher education programs organize their courses and field experiences are less important than what students in those programs can accomplish as a result.

• **Emphasis on assessment of outcomes.** Combined with this emphasis on outcomes is an emphasis on continuous assessment of professional growth in relation to these outcomes. Each set of standards is accompanied by expectations that higher education programs (or, in the case of National Board Certification, the Board) should use an organized, fair, and effective assessment system related to the standards. Evidence from such a system can be used not only for purposes of accreditation or National Board Certification but also to help professionals improve and to improve the programs in which they are enrolled.

• **Balanced attention to knowledge, skills, and dispositions.** Each of these standards documents recognizes that early childhood professionals need knowledge (concepts and background grounded in both the liberal arts and professional specialization), combined with practical skills and dispositions. For example, abstract or conceptual knowledge about mathematics alone does not give a teacher of 4-year-olds everything she needs to be effective. Yet technical skills alone—how to present a math-based activity

Opportunities to develop dispositions

Disposition outcomes should be considered in the same intentional and systematic fashion as knowledge and skill outcomes when designing and implementing both initial and advanced early childhood professional preparation programs. What opportunities will the program provide to allow candidates to acquire the knowledge and skills that are prerequisite to demonstrating dispositions? For example, the ability to think reflectively necessarily precedes the disposition to reflect on one's teaching. How will the program provide opportunities for candidates to see dispositions modeled by program faculty, other candidates, and early childhood professionals in the field? How will the program provide multiple planned opportunities for candidates to practice and demonstrate desired dispositions? When will opportunities to observe, practice, and demonstrate dispositions be provided throughout the program?

—John Johnston, University of Memphis

so that it will interest 4-year-olds—yield a shallow curriculum and poor results if the teacher lacks a sound mathematics knowledge base. Finally, if the teacher does not have professional dispositions (such as the belief that all children can learn), her well-conceptualized, well-taught math curriculum may benefit only a few children.

Linking the standards with a broader system of early childhood professional development

The standards in this book present a relatively comprehensive description of high-quality professional preparation and credentialing in colleges and universities and of certification of accomplished teachers who already have a college education and professional experience. However, the system of early childhood professional development is broader than that.

To be most effective, these standards need to be reflected in the content of community-based training, whether or not that training carries college credit. Such training is required in most states for staff in licensed child care programs. Ongoing training is also required for Head Start and Early Head Start staff, as well as for those working in public school kindergarten, prekindergarten, and the primary grades. Federal child care initiatives oblige states to create professional development plans, providing new opportunities for these standards to have a broader impact.

Another key component of the field's professional development system is the Child Development Associate credential. The CDA began as a noncredit, job-embedded credential but has increasingly been linked to college credit. With college credit, staff in Head Start and child care programs who are awarded the CDA may be better positioned to make the transition to associate and baccalaureate institutions. The CDA Competency Standards include six goals that closely align with the NAEYC standards for early childhood professional preparation. As these parts of the system become more connected, it will be important to emphasize the links between the CDA goals and the expected outcomes in the NAEYC standards for both associate degree and baccalaureate programs.

Additionally, all early childhood practitioners, whether or not they have degrees and certification, and whether or not their jobs require ongoing training, should experience continuing, in-depth, job-embedded professional development. This kind of professional development helps all practitioners—teacher aides, college faculty, directors, home visitors, and so on—to update their knowledge base, refine the skills that are most important in promoting children's development and learning, and reflect on their own growth. NAEYC's core standards and their key elements can easily serve as a guide for those planning ongoing staff development.

Changing children's lives through the standards— What public policies are needed?

These standards represent the early childhood field's best thinking about what young children need from their teachers and other professionals if they are to develop and learn to their full potential. Yet without public policies to support the implementation of these standards, the standards themselves will do little to affect outcomes for children and their families. What is needed?

• **Consistent teacher licensure in early childhood education.** In 1991 NAEYC and the Association of Teacher Educators (ATE) issued a position statement urging every state to have a uniform and distinctive birth–age 8 license for early childhood professionals (ATE & NAEYC 1991). However, few states have such a license (Ratcliff, Cruz, & McCarthy 1999), despite growing evidence of the value of specialized preparation for those working with young children (National Research Council 2001; Barnett 2003). As teacher shortages increase, they may accelerate the trend away from early childhood licensure in favor of generic credentials that lack relevant knowledge bases and field experiences.

• **Policies to support articulation.** Many people encounter barriers when they try to transfer early childhood education–related credits from community colleges to four-year institutions, or when they attempt to receive college credit for extensive training that has taken place outside the higher education system. The close alignment across NAEYC's associate degree, initial licensure, and advanced program standards (which also connect with the expectations of NBPTS), and the partnerships between NAEYC and CEC/DEC should make it easier to develop public policies to promote articulation, as a number of states have begun to do.

• **Policies to increase the cultural and linguistic diversity of early childhood professionals.** National surveys reinforce the obvious: the current workforce—predominantly white and non-Hispanic—does not reflect the racial, ethnic, and linguistic characteristics of today's young children and families (Early & Winton 2001). Many ethnically and linguistically diverse practitioners have begun their careers in community programs. These committed adults represent a pool of talented future leaders who can, with support, move into, through, and beyond the higher education system. Again, the linkages across levels and settings that are reflected in these standards should make it easier to create a connected system of preparation, removing rather than creating barriers.

• **Policies to increase compensation and improve working conditions.** Salaries, benefits, and working conditions create obstacles to the recruitment and retention of capable early childhood professionals who have the education and training to implement high-quality, evidence-based practices. The United States needs to emulate other countries that have created well-financed systems of early care and education (see OECD 2001). Then those who successfully complete higher education programs that follow the high standards of NAEYC and CEC/DEC, or who become National Board Certified Teachers, may be compensated fairly and will be more likely to remain in the profession.

Standards and portfolio documentation

At our institution we have used a portfolio development system for several years with initial candidates. Students begin their portfolio in their first course, as freshmen, and it grows and develops with them throughout the program. As a result of this process, our beginning teachers can articulate, "This is what I know and believe about children," and with the portfolio documentation they can say, "This is what I did and why I did it." Aligned first with NAEYC's 1994 Guidelines and now with the new standards, the portfolios have been a significant tool for our program's development.
—*Edyth Wheeler*, Towson University

Standards and the faculty

Faculty are simply overwhelmed by the resources they must expend to align program elements with the multitude of state and national expectations, and they often become disillusioned with the meaningfulness of standards. Rather than resulting in program improvement, programs can become fragmented and faculty may actively resist what they perceive as attempts at standardization.

I imagine there was a collective groan around the country at the announcement of a revision of NAEYC's standards! But I am witnessing a gradual reversal of any negativism as faculty become aware that NAEYC has reconceptualized the notion of standards. Rather than bogging faculty down in minutiae, NAEYC's five "core" standards provide a mechanism for rich faculty discussions about program quality and outcomes. Faculty are given license to spend their energy creating unique experiences suited to their particular context. The revised standards provide the potential to create quality programs with unity and coherence, not fragmentation; voice and identity, not standardization.

—*Debra Thatcher*,
Northern Michigan University

• **Policies to support and reward early childhood educators for achieving higher levels of education and specialized training.** People often begin working in early childhood education without specialized training and without a high level of formal education. Many have the ability and commitment to move forward in higher education and to gain licensure or other credentials. However, policies and resources to support these future leaders are often lacking. Promising examples of such policies are the efforts in 23 states to create T.E.A.C.H. Early Childhood Projects and other scholarships that support staff enrolled in higher education, as well as school districts' and others' financial support for early childhood professionals seeking National Board Certification (Gundling & Hyson 2002).

• **Policies to promote thoughtful connections and alignment across standards and settings.** The national standards represented in this book gain their effectiveness from being connected with, for example, state standards for early childhood professional preparation; core competencies for states' career development systems in early care and education; relevant standards of other professional associations (e.g., NCATE's standards for professional education units, the International Reading Association's standards for reading specialists); states' early learning standards that describe what young children should know and be able to do; and standards for high-quality programs for young children, as represented by NAEYC's early childhood program standards and accreditation criteria (NAEYC 1998, 2003).

• **Policies to create a research agenda focused on early childhood professional preparation.** We know a lot about the positive effects well-prepared early childhood professionals can have on children's lives, and about the knowledge, skills, and dispositions needed to produce those effects. However, we know much less about how programs should be organized and what combinations of courses, field experiences, and faculty expertise best prepare those professionals (Bredekamp 1996; National Institute on Early Childhood Development and Education 2000).

Research is needed to address a number of urgent questions. What specific sequences, requirements, critical experiences, support services, or other features of early childhood professional preparation programs ultimately make a difference for children? What kinds of pedagogy, such as strong focus on learning communities, continuous assessment of students' progress, problem-based or case study–based learning, might be most effective under which conditions? How might programs most effectively prepare adults with different educational experiences, cultures, and home languages? Are some standards-related competencies easier to influence than others? If so, which ones, and under what conditions? Investments in well-designed research can yield answers.

How can the standards be used to promote better outcomes for children?

The standards and other resources in this book can be used in a variety of ways that ultimately will lead to better outcomes for children. For example,

• At NCATE-affiliated institutions of higher education, the NAEYC early childhood program standards are used as guides for programs that seek to demonstrate compliance with the standards. (At present, only programs at the baccalaureate and graduate levels are eligible to participate in accreditation. In collaboration with others, NAEYC is moving toward implementing a system to accredit associate degree programs.)

• The NAEYC standards, along with other standards described in this book, may serve as guides for higher education programs that are not currently part of a voluntary accreditation system such as NCATE's. Faculty and students can discuss and review their programs in light of the relevant standards, as well as in light of the programs' unique missions and contexts. With or without formal accreditation, self-study is beneficial.

• As noted earlier, the standards may provide a framework for those outside the higher education system to use in developing training plans, designing state-level professional development systems, or aligning state or other competencies with national standards.

• Finally, the standards may serve as guides to advocates or to state or federal policy makers, outlining the key dimensions of professional preparation and ongoing professional development, as identified through a consensus-building process guided by research and professional values. Those dimensions, in turn, would be the focus of efforts to fund or create public policies to support the use of these standards.

References

ATE (Association of Teacher Educators) & NAEYC. 1991. Early childhood teacher certification guidelines: A position statement. *Young Children* 47 (1): 16–21.

Barnett, W.S. 2003. Better teachers, better preschools: Student achievement linked to teacher qualifications. *NIEER Policy Briefs. 2.* Online: http://nieer.org/resources/policybriefs/2.pdf

Bredekamp, S. 1996. Early childhood education. In *Handbook of research on teacher education,* 2d ed., eds. J. Sikula, T. Buttery, & E. Guyton, 323–47. New York: Simon & Shuster Macmillan.

Bredekamp, S., & C. Copple. 1997. *Developmentally appropriate practice in early childhood programs.* Rev. ed. Washington, DC: NAEYC.

Early, D.M., & P.J. Winton. 2001. Preparing the workforce: Early childhood teacher preparation at two- and four-year institutions of higher education. *Early Childhood Research Quarterly* 16: 285–306.

Gundling, R., & M. Hyson. 2002. Professional Development. National Board Certification: The next professional step? *Young Children* 57 (5): 60–61.

NAEYC. 1998. *Accreditation criteria and procedures of the National Association for the Education of Young Children.* 1998 ed. Washington, DC: Author.

NAEYC. 2003. Draft NAEYC early childhood program standards. Online: www.naeyc.org/accreditation/nextera.asp

NAEYC & NAECS/SDE (National Association of Early Childhood Specialists in State Departments of Education). 2003. Early childhood curriculum, assessment,

(continued on p. 14)

Teaching the NAEYC standards

In a series of articles for *Early Childhood Today* (fall 2002–spring 2003), I laid out plans for three workshops for early childhood professionals to present. I drew directly from the NAEYC Initial Licensure Standards for the workshop topics:
• Using Developmentally Effective Approaches
• Connecting with Children and Families
• Building Family and Community Relationships
Handouts are excerpted from the NAEYC standards. The workshops revolve around the handouts.

Early childhood program administrators or teacher educators at a university associated with an early childhood center, for example, can use these workshop outlines to set up training sessions about the standards for teachers in the center. When NAEYC standards are integrated into teacher training, they come to life for teachers.

—*Carol Seefeldt,*
University of Maryland

Blended program benefits

As an undergraduate with a bachelor's degree in elementary education, finding a job in my field was very difficult, but I was immediately pegged for an administrative position in early childhood education.

In a few days I realized I was in over my head. I was attempting to coordinate services for preschool-age children, with and without disabilities, by supervising teachers who had little or no formal training in the same field. I began reading everything I could find about early childhood education in the evenings. I enrolled in an interdisciplinary early childhood education program. Working full-time and . . .

Is Yours a Blended Program? Or Are You Developing One?

To be approved by NAEYC, programs that prepare early childhood professionals must provide their candidates with opportunities to develop the knowledge, skills, and dispositions necessary to meet the needs of all children, including children with disabilities and developmental delays.

However, some programs go beyond that level of attention to provide a "unified" or "blended" program with depth and focus both in general early childhood education *and* in early childhood special education. A blended early childhood professional preparation program combines all the elements called for in NAEYC's early childhood standards and those in CEC's early childhood special education standards in a curriculum that is planned, implemented, and evaluated by an interdisciplinary group of faculty and other individuals.

Blended programs may request review under a joint process involving both NAEYC- and CEC-trained reviewers that recognizes their distinctive nature.

Considering the following questions may help you decide whether the early childhood program at your institution—or a program you are designing—is a blended program.

Questions to consider:

• Does your state have a Blended or Unified Early Childhood license? It is not essential for your state to offer such a license in order for your institution to have a blended program. However, in many cases blended programs have been developed in response to state licensure. In some states students who graduate from a state-approved blended program automatically receive dual licensure in Early Childhood Education and Early Childhood Special Education.

• Do your general early childhood education faculty and your early childhood special education faculty *jointly* plan and implement the program?

Looking specifically at the NAEYC Initial Licensure standards (pp. 17–63) and at CEC's Content Standards and its Common Core (CC) and Early Childhood (EC) knowledge and skill base standards (pp. 129–138)—

• Do all candidates in your program receive *in-depth preparation* that leads to competence in both early childhood education and early childhood special education? Do your program's courses provide candidates with the knowledge and skills they need to support children who are typically developing *and* those with special needs? Do your program's internships offer in-depth experiences with children with *and* without disabilities?

• Are your program's candidates *assessed* against both early childhood education and early childhood special education standards, including the NAEYC standards, the CEC Common Core, and the CEC/DEC specialization standards?

In summary—

• Do all of your early childhood candidates complete a *common* program that prepares them for both general early childhood education and early childhood special education?

Next steps

If your program is a blended program—

• Submit your **blended special education/early childhood education** Program Report to NCATE for review by NAEYC in collaboration with CEC. This report should follow the NAEYC Initial Licensure Standards and Program Report Outline. It should also include responses to the CEC Content Standards. (The easiest way to respond to the CEC standards is to use Form A in the Guidelines for the Preparation of the Special Education Program Report, available on the CEC Website. Go to www.cec.sped.org, click on Search, then search for "Guidelines for Preparation of the Special Education Program Report.")

If your program is *not* a blended program, but you do offer both early childhood education and early childhood special education preparation, you should—

• Submit your **early childhood education** Program Report to NCATE for review by NAEYC.

• Submit your **early childhood special education** Program Report to NCATE for review by CEC.

Resources

Blanton, L.P., C.C. Griffin, J.A. Winn, & M.C. Pugach, eds. 1997. *Teacher education in transition: Collaborative programs to prepare general and special educators.* Denver: Love.

Heston, M.L., D. Raschke, C. Kliewer, L.M. Fitzgerald, & R. Edmiaston. 1998. Transforming teacher preparation in early childhood education: Moving to inclusion. *Teacher Education and Special Education* 21: 278–92.

Isenberg, J.P. 2000. The state of the art in early childhood professional preparation. In *New teachers for a new century: The future of early childhood professional preparation,* ed. National Institute on Early Childhood Development and Education, U.S. Department of Education, 17–58. Jessup, MD: U.S. Department of Education, ED Publishing.

Kemple, K.M., L.C. Hartle, V.I. Correa, & L. Fox. 1994. Preparing teachers for inclusive education: The development of a unified teacher education program in early childhood and early childhood special education. *Teacher Education and Special Education* 17: 38–51.

Kilgo, J., & M.B. Bruder. 1997. Creating new visions in institutions of higher education: Inter-disciplinary approaches to personnel preparation in early intervention. In *Reforming personnel preparation in early intervention: Issues, models, and practical strategies,* eds. P.J. Winton, J. McCollum, & C. Catlett, 81–102. Baltimore, MD: Brookes.

Lesar, S., S.M. Benner, J. Habel, & L. Coleman. 1997. Preparing general education teachers for inclusive settings: A constructivist teacher education program. *Teacher Education and Special Education* 20: 204–20.

Miller, P., L. Fader, & L. Vincent. 2000. Preparing early childhood educators to work with children who have exceptional needs. In *New teachers for a new century: The future of early childhood professional preparation,* ed. National Institute on Early Childhood Development and Education, U.S. Department of Education, 91–112. Jessup, MD: U.S. Department of Education, ED Publishing.

Miller, P.S., & V.D. Stayton. 1998. Blended interdisciplinary teacher preparation in early education and intervention: A national study. *Topics in Early Childhood Special Education* 18 (1): 49.

Sandall, S., M. McLean, & B. Smith. 2000. *DEC recommended practices in early intervention/early childhood special education.* Longmont, CO: Sopris West Educational Services.

Stayton, V.D., & J.A. McCollum. 2002. Unifying general and special education: What does the research tell us? *Teacher Education and Special Education* 25: 211–18.

Stayton, V.D., & P.S. Miller. 1993. Combining general and special education standards in personnel preparation programs: Experiences from two states. *Topics in Early Childhood Special Education* 13: 372–87.

Stayton, V.D., P.S. Miller, & L. Dinnebeil, eds. 2002. *Recommended practices in personnel preparation: Guidelines for early childhood special educators.* Longmont, CO: Sopris West Educational Services.

committing myself to this demanding program seemed impossible. However, I knew that if I did not commit myself, I would eventually drown.

Initially I thought because I already was "in the field," the program's field placement requirement was busywork and not applicable to me. However, the more hours I spent in them, the more I found I could apply the theory and strategies introduced in class. While challenging and sometimes frustrating, those field placements were an invaluable piece of my professional development— one that cannot be replaced with textbooks or theory.

—Beth Schaeffer, preschool teacher

and program evaluation—Building an accountable and effective system for birth through age eight. Draft joint position statement. Online: www.naeyc.org/resources/position_statements/Position_Statement_2003.pdf

National Association for Nursery Education. 1929. *Minimum essentials for nursery school education.* Chicago, IL: Author.

National Institute on Early Childhood Development and Education, U.S. Department of Education. 2000. *New teachers for a new century: The future of early childhood professional preparation.* Jessup, MD: U.S. Department of Education, ED Publishing.

National Research Council. 2001. *Eager to learn: Educating our preschoolers.* Eds. B. Bowman, M. Donovan, & M. Burns. Committee on Early Childhood Pedagogy. Commission on Behavioral and Social Sciences and Education. Washington, DC: National Academy Press.

OECD (Organisation for Economic Co-operation and Development). 2001. *Starting strong: Early education and care.* Paris, France: Author.

Peisner-Feinberg, E., M.R. Burchnal, R.M. Clifford, M.L. Culkin, C. Howes, S.L. Kagan, N. Yazejian, P. Byler, J. Rustici, & J. Zelazo. 2000. *The children of the Cost, Quality, and Outcomes Study go to school: Technical report.* Chapel Hill: University of North Carolina at Chapel Hill, Frank Porter Graham Child Development Center.

Ratcliff, N., J. Cruz, & J. McCarthy. 1999. *Early childhood teacher education licensure patterns and curriculum guidelines: A state-by-state analysis.* Washington, DC: Council for Professional Recognition.

National Association for the Education of Young Children

NAEYC

Contents

Introduction   17

Why have standards for early childhood professional preparation?   17

The context and scope of the early childhood field   18

Why revise now? Today's context for standards revisions   19

The process of standards revision   20

NAEYC's revised standards: What is the same?   21

NAEYC's revised standards: What's new?   22

Changes in format and terminology in NAEYC's revised standards   23

How programs will document compliance with NAEYC's standards   26

Transition to NAEYC's new standards and documentation of performance   26

Putting it back together: Linking the elements of high-quality early childhood practice   27

Some final thoughts   27

Standards Summary   29

Standards   30

Standard 1. Promoting Child Development and Learning   30

Standard 2. Building Family and Community Relationships   31

Standard 3. Observing, Documenting, and Assessing to Support
Young Children and Families   33

Standard 4. Teaching and Learning   35

Standard 5. Becoming a Professional   44

References and Resources   47

Appendix

A: Comparison of INTASC principles with related sections of
NAEYC Initial Licensure Standards   51

B: Rubrics, aligned with NAEYC's 2001 Initial Licensure Standards   52

C: Initial Licensure Standards Work Group   63

NAEYC Standards for Early Childhood Professional Preparation

Initial Licensure Programs

Approved by NAEYC Governing Board, July 2001

Approved by NCATE, October 2001

Introduction

Why have standards for early childhood professional preparation?

This document presents one part of NAEYC's standards for the preparation of early childhood professionals. The standards in this document are specifically intended for higher education programs that prepare practitioners at the "initial licensure" or certification level (usually a baccalaureate or master's degree). However, the standards, and the principles that these standards represent, are relevant to many other professional development settings. NAEYC recognizes and welcomes all those who teach young children—whatever their current education and experience—into the community of professional practice. NAEYC honors the commitment that draws so many talented people into this field, and we hope that these and other professional standards will help create a unified vision of excellence, with multiple, well-articulated professional pathways.

Standards and NAEYC's mission

Why should NAEYC have standards for the preparation of early childhood professionals? NAEYC's mission is to improve the quality of services for children from birth through age 8. Over the years, NAEYC has supported that mission through its leadership in developing position statements, guidelines, and standards on behalf of the profession. Collaboratively devel-

oped standards can provide a solid, commonly held foundation from which diverse structures may arise, incorporating the wisdom of local communities, families, and practitioners.

Connecting with others through standards

By developing and revising standards for early childhood professional preparation, NAEYC connects its vision of excellence with that of many other groups that are concerned about teacher preparation and performance. The National Council for Accreditation of Teacher Education (NCATE) has general, or "unit," standards that describe the kinds of knowledge, skills, and dispositions that *all* well-prepared education professionals should possess.

NAEYC's "program" standards are closely aligned with those of NCATE but provide specific guidance about the preparation of early childhood professionals. Other NCATE-affiliated groups, including specialty professional associations like NAEYC but in elementary education, special education, reading, mathematics, science, and social studies, set their own expectations for high-quality professional preparation. NAEYC collaborates with those groups and works to coordinate its standards with theirs. NAEYC works especially closely with the Division for Early Childhood (DEC) of the Council for Exceptional Children (CEC) to ensure that our standards complement and support one another, so that all early childhood teachers are well prepared to teach young children with and without developmental delays or disabilities.

Teacher preparation standards and positive outcomes for children

Finally, NAEYC's standards for professional preparation are part of a larger set of expectations, or standards, that together form an image of what is required if all young children are to receive the kind of early education they need and deserve.

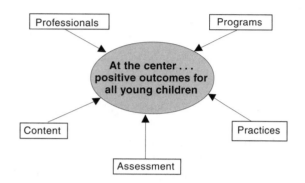

Yet standards cannot be rigid or "one size fits all." As the diagram above suggests, NAEYC's expectations—for children, for professionals, for programs, for teaching practices, for curriculum content, and for assessment—are always embedded within the context of specific cultures and communities. Within those contexts, young children are at the center of all of NAEYC's efforts to set standards in early childhood education. If we intend to help all young children develop and learn well, we need high expectations for the programs they attend (see NAEYC's *Accreditation Criteria and Procedures for Early Childhood Programs* [1998]), for the practices used by their teachers (see NAEYC's *Developmentally Appropriate Practice in Early Childhood Programs* [Bredekamp & Copple 1997]), and for the approaches used in early childhood curriculum content and assessment (see NAEYC's *Reaching Potentials*, Vols. 1 and 2 [Bredekamp & Rosegrant 1992, 1995]). And we need high expectations for the preparation and performance of early childhood professionals—expectations that are articulated in this document. Indeed, as the picture shows, all of these expectations are linked, and all are needed to support young children's development and learning. Finally, we need a system for financing early education—a system that ensures the resources needed to build an infrastructure for excellence.

The context and scope of the early childhood field

Context

As emphasized in NAEYC's last standards publication (NAEYC 1996a) and elsewhere (e.g., NAEYC's 1997 position statement *Licensing and Public Regulation of Early Childhood Programs*), the field of early childhood education differs in significant ways from other domains of education, although it also shares common elements. As compared with elementary and secondary teachers, early childhood professionals work in many settings—not just public schools but also child care programs, private preschools and kindergartens, early intervention programs including Head Start and Early Head Start, family support and home-based programs, and so on. Similarly, the professional roles assumed by early childhood professionals are far more varied than those typical in elementary and secondary education—including roles as lead teachers, mentor teachers, education coordinators, early childhood trainers, inclusion specialists, resource and referral staff, technical assistance specialists, early childhood technology specialists, early interventionists, and home visitors. Even at institutions where the majority of graduates take teaching positions in public schools, high-quality early childhood professional preparation programs convey to candidates the range and complexity of those roles, most of which involve significant collaboration across professions, as well as collaboration with young children's families.

Scope

NAEYC continues to define the "early childhood" period as spanning the years from birth through age 8. As in past editions of its standards, NAEYC recognizes that within that range, early childhood professionals—and the programs that prepare them—may choose to specialize within the early childhood spectrum (infants/toddlers, preschool, or kindergarten/primary). Teacher licensure complicates the picture, since states' definitions of the early childhood age span and its subdivisions vary greatly (McCarthy, Cruz, & Ratcliff 1999).

Specialization can be valuable, but NAEYC believes that all early childhood professionals should have a broad knowledge of development and learning across the birth–age 8 range; that they should be familiar with appropriate curriculum and assessment approaches across that age span; and that they should have in-depth knowledge and skills in at least two of the three subperiods listed above. The reason is clear: Without knowing about the *past* and the *future* (the precursors to children's current development and learning, and the trajectory they will follow in later years), teachers cannot design effective learning opportunities within their specific professional "assignment." In addition, today's inclusive early childhood settings—those that include young children with developmental delays and disabilities—require knowledge of an even wider range of development and learning than was needed in many classrooms of the past.

Two specific challenges face programs as they prepare early childhood professionals within the birth–age 8 range. First, even programs that emphasize the upper end of the age range may not adequately prepare candidates in the critical content or subject matter areas needed to build children's academic success. Literacy is only one example: National reports (e.g., National Institute of Child Health and Human Development 2000) repeatedly fault teacher education for failing to provide candidates with research-based knowledge about reading and in-depth practical experience. But a second, equally important concern is the tendency for teacher education programs to give inadequate attention to children's critical early years, especially the birth–age 3 period. National studies (e.g., Whitebook, Howes, & Phillips 1989, 1998) show that quality is lowest for infant-toddler child care programs, despite what is known about the importance of that period for children's later language, cognitive, and social-emotional development. Candidates who take positions in infant-toddler care but whose preparation has slighted that period may fail to support children's learning and development because the curriculum and teaching strategies they were taught to use are more effective with older children. NAEYC's standards attempt to address both of these challenges.

Why revise now? Today's context for standards revisions

NAEYC last approved standards (then called "guidelines") for initial licensure programs in 1994. Why revise so soon? The new century brings new challenges (see, e.g., National Institute on Early Childhood Development and Education 2000). Profound changes drive NAEYC's standards revision process.

Changes in the knowledge base of the early childhood field

First, the knowledge base for the early childhood field has expanded substantially since the mid-1990s. Long-term follow-up studies from the Chicago Parent-Child Centers, the Abecedarian Project, the Perry Preschool Project, and the Cost, Quality, and Outcomes Project continue to demonstrate the importance of high-quality early experiences in homes, classrooms, and communities (Barnett, Young, & Schweinhart 1998; Peisner-Feinberg et al. 1999; Campbell et al. 2002; Reynolds et al. 2001). Major reports from committees of the National Research Council have synthesized research on the science of learning (1999), early literacy (1998), early childhood pedagogy and content (2001b), and integrated child development knowledge (National Research Council and Institute of Medicine 2000).

Changes in contexts for early childhood education

Recent years have seen increases in the number of state-funded prekindergarten programs, with more than 40 states now having some investment in that form of early education. Public school involvement in early childhood education has brought with it an increased attention to standards and accountability—as has Head Start's Child Outcomes Framework. Early Head Start has become a major form of early intervention for infants and toddlers, with both center- and home-based models implemented around the country. And inclusive early childhood programs, although certainly in place at the time of NAEYC's last revision of its standards, are even more widespread now and welcoming young children with increasingly challenging disabilities and medical conditions. Technology, too, has changed the context for young children both at home and at school, expanding learning opportunities as well as professional challenges.

Changes in early childhood demographics

The face of America is rapidly changing. In three states including California, European-Americans are no longer the majority group. U.S. babies born today will reach adulthood in a country in which no one ethnic group predominates. By the year 2005, children and adolescents of color will represent 40 percent of all U.S. school children. The largest proportion of individuals with disabilities is found in the preschool population. Thus, tomorrow's early childhood teachers must be prepared to serve and to value a far more diverse group of young children and families than at any time in the past. In addition, the profession needs to recruit many more early childhood professionals who themselves share children's cultures and home languages. Institutions of higher education urgently need to create policies, incentives, and resources to recruit diverse teacher candidates and teacher education faculty and to provide ongoing support.

Changes in states' involvement in setting teacher preparation standards

Education reform is placing even greater emphasis on the preparation of teachers, with national reports pointing to inadequate preparation of teachers in areas including literacy (Committee 1998; National Institute of Child Health and Human Development 2000), knowledge of child development and of other content areas (National Research Council 2001b), knowledge of children's mental health and relationship issues (Child Mental Health 2000), and knowledge of the importance of family involvement (Shartrand et al. 1997; Epstein, Sanders, & Clark 1999). States have become increasingly involved in setting standards for higher education institutions and for entry into the profession. In that process, more states have forged partnerships with NCATE, and increasingly with NAEYC. Those changes are resulting in closer ties between national and state standards for early childhood teacher preparation.

Changes in general standards for teacher education

In 1997, NCATE undertook a major revision of its standards for "professional education units"—schools, colleges, or departments of education or entire institutions that engage in teacher preparation. The new performance-based standards, announced in May 2000, present an image of what competent professional education candidates should know and be able to do. NCATE grouped its previous standards into a smaller number of categories, and added rationales, or "explanations," of each standard, "critical elements" of that standard, and "rubrics" that describe different levels of performance with respect to each element. The nature of the evidence that institutions must provide in order to document compliance with the NCATE standards has changed dramatically. "Inputs" (courses, credits, hours) are far less important sources of evidence than are multiple, aggregated indicators of "outputs"—the results a particular program can demonstrate, in the quality of the teachers it produces and in their positive effects on children's learning.

As an NCATE constituent member, NAEYC has engaged in a similar process, aiming to make its standards even more performance-based; better supported by explanatory narratives, rubrics, and references; and even more focused on candidates' effects on the young children with whom they work.

The process of standards revision

As with all its revisions of position statements and other materials, NAEYC engaged in a comprehensive process to revise its standards for early childhood professional preparation at the initial licensure level. Important features of that process were as follows:

• NAEYC began by soliciting comments concerning strengths and gaps in its 1994 initial certification Guidelines, using conference sessions and electronic response options.

• In drafting revisions, NAEYC worked closely with NCATE and a number of NCATE's other specialty organizations. In particular, NAEYC's revisions were influenced by the work of the multidisciplinary group (which included an

NAEYC representative) that drafted the new NCATE/ACEI Program Standards for Elementary Teacher Preparation. NCATE intended the work of that group to provide a model for its other specialty organizations. The format of the elementary standards document and NAEYC's desire to create a more coherent relationship between elementary and early childhood standards influenced NAEYC's revisions.

• NAEYC worked collaboratively with other professional groups that were also revising their standards, including with the Early Childhood/ Generalist committee of the National Board for Professional Teaching Standards (NBPTS) and with the Division for Early Childhood of the Council for Exceptional Children.

• NAEYC consulted with other groups that have a stake in standards for early childhood professional preparation. Those groups included the National Association for Early Childhood Teacher Educators (NAECTE); the American Associate Degree Early Childhood Educators (ACCESS); the National Association of Early Childhood Specialists in State Departments of Education (NAECS/SDE); and the Council for Professional Recognition. These are only a few of the groups with which NAEYC has continuing discussion about our collective work in developing appropriate, high expectations for professional preparation.

• In developing sections of NAEYC's standards in specific subject areas and other specialized areas of professional preparation, NAEYC consulted with specialists affiliated with related organizations including the National Association for Bilingual Education (NABE); the National Council of Teachers of Mathematics (NCTM); the National Association for Music Education (MENC); the International Reading Association (IRA); NAEYC's own Technology and Young Children Interest Forum; and ZERO TO THREE.

• NAEYC's revisions also align with general principles and standards in teacher education. The INTASC principles (Interstate New Teacher Assessment and Support Consortium) were specifically examined for congruence with NAEYC's standards. Those principles, intended for all beginning teachers, are fully consistent with NAEYC's standards. Many states have specifically adopted the INTASC principles, and so it is important that all specialty organizations share that common framework, while also setting forth their own professional expectations. Appendix A presents a framework for comparison of the INTASC principles with related sections of the NAEYC standards.

• Using those and other sources of insight, a subcommittee of NAEYC's Professional Development Panel and NAEYC staff identified areas for revision and appropriate formats for revision, and completed a first draft of a new Initial Licensure Standards document.

• It and later drafts were discussed at NAEYC conference sessions over the next two years; they also were posted on NAEYC's Website for comment. Revisions were made on the basis of feedback from the groups listed above and others.

• NAEYC's Governing Board reviewed a final revision of this Initial Licensure Standards document and voted approval of its substance in July 2001.

• NCATE approval came in October 2001, beginning an 18-month transition for higher education programs to the new NAEYC standards and to a new, performance-based system of documentation. After Spring 2003, all institutions seeking NCATE accreditation for their initial licensure programs must respond to these standards, with full implementation of the performance assessment system in 2005.

NAEYC's revised standards: What is the same?

For readers who are familiar with NAEYC's 1994 initial certification Guidelines, the new format will seem different, but they also will find much here that affirms that previous document's central focus.

The scope of early childhood

These Initial Licensure Standards continue to encompass the birth–age 8 range. They also affirm and emphasize the diversity of settings in which early childhood professionals work.

Beliefs, commitments, struggles

The Early Childhood–Grade 4 program stands on the same four pillars on which we base our overall unit in education: (1) our belief that at its best, teaching is a form of inquiry that involves reflective practice; (2) our commitment to preparing teachers who view inclusion as a strength; who believe that under the right conditions all children can become successful learners; and who value continuous learning for themselves and their colleagues; (3) our struggle to ensure that programs address not only the technical level of competence but also clinical, personal, and critical levels of competence; and (4) our belief that teaching is shaped by key knowledge bases that together provide the supports that establish and extend practice, provide the substance for what teachers do, and provide the source of authority for their work.
— Trinity University, NCATE/NAEYC Program Report

The liberal arts

In keeping with the spirit of educational standards articulated by professional organizations such as NAEYC and by the Illinois State Board of Education, our early childhood education candidates experience a broad general-education curriculum.

This curriculum includes an extensive and integrated knowledge base, methods of birth–third grade teaching using the best practices for teaching all children in a technological and interdependent society, and continuous opportunities to apply theory to practice through varied and intensive field experiences. All efforts in the teacher education program rest firmly on the college's history of melding the liberal arts with preparation for meaningful work.
— Elmhurst College, NCATE/NAEYC Program Report

Child development is key

All aspects of the early childhood education program are guided by a child development frame of reference. Solid grounding in child development is the beginning point for all program development and candidates' learning opportunities. Curriculum and pedagogy are tempered by the need to comply with state content mandates. Emphasis is on using knowledge about children as the filter for appropriate and meaningful academic content. A commitment to child development is the screen through which planning, curriculum, classroom management, and interactions with children and families are viewed.
— James Madison University, NCATE/NAEYC Program Report

Significant values and emphases

These Initial Licensure Standards continue to give weight to the core professional values and emphases in the 1994 Guidelines. For example, children's play is explicitly acknowledged as a powerful influence on early development and learning. Child development knowledge is accorded great importance as a basis for professional decisions. Active and integrated learning, engaging children's minds in real-life, meaningful issues, are again important themes. Reciprocal relationships with families continue to be highly valued. Children's cultures and communities were emphasized in the earlier Guidelines and continue to be prominent in this document. Professional knowledge and skills in ethical practices and in policy advocacy again receive strong emphasis.

Finally, five of the major categories of professional competence from the 1994 Guidelines (i.e., Child Development and Learning; Curriculum Development and Implementation; Family and Community Relationships; Assessment and Evaluation; and Professionalism) remain, although with some differences in wording. Well-chosen and well-supervised field experiences, which in 1994 was a sixth category, continue to be seen as essential learning tools for early childhood teacher candidates.

NAEYC's revised standards: What's new?

Some of the differences between the 1994 Guidelines and these revised standards have to do with shifts in emphasis or clarifications in emphasis, reflecting changes in the early childhood knowledge base and among the children and families served in early childhood programs. Areas of difference:

Enhanced emphasis on linguistic and cultural diversity

These new Initial Licensure Standards maintain the Guideline's emphasis on diversity, but make the emphasis even more explicit.

Enhanced emphasis on inclusion

Those familiar with the 1994 Guidelines will find the same commitment to inclusion, but throughout this document there is now substantially greater explicitness about the knowledge and skills necessary to serve children with developmental delays and disabilities.

Enhanced emphasis on subject matter

While continuing to emphasize child development knowledge, in-depth integrated curriculum, and the central value of play in the lives of children, these standards now are more specific about what candidates should know and be able to do in academic disciplines or subject matter areas (understanding of content/core concepts/ tools of inquiry, and applications in curriculum development). This document explicitly links that subject matter knowledge to national professional standards and to other key resources. While all candidates should have essential subject matter knowledge, these standards now make clear that different areas of specialization (e.g., infant/toddler and preschool specialization vs. kindergarten/primary) may call for different levels of knowledge and skill.

Enhanced emphasis on communities in which children live

This revision continues to emphasize candidates' knowledge of young children's families, but it adds greater understanding of the *communities* in which children live and the importance of embedding early childhood education within particular community settings.

More emphasis on the complexity of assessment issues in today's educational settings

Assessment has been a critically important area for professional preparation in the past. This revision is even more explicit about the challenges of appropriate, effective early childhood assessment in the context of high-stakes testing, increasing diversity and inclusion in early childhood programs, and ethical responsibilities.

More explicit emphasis on a "continuum of teaching strategies" and developmentally effective approaches

Consistent with recent NAEYC publications (e.g., Bredekamp & Copple 1997), this revision emphasizes the varied approaches to teaching that competent early childhood professionals need to know. Candidates are expected to draw from a continuum of strategies and tools in order to support the learning and development of all children.

Field experiences emphasized and integrated throughout the standards

In the previous Guidelines, "Field Experiences" constituted a separate major category of professional competence. These standards instead consider such experiences to be centrally important within each of the other five "core" standards categories. It is through field experiences that candidates are best able to translate knowledge into deep understanding and professional skills.

As NCATE points out, its new standards (and NAEYC's, as well) require much closer partnership between institutions of higher education and community education settings than often has been the case in the past. With NCATE's and NAEYC's increased emphasis on assessment and evaluation of candidate performance, field experiences become a central component of the institution's assessment system. Further, the quality of those experiences, as documented in candidate performance, becomes a critical part of the evidence used by program reviewers.

Changes in format and terminology in NAEYC's revised standards

Besides the changes in emphasis outlined above, readers who are familiar with the previous Guidelines will see many changes in format and terminology here. Those changes are intended to focus on the "big picture" of early childhood professional preparation; highlight the rationale and knowledge base that undergird each standard; and provide institutions with a sense of what might constitute distinct levels of candidate performance or evidence within each area.

Standards are written more concisely

Building on the previous Guidelines, these standards now are organized into five core categories: Promoting Child Development and Learning; Building Family and Community Relationships; Observing, Documenting, and Assessing to Support Young Children and Families; Teaching and Learning; and Becoming a Professional.

Note that the categories now are stated actively, reflecting the performances expected of candidates. For each category, one standards statement, of no more than a few sentences, captures the essential features of that standard (a variation is Standard 4, which due to its complexity comprises one overall standard and four sub-standards).

Expectations for candidates are worded in more strongly "performance-based" language

What should competent early childhood professionals know and be able to do? In the previous Guidelines, NAEYC had already moved toward using performance language. This revision adopts and extends that language.

Each standard is followed by a "supporting explanation"

In this revision, NAEYC attempts to help readers understand the "why" behind each standard. Therefore, each standards statement is followed by a narrative discussion of the knowledge base and professional values that support that particular standard. Those supporting explanations also provide more detail than do the brief standards statements about the competencies that candidates should demonstrate, and about why a standard is important in preparing capable early childhood professionals.

Supporting explanations are followed by "key elements" of that standard

This document identifies the key elements of each standard and of that standard's supporting explanation. The key elements are presented as concise, bulleted points that identify that standard's critical components as represented in the standard itself and as elaborated in its supporting explanation.

Each key element is aligned with "rubrics"

The rubrics are a set of descriptions of what would be expected at each of three levels of candidate performance, including candidate knowledge, skills, and dispositions: "Exceeds Expectations" (program evidence of candidates' exceptional performance in that element of the standard, beyond what one would typically

Multisite PDS

The university's professional development school (PDS) reflects the birth–age 8 span of early childhood by linking four child care centers with four elementary schools, the local community college early childhood program, and the child development program at a high school. This large, multisite PDS provides internships and field placements.

In addition, through a grant from the state, our regular undergraduate courses are offered to staff in centers pursuing NAEYC early childhood program accreditation. The courses are taught by center directors, all of whom have master's degrees, with our faculty providing additional support.

Making this model of university teacher education available without cost to child care staff is a step toward staff advancement; having credentialed directors do adjunct teaching is a desirable career advancement for them, as well.

—University of Maryland, Baltimore County, NCATE/NAEYC Program Report

Children in context

Faculty expect candidates to work with children and families in ways that reflect their understanding of the child as a whole person in the family/community context, rather than as a mere consumer of academic skills.

—James Madison University, NCATE/NAEYC Program Report

expect of beginning professionals); "Meets Expectations" (program evidence of satisfactory performance from well-prepared candidates); and "Does Not Yet Meet Expectations" (program evidence fails to show adequate performance).

Like the rubrics that NCATE developed for its unit-level accreditation, NAEYC's rubrics are intended to help teacher educators and institutions to think about what kinds of evidence would be needed to document various levels of performance. The rubrics appear in Appendix B.

References address each standard.

Items in the References and Resources section include standards documents written by other professional groups, syntheses of relevant research, significant work on early childhood pedagogy, valuable Websites, and other resources intended to help programs find relevant information. Most items are keyed to one or more of the standards.

Some notes on the terminology used in this document

"**Candidates**" refers to those who are preparing for professional positions serving young children and their families. In this Initial Licensure Standards document, candidates are assumed to be preparing for initial licensure in a four- or five-year higher education program.

"**All children**" means *all*: children with developmental delays or disabilities, children who are gifted and talented, children whose families are culturally and linguistically diverse, children from diverse socioeconomic groups, and other children with individual learning styles, strengths, and needs. (Note that NAEYC uses the term *children,* rather than *students,* to reflect the focus on all aspects of development and learning and to remind ourselves that children have identities outside of their classroom roles.)

The term "**field experiences**" includes observations, field work, practica, and student teaching or other "clinical" experiences such as home visiting.

"**Know**" refers to candidates' possession of key information; "**understand**" includes analysis and reflection; "**use**" refers to application in practice, always soundly based on professional knowledge.

Using NAEYC's rubrics in field experiences

Standard 4. Teaching and Learning

Evidence is drawn from instructors'/supervisors' observational notes and from assignments such as written reflection papers completed for course assignments. Note that this is a course that precedes student teaching, so candidates do not have opportunities to plan and enact extensive lessons or series of lessons.

Key element 4a. Knowing, understanding, and using positive relationships and supportive interactions

Does Not Yet Meet Expectations—The candidate focuses narrowly on curricular content, such as ways of introducing children to literacy. She/he does not apply the information from readings about the crucial role of relationships in teaching and learning. She/he does not take opportunities to interact with the other adults in her/his field site.

Meets Expectations—The candidate attempts to balance the focus on content and the focus on communicating with children and adults to establish working relationships. He/she appears to be sensitive to the needs of all children to seek relationships, and attempts to communicate with children who do not initiate conversations with him/her. He/she is knowledgeable about the roles of the different adults in his/her field sites.

Exceeds Expectations—The candidate uses observational skills while establishing relationships with children and adults. The skills are demonstrated in discussion comments and reflections papers. The candidate attempts to interact with all children, including English-language learners whose communication is a combination of words and gestures. She/he establishes relationships with other adults by asking questions about the school and commenting on individual children and their activities.

—Teachers College, Columbia University, NCATE/NAEYC Program Report

The term "**culture**" includes ethnicity, racial identity, economic class, family structure, language, and religious and political beliefs, which profoundly influence each child's development and relationship to the world.

How programs will document compliance with NAEYC's standards

A higher education institution applying for NCATE accreditation must submit documentation about its compliance with standards for the unit overall and for all specialty programs in which it prepares education professionals. NAEYC is the NCATE specialty professional association (SPA) for early childhood programs. Thus, if an NCATE-affiliated institution has an early childhood professional preparation program, it must submit materials for review by NAEYC (unless the institution has a state partnership approved by NCATE and NAEYC allowing state-level review of its early childhood program).

Both at the unit and the specialty program levels, the kinds of evidence required under NCATE's new performance-based assessment system differ in substantial ways from the documentation that was previously required. The details of the process at the unit level may be found on NCATE's Website at www.ncate.org.

To align with but not duplicate that documentation, the specialty organizations (i.e., NAEYC, Council for Exceptional Children, National Council of Teachers of Mathematics, etc.) have drafted guidance for institutions concerning evidence required under the specialty organizations' standards. That information may be found on NCATE's Website at www.ncate.org/ standard/interimsasbstand.pdf; see the attachment to that document, pp. 16–17.

Briefly, however, NAEYC expects institutions to provide documentation that includes:

• a description of the institutional and professional context within which the program operates

• an organized system by which the program tracks candidate performance across time, including positive effects on children

• a description of the kinds of evidence that the program collects to document candidate performance in relation to the standards, with emphasis on multiple assessments in authentic contexts such as field experiences

• summarized evidence of candidates' performance using those assessments, with samples of candidate work at varying levels of performance

• evidence that the information is used for continuous program improvement.

Transition to NAEYC's new standards and documentation of performance

The Initial Licensure Standards for early childhood teacher preparation in this document were approved by NAEYC's Governing Board in July 2001 and by NCATE in October 2001. The next 18 months were a period of phasing in the new standards and the performance assessment system, during which initial licensure programs had the option of documenting compliance either with the 1994 Guidelines or the new standards. Effective Spring 2003, all institutions submitting Program Reports as part of NCATE accreditation of initial licensure early childhood programs must demonstrate compliance with NAEYC's 2001 standards as described in this document.

NCATE and the SPAs, including NAEYC, have also adopted a timeline for the transition to fully performance-based program review, with all NCATE institutions to have fully functioning assessment systems by 2005. Details of the transition timeline are available on NCATE's Website at www.ncate.org. The use of candidate performance evidence by NAEYC also will be phased in over time, as institutions develop their own capacity. NAEYC's timetable for transition to a fully operational assessment system is available on its Website at www.naeyc.org.

Thus, the transition to use of NAEYC's revised standards and to a new system by which institutions and their specialty programs document performance is a gradual and developmental process—both for institutions and for candidates.

A developmental process for institutions

NCATE, NAEYC, and other professional organizations wish to work in a supportive way with institutions, to help them in the transition to new standards and assessment systems. The processes of self-study and of developing performance assessment systems are both valuable aspects of that transition, and time was built in for those tasks.

A developmental process for candidates

NAEYC's standards, key elements, and rubrics are intended to focus on the competencies expected of *beginning* early childhood professionals who have been prepared in baccalaureate or master's programs. Becoming an accomplished early childhood practitioner takes time. While setting high expectations for candidate performance, we need to keep in mind the developmental nature of professional growth, which continues long after the candidate completes preservice education. We should also acknowledge the diverse routes taken by early childhood teacher candidates, many of whom have spent years serving children and families before entering higher education. Their wealth of experience and their commitment require recognition, as well as adaptation of some aspects of the higher education experience.

Putting it back together: Linking the elements of high-quality early childhood practice

When we try to identify the important categories of expectations for early childhood teacher candidates, we are forced to separate the complex elements of early childhood practice into what may seem to be artificial categories. How can one really separate a category such as "Becoming a Professional" from "Promoting Child Development and Learning"? In turn, how can one separate "Promoting Child Development and Learning" from "Building Relationships with Families and Communities"? All are interconnected. Listening to an orchestra playing a symphony, one hears the whole, not each individual instrument. Hearing each part played separately fails to convey the complexity and beauty of the whole. In the same way, when we watch a skilled early childhood teacher at work, it is difficult to identify each separate element of her practice. Yet the separation is necessary in order to write standards that can be understood and applied in preparing early childhood professionals.

As higher education programs use these standards to develop programs and to document teacher candidates' performance, NAEYC hopes the symphony will be heard above the separate parts. Often the performance of teacher candidates (and of experienced teachers) shows exemplary knowledge and skills in several standards categories simultaneously. For example, a student teacher might involve children in a project about their own hands, simultaneously showing her competence in supporting their physical skills; their scientific understandings; their insight into culture and language ("How many words do we know for *hand* or *finger?*—And what wonderful colors our hands are!"); her skills in assessing children's fine motor skills; and her support of early writing. For future early childhood teachers, learning is seamless and integrated, in the same way that learning is for young children.

Some final thoughts

Avoiding "mile wide and inch deep" professional preparation

As is evident from this introduction and from the standards that follow, both the standards themselves and the kinds of evidence needed to document candidate performance are more challenging and complex than in the past. To help all young children develop and learn, early childhood candidates require a great deal of knowledge, understanding, and skill in multiple domains, linked with dispositions that support candidates' actions. However, NAEYC would not wish to see programs substitute breadth for depth, nor sacrifice deep understanding for superficial coverage of topics. To avoid that risk, NAEYC suggests several strategies:

• While attending to the full birth–age 8 range, programs may, as in the past, elect to specialize in sub-periods—e.g., infancy through preschool, or preschool/kindergarten/primary. Such specialization has implications for, for example, the level at which candidates must know and be able to implement curriculum in specific academic areas such as science or social studies. However, every candidate needs to know the basics of how young children gain understanding of those concepts and should be able to implement essential foundational experiences. In addition, all candidates need in-depth knowledge of early language and literacy, due to its long-term significance across multiple academic and developmental areas.

• Programs may—and should—emphasize "learning how to learn," helping candidates gain access to credible, research-based resources to support their work. Such resources, important both in academic subject matter areas and in addressing issues of disability and diversity, may include print and non-print resources such as journals, videos, and Websites, as well as persons with relevant expertise at the school or in the community.

Standards as a vision

With good reason, many educators have become wary of standards. At times, standards have constricted learning and have encouraged a one-size-fits-all mentality. But standards can also be visionary and empowering, for children and professionals alike. NAEYC hopes its standards for professional preparation can provide something more valuable than a list of rules for programs to follow.

The five brief standards statements in this document offer a shared vision of early childhood professional preparation. But to make the vision real, the details must be constructed uniquely and personally, within particular communities of learners. Good early childhood settings may look very different from one another. In the same way, good professional preparation programs may find many pathways to help candidates meet high standards, so that they can effectively support young children and their families.

Standards Summary

Standard 1. Promoting Child Development and Learning

Candidates use their understanding of young children's characteristics and needs, and of multiple interacting influences on children's development and learning, to create environments that are healthy, respectful, supportive, and challenging for all children.

Standard 2. Building Family and Community Relationships

Candidates know about, understand, and value the importance and complex characteristics of children's families and communities. They use this understanding to create respectful, reciprocal relationships that support and empower families, and to involve all families in their children's development and learning.

Standard 3. Observing, Documenting, and Assessing to Support Young Children and Families

Candidates know about and understand the goals, benefits, and uses of assessment. They know about and use systematic observations, documentation, and other effective assessment strategies in a responsible way, in partnership with families and other professionals, to positively influence children's development and learning.

Standard 4. Teaching and Learning

Candidates integrate their understanding of and relationships with children and families; their understanding of developmentally effective approaches to teaching and learning; and their knowledge of academic disciplines to design, implement, and evaluate experiences that promote positive development and learning for all children.

Sub-Standard 4a. Connecting with children and families

Candidates know, understand, and use positive relationships and supportive interactions as the foundation for their work with young children.

Sub-Standard 4b. Using developmentally effective approaches

Candidates know, understand, and use a wide array of effective approaches, strategies, and tools to positively influence children's development and learning.

Sub-Standard 4c. Understanding content knowledge in early education

Candidates understand the importance of each content area in young children's learning. They know the essential concepts, inquiry tools, and structure of content areas including academic subjects and can identify resources to deepen their understanding.

Sub-Standard 4d. Building meaningful curriculum

Candidates use their own knowledge and other resources to design, implement, and evaluate meaningful, challenging curriculum that promotes comprehensive developmental and learning outcomes for all young children.

Standard 5. Becoming a Professional

Candidates identify and conduct themselves as members of the early childhood profession. They know and use ethical guidelines and other professional standards related to early childhood practice. They are continuous, collaborative learners who demonstrate knowledgeable, reflective, and critical perspectives on their work, making informed decisions that integrate knowledge from a variety of sources. They are informed advocates for sound educational practices and policies.

Standards

A child study assignment

Students conduct a semester-long child study of a preschooler or kindergartner in order to (a) strengthen their skills as observers, describers, and interpreters of the worlds of childhood and learning; (b) expand their knowledge of child development; (c) begin to learn how to support and assess young children's literacy development; and (d) study whether and how the early childhood classroom context exemplifies the qualities of a strong program and supports children's language and culture.

We revised the child study to provide candidates with a more focused opportunity to think carefully about how a child's multiple contexts shape her or his development and learning. When we have the aggregate data from the revised child study and the Early Childhood–Grade 4 certification exam, we will further revise the assignment as needed.

—Trinity University, NCATE/NAEYC Program Report

Child development in action

In one course, small groups of candidates prepare presentations on the stages of oral language development from birth through age 5, the acquisition of a second language by young children, and stages of emergent and early literacy. In addition, candidates observe two children under age 2, in two different settings, to study adult interaction around language development. Candidates then reflect on their observations in terms of theories of language acquisition.

—University of Maryland, Baltimore County, NCATE/NAEYC Program Report

Typical and atypical development

The program ensures that candidates' field placements offer a wide range in both diversity of children's backgrounds and their age levels. Because many children who have special needs have not yet been identified in preschool or kindergarten classrooms, candidates have multiple opportunities to work with young children who may be developing atypically, prior to formal identification. Thus candidates' understanding of typical development and behavior forms the basis for recognition of atypical development.

—James Madison University, NCATE/NAEYC Program Report

Standard 1. Promoting Child Development and Learning

Candidates use their understanding of young children's characteristics and needs, and of multiple interacting influences on children's development and learning, to create environments that are healthy, respectful, supportive, and challenging for all children.

Supporting explanation

The early childhood field has historically been grounded in a child development knowledge base, and early childhood programs have aimed to support a broad range of positive developmental outcomes for all young children. Although the scope and emphasis of that knowledge base have changed over the years, and although early childhood professionals recognize that other sources of knowledge are also important influences on curriculum and programs for young children, early childhood practice continues to be deeply linked with a "sympathetic understanding of the young child" (Elkind 1994).

In basing their practice in child development, however, well-prepared early childhood professional candidates go beyond narrow or outdated developmental concepts. Their **knowledge and understanding of young children's characteristics and needs** encompasses multiple, interrelated areas of children's development and learning—including physical, cognitive, social, emotional, language, and aesthetic domains, play, activity, and learning processes, and motivation to learn—and is supported by coherent theoretical perspectives and by current research. Candidates also understand and apply their understanding of the many influences on young children's development and learning, and of how those influences may interact to affect development in both positive and negative ways. Candidates emphasize—both in their conceptual understanding and in their work with children—the **multiple influences on development and learning.** Those influences include the cultural and linguistic contexts for development, children's close relationships with adults and peers, economic conditions of children and families, health status and disabilities, children's individual developmental variations and learning styles, opportunities to play and learn, technology and the media, and family and community characteristics. Candidates also understand the potential influence of early childhood programs, including early intervention, on short- and long-term outcomes for children.

Candidates' competence is demonstrated in their ability to **use developmental knowledge to create healthy, respectful, supportive, and challenging learning environments** for all young children (including curriculum, interactions, teaching practices, and learning materials). Such environments reflect four critical features. First, the environments are *healthy*—that is, candidates possess the knowledge and skills needed to promote young children's physical and psychological health, safety, and sense of security. Second, the environments reflect *respect*—for each child as a feeling, thinking individual and then for each child's culture, home language, individual abilities or disabilities, family context, and community. In respectful environments, candidates model and affirm antibias perspectives on development and learning. Third, the learning environments created by early childhood teacher candidates are *supportive*—candidates demonstrate their belief in young children's ability to learn, and they show that they can use their understanding of children's development to help each child understand and make meaning from her or his experiences through play, spontaneous activity, and guided investigations. Finally, the learning environments that early childhood candidates create are appropriately *challenging*—in other words, candidates apply their knowledge of contemporary theory and research to construct learning environments that provide achievable and "stretching" experiences for all children—including children with special abilities and children with disabilities or developmental delays.

Key elements of Standard 1

1a: Knowing and understanding young children's characteristics and needs

1b: Knowing and understanding the multiple influences on development and learning

1c: Using developmental knowledge to create healthy, respectful, supportive, and challenging learning environments

Rubrics for these key elements, outlining distinct levels of candidate performance and program evidence, appear in Appendix B.

Standard 2. Building Family and Community Relationships

Candidates know about, understand, and value the importance and complex characteristics of children's families and communities. They use this understanding to create respectful, reciprocal relationships that support and empower families, and to involve all families in their children's development and learning.

Supporting explanation

Because young children's lives are so embedded in their families and communities, and because research indicates that successful early childhood education depends upon partnerships with families and communities, early childhood professionals need to thoroughly understand and apply their knowledge in this area.

First, well-prepared candidates possess **knowledge and understanding of family and community characteristics,** and of the many influences on families and communities. Family theory and research provide a knowledge base. Socioeconomic conditions; family structures, relationships, stresses, and supports (including the impact of having a child with special needs); home language; cultural values; ethnicity; community resources, cohesiveness, and organization—knowledge of these and other factors creates a deeper understanding of young children's lives. The knowledge is critical to candidates' ability to help children learn and develop well.

Second, candidates possess the knowledge and skills needed to **support and empower families through respectful, reciprocal relationships.** Candidates understand how to build positive relationships, taking families' preferences and goals into account and incorporating knowledge of families' languages and cultures. Candidates demonstrate respect for variations across cultures in family strengths, expectations, values, and childrearing practices. Candidates consider family members to be resources for insight into their children, as well as resources for curriculum and program development. Candidates know about and demonstrate a variety of communication skills to foster such relationships, emphasizing informal conversations while also including such approaches as exchanging e-mails and posting information and children's work on the Web, with print copies sent home for families without Web access.

In their work, early childhood teacher candidates support and empower diverse families, including those whose children have disabilities or special characteristics or learning needs; families who are facing multiple challenges in their lives; and families whose languages and cultures may differ from those of the early childhood professional. Candidates also understand that their relationships with families include assisting families in finding needed resources, such as mental health services, health care, adult education, English language instruction, and economic assistance, that may contribute directly or indirectly to their children's positive development and learning. Well-prepared early childhood candidates are able to identify such resources and know how to connect families with services, including help with planning transitions from one educational or service system to another.

Finally, well-prepared candidates possess essential skills to **involve families and communities in many aspects of children's development and learning.** They understand and value the role of parents and other important family members as children's primary teachers. Candidates understand how to go beyond parent conferences to engage families in curriculum planning, assessing of children's learning, and planning for children's transitions to new programs. When their approaches to family involvement are not effective, candidates evaluate and modify those approaches rather than assuming that families "are just not interested."

Diverse learners

Early Childhood–Grade 4 teacher candidates largely complete their undergraduate and graduate fieldwork at one of two professional development schools: Hawthorne Elementary School or Walzem Elementary School. Both schools provide a full-day kindergarten and have a bilingual program; additionally, Hawthorne has a preschool program. Both schools serve Latino children from economically depressed areas of San Antonio. Trinity students have rich opportunities to cultivate the knowledge, skills, and dispositions needed to work with learners from a diversity of backgrounds.

—Trinity University,
NCATE/NAEYC Program Report

Families and professionals

At the University of Colorado, Boulder, early childhood education and communication disorders students learn firsthand the art of family-professional collaboration. Families of young children with disabilities partner with faculty members in designing, delivering, and evaluating course work. Students spend time in the homes of families, learning from these "master teachers'" about the daily demands of family life.

—University of Colorado, Boulder

Diverse communities

Early childhood and early childhood special education students at George Mason University have field experience in a wide array of community settings, ranging from homeless shelters to WIC offices. Opportunities to work with interpreters are also part of their preparation for working with children and families from culturally and linguistically diverse backgrounds.

—George Mason University

Key elements of Standard 2

2a: Knowing about and understanding family and community characteristics

2b: Supporting and empowering families and communities through respectful, reciprocal relationships

2c: Involving families and communities in their children's development and learning

Rubrics for these key elements, outlining distinct levels of candidate performance and program evidence, appear in Appendix B.

Standard 3. Observing, Documenting, and Assessing to Support Young Children and Families

Candidates know about and understand the goals, benefits, and uses of assessment. They know about and use systematic observations, documentation, and other effective assessment strategies in a responsible way, in partnership with families and other professionals, to positively influence children's development and learning.

Supporting explanation

Although definitions vary, in these standards the term "assessment" includes all methods through which early childhood professionals gain understanding of children's development and learning. Observation, documentation, and other forms of assessment are central to the practice of all early childhood professionals. Ongoing, systematic observations and other informal and formal assessments enable candidates to appreciate children's unique qualities, to develop appropriate goals, and to plan, implement, and evaluate effective curriculum. Although assessment may take many forms, early childhood candidates demonstrate its central role by embedding assessment-related activities in curriculum and in daily routines, so that assessment becomes a habitual part of professional life. Even as new professionals, they feel empowered by assessment rather than viewing assessment as a necessary evil imposed by others.

Well-prepared early childhood candidates recognize the central role that appropriate assessment plays in the design of effective programs and practices for young children. They can explain the central **goals, benefits, and uses of assessment.** In considering the goals of assessment, candidates articulate and apply the concept of "alignment"—good assessment is consistent with and connected to appropriate goals, curriculum, and teaching strategies for young children. At its best, assessment is a positive tool that supports children's development and learning, and that improves outcomes

for young children and families. Positive assessment identifies the strengths of families and children; through appropriate screening and referral, assessment may also result in identifying children who may benefit from special services. Candidates are able to explain such positive uses of assessment and exemplify them in their own work, while also showing awareness of the potentially negative uses of assessment in early childhood programs and policies.

Early childhood assessment includes **observation and documentation, plus other appropriate assessment strategies.** Effective teaching of young children begins with thoughtful, appreciative, systematic observation and documentation of each child's unique qualities, strengths, and needs. Observing young children in classrooms, homes, and communities helps candidates develop a broad sense of who children are—as individuals, as group members, as family members, as members of cultural and linguistic communities. Observation gives insight into how young children develop and how they respond to opportunities and obstacles in their lives. Because spontaneous play is such a powerful window on all aspects of children's development, well-prepared candidates create opportunities to observe children in playful situations as well as in more formal learning contexts. All behavior has meaning, and well-prepared candidates demonstrate skill in reading young children's behavior cues; the skill is especially important for infants and toddlers and for children whose verbal abilities are limited. Candidates demonstrate skills in conducting systematic observations, interpreting those observations, and reflecting on their significance.

With observation and documentation as their foundation, well-prepared candidates know about a wide range of assessment tools and approaches. More than reciting a list of assessment strategies, early childhood candidates can explain the connections between specific assessment approaches and specific educational and developmental goals. They can also identify the characteristics, strengths, and limitations of specific assessment tools and strategies, including the use of technologies such as videotape and electronic record keeping. New practitioners are not assessment specialists; however, they do understand essential distinctions and definitions

Inquiry

In our teacher education program we have created course work and experiences intended to develop teachers who see themselves as researchers and who have solid skills in applying the inquiry process to their work with children and families. In the first few semesters of the program we focus on what it means to engage in ongoing inquiry. We begin with honing students' *observation* skills—learning when and how to observe and how to document their observations. We support their development of a strong knowledge base about children, families, and schooling, which helps them form their *interpretative* lens. Finally, we guide them in developing *reflective* capacities to make meaning of their observations so they can apply their interpretations to their practice of curriculum planning, assessment, and accountability.

—Nancy Barbour,
Kent State University

Assessment and portfolio development

In a course I teach at the Harvard Graduate School of Education, students learn about documentation and assessment by focusing on science and literacy learning in children ages 3 through 8 years. Students review children's work samples and conversations for evidence of early science or literacy development.

Each student focuses intensively on one young child and constructs, presents, and submits a portfolio that traces the child's development of specific science or literacy concepts across the semester. Portfolios include
• *Background information* on the child, to give the reader a reasonable picture of what is known about the child's learning
• *Significant records* of the child's early science/literacy learning, collected over the semester
• *Description* of the context in which the documents were created and collected
• *Analysis* of what the documents reveal about the child's science learning
• *Analysis* of how instructional practice was, or might have been, influenced by what was revealed in the documents
• *Reflection* on how the process of documentation has or has not helped to enhance the student's understanding of children's learning and to improve instruction.

—Jacqueline Jones,
Educational Testing Service (ETS)

(e.g., *screening, diagnostic assessment, standardized testing, accountability assessment*) and are familiar with essential concepts of reliability and validity and other psychometric concepts. Their understanding helps them in selecting appropriate formal assessment measures, critiquing the limitations of inappropriate measures, and discussing assessment issues as part of interdisciplinary teams. Within the classroom or program setting, candidates demonstrate skills in using varied assessments that are appropriate to their goals and children's characteristics, with emphasis on curriculum-embedded, performance assessments.

Many young children with disabilities are included in early childhood programs, and early identification of children with developmental delays or disabilities is very important. All beginning professionals, therefore, need essential knowledge about how to collect relevant information, including appropriate uses of screening tools and play-based assessments, not only for their own planning but also to share with families and with other professionals. Well-prepared candidates are able to choose valid tools that are developmentally, culturally, and linguistically appropriate; use the tools correctly; adapt tools as needed, using assistive technology as a resource; make appropriate referrals; and interpret assessment results, with the goal of obtaining valid, useful information to inform practice and decision making.

Although assessment can be a positive tool for early childhood professionals, it has also been used in inappropriate and harmful ways. Well-prepared candidates understand and practice **responsible assessment.** Candidates understand that responsible assessment is ethically grounded and guided by sound professional standards. It is collaborative and open. Responsible assessment supports children, rather than being used to exclude them or deny them services. Candidates demonstrate understanding of appropriate, responsible assessment practices for culturally and linguistically diverse children and for children with developmental delays, disabilities, or other special characteristics. Finally, candidates demonstrate knowledge of legal and ethical issues, current educational concerns and controversies, and appropriate practices in the assessment of diverse young children.

Many aspects of effective assessment require collaboration with families and with other professionals. Such **assessment partnerships,** when undertaken with sensitivity and sound knowledge, contribute positively to understanding children's development and learning. Both family members and, as appropriate, members of interprofessional teams may be involved in assessing children's development, strengths, and needs. As new practitioners, candidates may have had limited opportunities to experience such partnerships, but they demonstrate essential knowledge and core skills in team building and in communicating with families and colleagues from other disciplines.

Key elements of Standard 3

3a: Understanding the goals, benefits, and uses of assessment

3b: Knowing about and using observation, documentation, and other appropriate assessment tools and approaches

3c: Understanding and practicing responsible assessment

3d: Knowing about assessment partnerships with families and other professionals

Rubrics for these key elements, outlining distinct levels of candidate performance and program evidence, appear in Appendix B.

Standard 4. Teaching and Learning

Candidates integrate their understanding of and relationships with children and families; their understanding of developmentally effective approaches to teaching and learning; and their knowledge of academic disciplines to design, implement, and evaluate experiences that promote positive development and learning for all young children.

• Sub-Standard 4a. Connecting with children and families

• Sub-Standard 4b. Using developmentally effective approaches

• Sub-Standard 4c. Understanding content knowledge in early education

• Sub-Standard 4d. Building meaningful curriculum

Standard 4 is complex, with four Sub-Standards, because teaching and learning with young children is a complex enterprise, and its details vary depending on children's ages, characteristics, and the settings within which teaching and learning occur. Well-prepared early childhood professionals construct curriculum and program content from multiple sources. As described below, the early teaching and learning experiences that will support all children's success must be grounded in four interrelated elements: (a) positive relationships and supportive interactions; (b) a broad repertoire of appropriate, effective teaching/learning approaches; (c) essential content knowledge and familiarity with significant resources in specific academic disciplines; and (d) skills in developing, implementing, and evaluating curriculum that integrates those elements to promote positive outcomes. Especially when planning curriculum and teaching strategies for young children with developmental delays or disabilities or are learning English, well-prepared candidates know about and have the skills to collaborate with professionals from other disciplines (e.g., special education, school psychology, speech and language).

The following subsections describe each of the four sub-standards of the Teaching and Learning standard in detail.

Sub-Standard 4a. Connecting with Children and Families

Candidates know, understand, and use positive relationships and supportive interactions as the foundation for their work with young children.

Supporting explanation

Throughout the years that children spend in educational settings, their successful learning is dependent not just on "instruction" but also on personal connections with important adults who support and facilitate their learning. It is through those connections that children develop not only academic skills but also positive learning dispositions and confidence in themselves as learners. Infants learn about the world through their relationships with their primary caregivers. Responsiveness in caregiving creates the conditions within which very young children can explore and learn about their world. Candidates who plan to work with children of any age must have skill in creating responsive relationships, although the nature of those relationships differs as children develop. The close attachments children develop with their teachers/caregivers, the expectations and beliefs that adults have about children's capacities, and the warmth and responsiveness of adult-child interactions are powerful influences on positive developmental and educational outcomes.

Early childhood candidates demonstrate that they understand the theories and research that support the importance of relationships and high-quality interactions in early education. In their practice, they display warm, nurturing interactions with individual children and their families, communicating genuine liking for and interest in young children's activities and characteristics.

Candidates demonstrate the essential dispositions and skills to develop positive, respectful relationships with children whose cultures and languages may differ from their own, as well as with children who may have developmental delays, disabilities, or other learning challenges. In making the transition from family to a group context, very young children need continuity between the caregiving practices of family members and those used by professionals in the early childhood setting. Their feelings of safety and confidence depend on that continuity. Candidates know the cultural practices and contexts of the young children they teach, and they adapt practices to be culturally sensitive. With older children, candidates continue to emphasize cultural sensitivity while also developing culturally relevant knowledge and skills in important academic domains.

Sub-Standard 4b. Using Developmentally Effective Approaches

Candidates know, understand, and use a wide array of effective approaches, strategies, and tools to positively influence young children's development and learning.

Supporting explanation

Early childhood professionals need appropriate, effective approaches to help young children learn and develop well. Candidates must ground their curriculum in a set of core approaches to teaching that are supported by research and are closely linked to the processes of early development and learning. In a sense, those approaches *are* the curriculum for infants and toddlers, although academic content can certainly be embedded in each of them. With older children, the relative weight and explicitness of subject matter or academic content become more evident in the curriculum, and yet the core approaches or strategies remain as a consistent framework.

Although this subsection describes many of those approaches, they are not merely a list from which early childhood professionals may pick at random. Well-prepared candidates' professional decisions about approaches to early childhood teaching and learning are based on understanding of children as individuals and (in most cases) as part of a group, and on alignment with important educational and developmental goals. A flexible, research-based "continuum of teaching strategies" is the best support for children's developmental and educational needs.

Well-prepared early childhood candidates understand and effectively use the following approaches, strategies, and tools to promote young children's development and learning:

Fostering oral language and communication. Early childhood candidates embed every aspect of the curriculum within the context of rich oral language and other communication strategies, using technology as needed to augment communication for children with disabilities. Both verbal and nonverbal communication create links with children from infancy onward, not only supporting close relationships but also creating the foundations for literacy and cognitive development and later academic competence.

Drawing from a continuum of teaching strategies. Well-prepared candidates display a broad range of interactive and instructional skills. They understand and use teaching approaches that span a continuum from child-initiated to adult-directed learning, and from free exploration to scaffolded support or teacher modeling. In selecting the approaches, candidates demonstrate that they are basing their selection on knowledge of individual children, on research evidence, and on understanding of appropriate, challenging teaching and learning goals.

Making the most of the environment and routines. Especially for the youngest children, the curriculum *is* the physical and social environment and in particular the daily routines of feeding, bathing, napping, and playtime. Candidates know the power of the environment to foster security and to support exploration, and they create physical environments and routines that offer predictability as well as opportunities for oral language development, social interaction, and investigations.

Candidates demonstrate understanding and skill in setting up all aspects of the indoor and outdoor environment to promote learning and development. Well-designed learning or activity centers can offer young children extensive opportunities to manipulate objects, build, paint, listen to stories or music, read, write, and challenge themselves. Candidates' work displays their skills in designing such centers and other features of the environment to support specific goals (including IEP and IFSP goals) and to expand children's learning. Well-prepared candidates also demonstrate skill in selecting and adapting bias-free, culturally relevant learning materials that support learning by all children, including those with developmental delays or disabilities. Daily, weekly, and longer-term schedules designed by candidates also provide evidence that candidates can apply their understanding of young children's need for balance, order, depth, variety, and challenge.

Capitalizing on incidental teaching. Because so much of young children's learning takes place informally and spontaneously, early childhood practitioners must be skilled at "incidental teaching," identifying and taking advantage of informal opportunities to build children's language, concept development, and skills. For those candidates preparing specifically to work with infants and toddlers, this will be the primary approach to teaching, but all candidates require skills in this area if they are to be effective. Depending on children's ages and program settings, candidates use diapering, meals, cleanup times, outdoor play, dressing, and other routines and transitions to support children's learning. Engaging conversations, thought-provoking questions, provision of materials, and spontaneous activities are all evident in candidates' repertoire of teaching skills.

A community of learners

We begin by asking candidates to study the development of a community of learners in their classroom. Our intention is to have them study relationships and how teachers facilitate relationships within the community. Candidates are asked to examine some type of relationship development (partners, small groups, or even whole groups) and document the process over time.

—*Nancy Barbour*,
Kent State University

Home away from home

Horrell Hill Elementary, a prekindergarten through fifth-grade public school, is a home away from home for Early Childhood MAT students. They spend several days each week during their fall semester learning the what, why, and how-to's of teaching language arts, mathematics, science, and social studies to young children—and Horrell Hill is their learning laboratory.

—*Nancy Freeman*,
University of South Carolina

Focusing on children's characteristics, needs, and interests. Another developmentally effective approach is to focus on children's individual characteristics, cultures, temperaments, and central developmental concerns, using families as important sources of insight. Again, such practices form the heart of teaching and learning for infants and toddlers, yet they are also effective approaches for children at the upper end of the early childhood period. And the focus on children's needs is also at the center of good practices for young children with disabilities, whose IEPs and IFSPs are based on individual and family goals. Well-prepared early childhood candidates keep the child as the center, while also paying close attention to important standards and learning outcomes, connecting new learning with children's prior knowledge and areas of individual fascination.

Linking children's language and culture to the early childhood program. Before they come to school, all children learn and develop in their own unique and highly diverse linguistic, social, and cultural context. When previous learning and development are nurtured in early education programs, the overall benefits of early education are enhanced. Recognizing and using the child's and family's primary language ensures that early childhood education adds to and does not subtract from previous experiences at home and in the community. In implementing effective approaches to teaching and learning, candidates demonstrate that they use linguistic and cultural diversity as resources, rather than seeing diversity as a deficit or problem.

Teaching through social interactions. Because so much of children's learning takes place in a social context, their peer group can be viewed as a teaching tool. When working with groups of children, candidates show competence in promoting positive social interactions and—depending on children's ages and social skills—engaging children in parallel or collaborative learning activities. Candidates understand that children who have limited social skills or who are rejected by others may have difficulty in other areas, and so candidates actively work to increase social competence in all children, treating this as an educational priority. Even as beginning teachers, they show a commitment to creating learning communities within early childhood classrooms, where children help and care for one another.

Creating support for play. All early childhood professionals must demonstrate competence in using play as a foundation for young children's learning from infancy through the primary grades. Although most children play spontaneously, well-prepared candidates can create and support environments that enrich and extend children's play, knowing when to intervene with questions, suggestions, and challenges. Especially for children with disabilities and developmental delays, candidates explicitly model and facilitate appropriate play and social interactions. Candidates create and support play experiences that reflect gender equity, respect for cultural diversity, and principles of nonviolence. Candidates demonstrate understanding of the value of play in itself, as a way for children to make sense of their experiences and to develop a wide range of skills.

Addressing children's challenging behaviors. "Classroom management" is the greatest difficulty reported by most novice practitioners. Well-prepared early childhood candidates demonstrate understanding of the multiple, underlying causes of children's challenging behaviors. Early childhood candidates demonstrate a varied repertoire of research-based guidance approaches to meet individual children's needs. Their work shows that they understand the importance of a supportive, interesting classroom environment and relationships as ways to prevent many challenging behaviors. In implementing guidance approaches, candidates aim to develop children's self-regulation and respect for others. Candidates also demonstrate knowledge and essential skills to meet the special needs of children whose behavioral difficulties are related to disabilities, family or community violence, or other stressful circumstances.

Supporting learning through technology. Rather than being merely an enrichment or add-on to the curriculum, technology has taken a central place in early childhood programs. Candidates demonstrate sound knowledge and skills in using technology as a teaching and learning tool. Appropriate technology, including computer software, digital or Web content, cameras, and other peripherals, can support and expand young children's learning, including (through assistive technology) the learning of many children with disabilities. Candidates display awareness of the benefits and potential risks of technology, as well as issues of economic and gender equity in distribution of technology resources. Candidates demonstrate knowledge about how to combine appropriate software with other teaching tools to integrate and reinforce learning.

Using integrative approaches to curriculum. Skills in developing integrated, thematic, or emergent curriculum are evident in the work of well-prepared early childhood candidates. Those skills go well beyond implementing prepackaged, superficial units of study about seasons and holidays. Depending on children's ages and developmental levels, an integrated "project approach" to teaching and learning frequently allows children to immerse themselves for extended periods in the study of a topic of high interest to an entire class or a small group. Candidates with strong subject-matter knowledge (as discussed in Sub-Standard 4c) can embed valuable content from mathematics, the arts, literacy, social studies, and other areas in such thematic studies.

Sub-Standard 4c. Understanding Content Knowledge in Early Education

Candidates understand the importance of each content area in young children's learning. They know the essential concepts, inquiry tools, and structure of content areas including academic subjects and can identify resources to deepen their understanding.

Supporting explanation

Good early childhood curriculum does not come out of a box or a teacher-proof manual. Early childhood professionals have an especially challenging task in developing effective curriculum. As suggested in Standard 1, well-prepared candidates ground their practice in a thorough, research-based understanding of young children's *development and learning processes*. In developing curriculum, they recognize that every child constructs knowledge in personally and culturally familiar ways. In addition, in order to

make curriculum powerful and accessible to all, well-prepared candidates develop curriculum that is free of biases related to ethnicity, religion, gender, or ability status—and, in fact, the curriculum actively counters such biases.

Content areas for early childhood

But these tasks are only part of the challenge. Guided by standards for early learning that are effective (NAEYC & NAECS/SDE 2002), the teacher of children from birth through age 8 must also be well versed in the essentials of many academic disciplines and content areas. And because children are encountering those content areas for the first time, early childhood professionals set the foundations for later understanding and success. Well-prepared candidates choose their approaches to the task depending on the ages and developmental levels of the children they teach. With the youngest children, early childhood candidates emphasize the key experiences that will support later academic skills and understandings—with great reliance on the core approaches and strategies described in Sub-Standard 4b and with great emphasis on oral language and the development of children's background knowledge. Working with somewhat older or more skilled children, candidates also identify those aspects of each subject area that are critical to children's later academic competence. With all children, early childhood professionals support later success by modeling engagement in challenging subject matter and by building children's faith in themselves as young learners—as young mathematicians, scientists, artists, readers, writers, historians, economists, and geographers (although children may not think of themselves in such categories).

Going beyond conveying isolated facts, then, well-prepared early childhood candidates possess the kind of content knowledge that focuses on the "big ideas," methods of investigation and expression, and organization of the major academic disciplines. Thus, the early childhood professional knows not only *what* is important in each content area but also *why* it is important—how it links with earlier and later understandings both within and across areas. The following sections outline some of this essential understanding in each major discipline.

Improving literacy content

The redesign of the preK–3 program to enhance its literacy content was influenced by external sources and feedback from cooperating teachers, student teaching supervisors, former student teachers, and alumni. Feedback on surveys from candidates completing selected semesters also guided the redesign. For example, it is clear from candidates' comments for several semesters running that they were not developing competencies adequate for feeling comfortable with literacy instruction. For those candidates, the seminar attached to their student teaching experiences targeted additional literacy instruction and support.

—James Madison University,
NCATE/NAEYC Program Report

Storybooks and math

The children were very interested in the [storybook's] illustrations and had many questions or comments about them. For instance, several children remembered that the story said Snow White was seven years old when she left the forest. They thought that the picture of her made her look 18 years old, and I agree. This was a small detail that several of the children remembered. I think they must have been comparing her age with theirs to remember her age.

—student teacher journal entry, University of Maryland,
Baltimore County, NCATE/NAEYC Program Report

However, early childhood educators cannot be experts in everything. Because of its central place in later academic competence, the domain of language and literacy requires in-depth research-based understanding and skill. Mathematics, too, is increasingly recognized as an essential foundation. Yet because early childhood professionals must be acquainted with such a breadth of content knowledge, additional resources are needed to supplement the basic knowledge of beginning practitioners. Items in the References and Resources section of this document, especially the professional association standards documents, offer greater depth and detail in all these content areas.

Common features in candidates' work across content areas. Well-prepared candidates demonstrate certain competencies that cut across content areas or academic disciplines. Certain "basics" are common features in candidates' work, whether they are developing curriculum in language and literacy, the arts, mathematics, physical activity and physical education, science, or social studies.

Well-prepared early childhood candidates understand the importance of each content area in children's development and learning. They demonstrate essential knowledge of the developmental foundations of children's interest in, and understanding of, each content area (i.e., how children's cognitive, language, physical, social, and emotional development influence their ability to understand and benefit from curriculum in each content area—as well as how that curriculum may support development in each domain). Candidates observe and describe the early roots of children's interest and capacities in each content area, and they know how early childhood programs can build on those interests. They demonstrate the essential knowledge and skills needed to provide appropriate environments that support learning in each content area for all children, beginning in infancy (through foundational developmental experiences) and extending through the primary grades—although the nature and depth of their knowledge and skills will vary depending on which sub-periods of early childhood their program emphasizes. Candidates demonstrate basic knowledge of the research base underlying each content area and they demonstrate basic knowledge of the core concepts and standards of professional organizations in each content area, relying on sound resources for that knowledge. Finally, candidates demonstrate that they can analyze and critique early childhood curriculum experiences in terms of the relationship of the experiences to the research base and to professional standards.

Language and literacy. Early language and literacy form the basis for much later learning, and well-prepared candidates possess extensive, research-based knowledge and skill in the area, regardless of the age group or setting in which they intend to practice.

Listening, speaking, reading, and writing are integrated elements. Verbal and nonverbal communication in its diverse forms, combined with competence as a reader and writer, are essential for children's later development. Even as infants and toddlers, children are building the foundations for literacy through early experiences.

Candidates—including those who are not currently teaching linguistically diverse young children—also demonstrate knowledge of second-language acquisition and of bilingualism. They know the home language environments of the children they teach and the possible effects on children when their classroom environment does not reflect the home language. Candidates know the sociopolitical contexts of major language groups and how those may affect children's motivation to learn English. Candidates understand the benefits of bilingualism and the special needs of young English language learners (ELLs), building on the home language systems that children already have developed and assisting them to add a second language to their repertoire. For young ELLs who are learning to read, candidates use, adapt, and assess research-based literacy activities and teaching methods that build on prior knowledge and support successful transitions for those learners.

Candidates are able to articulate priorities for high-quality, meaningful language and literacy experiences in early childhood, across a developmental continuum. Across the years from infancy through third grade, those experiences should help children to, for example:

• Explore their environments and develop the conceptual, experiential, and language foundations for learning to read and write

• Develop their ability to converse at length and in depth on a topic in various settings (one-on-one with adults and peers, in small groups, etc.)

• Develop vocabulary that reflects their growing knowledge of the world around them

• Use language, reading, and writing to strengthen their own cultural identity, as well as to participate in the shared identity of the school environment

• Associate reading and writing with pleasure and enjoyment, as well as with skill development

• Use a range of strategies to derive meaning from stories and texts

• Use language, reading, and writing for various purposes

• Use a variety of print and non-print resources

• Develop basic concepts of print and understanding of sounds, letters, and letter-sound relationships

The arts: Music, creative movement, dance, drama, and art. Even before children can speak, they move, gesture, and respond to color, sound, and rhythm. Their joy in the "hundred languages of children" shows the value of the arts in early childhood, both as important ends in themselves and as tools for success in other areas.

Candidates are able to articulate priorities for high-quality, meaningful arts experiences in early childhood, across a developmental continuum. Depending on children's ages and other characteristics, those experiences should help children to, for example:

• Interact musically with others

• Express and interpret understandings of their world through structured and informal musical play

• Sing, play, and create music

• Respond to expressive characteristics of music—rhythm, melody, form—through speaking, singing, moving, and playing simple instruments

• Use music to express emotions, conflicts, and needs

• Move expressively to music of various tempos, meters, modes, genres, and cultures to express what they feel and hear

• Understand and apply artistic media, techniques, and processes

• Make connections between visual arts and other disciplines

Mathematics. Strong mathematical foundations are associated with later academic competence, but international comparisons have found American mathematics education to be seriously deficient. Yet for curious young children, mathematics is a powerful, exciting tool to use in making sense of their world.

Mathematics instruction should be guided by the principles and standards developed by the National Council of Teachers of Mathematics (NCTM) and by the joint position statement of NAEYC and NCTM (2002). Early childhood candidates apply the principles that guide all mathematics instruction, as well as the specific NCTM standards for preK–grade 2. The standards are based on the belief that "students learn important mathematical skills and processes with *understanding*" (NCTM 2000, ix). According to NCTM, understanding develops through interaction with materials, peers, and supportive adults in settings where students have opportunities to construct their own relationships when they first meet a new topic.

As outlined by NCTM, well-prepared candidates understand and apply the following six principles, or "themes," of mathematics instruction:

• *Equity*: high expectations and strong support for all children

• *Curriculum*: more than a collection of activities: coherent, focused on important mathematics, and well integrated across grades and developmental levels

• *Teaching*: understanding what children already know and need to learn, and challenging and supporting them to learn it well

• *Learning*: children must learn with understanding, building new mathematical knowledge from experience and prior knowledge

• *Assessment*: should support the learning of important mathematics and give useful information to teachers and children

• *Technology*: is essential in teaching and learning mathematics; a tool to enhance learning

In addition to those principles, candidates understand which concepts and skills are developmentally appropriate for preK–grade 2 children in each of five content areas—operations, algebra, geometry, measurement, data analysis, and probability—as well as in the five process areas of problem solving, reasoning and proof, connections, communication, and representation. Early childhood candidates are able to link those two sets of standards together so that the process standards are used in teaching and learning mathematical content.

Physical activity and physical education. For young children, moving and exploring what their bodies can do are essential elements of early learning. All children, with and without disabilities, set themselves physical challenges and investigate the frontiers of their physical capacities. Candidates are able to articulate priorities for high-quality, meaningful physical activity and physical education experiences in early childhood, across a developmental continuum. Depending on children's ages and other characteristics, those experiences should help children to, for example:

• Have varied, repeated experiences with functional movement and manipulation

• Demonstrate progress toward mature forms of selected physical skills

• Try new movement activities and skills

• Use feedback to improve performance

• Experience and express pleasure from participation in physical activity

• Apply rules, procedures, and safe practices

• Gain competence to provide increased enjoyment in movement

In promoting children's physical development, candidates are aware of cultural differences and gender expectations. They know when to respect children's and families' preferences regarding dress for physical activity and level of participation, and when to make adaptations to help children meet physical goals, yet support culturally sensitive practices.

Science. Although their investigations may not be systematic and their ideas and questions may not be scientifically accurate, young children's intense curiosity and love of hands-on exploration give them much in common with more mature scientists. Early childhood offers unique opportunities to explore phenomena using skills of scientific inquiry, cultivate scientific dispositions, and build a foundation for understanding core scientific concepts.

Candidates are able to articulate priorities for high-quality, meaningful science experiences in early childhood, across a developmental continuum. Focused exploration of meaningful content (for example, the growth and development of a plant over time, or investigation of the properties of water at a water table) supports early scientific understanding. Depending on children's ages and other characteristics, those experiences should help children to, for example:

• Raise questions about objects and events around them

• Explore materials, objects, and events by acting upon them and noticing what happens

• Make careful observations of objects, organisms, and events using all their senses

• Describe, compare, sort, classify, and order in terms of observable characteristics and properties

• Use a variety of simple tools to extend their observations (e.g., hand lens, measuring tools, eye dropper)

• Engage in simple investigations including making predictions, gathering and interpreting data, recognizing simple patterns, and drawing conclusions

• Record observations, explanations, and ideas through multiple forms of representation

• Work collaboratively with others, share and discuss ideas, and listen to new perspectives

Social studies. The social studies area presents special challenges to early childhood education. Because core concepts may be abstract or distant in time or space, providing many hands-on experiences is difficult yet essential for children's interest and understanding. Candidates are able to articulate priorities for high-quality, meaningful social studies experiences in early childhood, across a developmental continuum. Depending on children's ages and other characteristics, those experiences should help children to, for example:

Geography

• Make and use maps to locate themselves in space

• Observe the physical characteristics of the places in which they live and identify landforms, bodies of water, climate, soils, natural vegetation, and animal life of that place

History

• Use the methods of the historian, identifying questions, locating and analyzing information, and reaching conclusions

• Record and discuss the changes that occur in their lives, recalling their immediate past

Economics

• Develop awareness of the difference between wants and needs (the concept of scarcity)

• Develop interest in the economic system, understanding the contributions of those who produce goods and services

Social relations/Civics

• Become a participating member of the group, giving up some individuality for the greater good

• Recognizing similarities among people of many cultures

• Respecting others, including those who differ in gender, ethnicity, ability, or ideas

• Learn the principles of democracy, working cooperatively with others, sharing, and voting as they solve problems

Sub-Standard 4d: Building Meaningful Curriculum

Candidates use their own knowledge and other resources to design, implement, and evaluate meaningful, challenging curriculum that promotes comprehensive developmental and learning outcomes for all young children.

Supporting explanation

In their work with young children, candidates demonstrate that they can draw upon all the preceding tools—relationships with young children and families; appropriate, effective approaches to early childhood teaching and learning; and meaningful content in the academic disciplines—to design, implement, and evaluate curriculum for young children. The complexity of the process requires candidates, as well as experienced teachers, to go beyond their own basic knowledge to identify and use high-quality resources, including books, standards documents, Web resources, and individuals who have specialized content expertise, in developing early childhood curriculum. Curriculum planning starts with clear, appropriate goals and desired outcomes for children. Although national or state standards or desired expectations may influence curriculum in positive ways, several larger goals are also important guides:

Security and self-regulation. Appropriate, effective curriculum creates a secure base from which young children can explore and tackle challenging problems. Well-implemented curriculum also helps children become better able to manage or regulate their expressions of emotion and, over time, to cope with frustration and manage impulses effectively, rather than creating high levels of frustration and anxiety.

Problem-solving and thinking skills. Candidates who have skills in developing and implementing meaningful, challenging curriculum will also support young children's ability—and motivation—to solve problems and think well.

Academic and social competence. Because good early childhood curriculum is aligned with young children's developmental and learning styles, it supports the growth of academic and social skills.

With these goals in mind, candidates develop curriculum to include both planned and spontaneous experiences that are developmentally appropriate, meaningful, and challenging for all young children, including those with developmental delays or disabilities; that address cultural and linguistic diversities; that lead to positive learning outcomes; and that—as children become older—develop positive dispositions toward learning within each content area.

Depending on children's ages and program settings, candidates demonstrate skill in building curriculum from relationships, daily interactions, and routines (the core elements of infant/toddler curriculum); in integrating academic disciplines with other content in an emergent, interdiscipli-

nary, or thematic curriculum; and (especially for older children) in providing focused learning opportunities within a specific content area.

Candidates demonstrate that they can implement plans in organized yet flexible ways, adapting the curriculum to meet the interests and needs of diverse children while proactively supporting their learning. They demonstrate essential skills in evaluating the curriculum in light of their own goals and of children's engagement in learning activities, and they modify curriculum in light of their own evaluation and feedback from supervisors.

Key elements of Standard 4

4a: Knowing, understanding, and using positive relationships and supportive interactions

4b: Knowing, understanding, and using effective approaches, strategies, and tools for early education

4c: Knowing and understanding the importance, central concepts, inquiry tools, and structures of content areas or academic disciplines

4d: Using own knowledge and other resources to design, implement, and evaluate meaningful, challenging curriculum to promote positive outcomes

Rubrics for these key elements, outlining distinct levels of candidate performance and program evidence, appear in Appendix B.

Standard 5. Becoming a Professional

Candidates identify and conduct themselves as members of the early childhood profession. They know and use ethical guidelines and other professional standards related to early childhood practice. They are continuous, collaborative learners who demonstrate knowledgeable, reflective, and critical perspectives on their work, making informed decisions that integrate knowledge from a variety of sources. They are informed advocates for sound educational practices and policies.

Supporting explanation

The early childhood field has a distinctive history, values, knowledge base, and mission. Early childhood professionals, including beginning teachers, have a strong **identification and**

involvement with the early childhood field, to better serve young children and their families. Well-prepared candidates understand the nature of a profession. They know about the many connections between the early childhood field and other related disciplines and professions with which they may collaborate while serving diverse young children and families. Candidates are also aware of the broader contexts and challenges within which early childhood professionals work and might work in the future.

Because young children are at such a critical point in their development and learning, and because they are vulnerable and cannot articulate their own rights and needs, early childhood professionals have compelling responsibilities to **know about and uphold ethical guidelines and other professional standards.** The profession's code of ethical conduct guides the practice of responsible early childhood educators. Well-prepared candidates are very familiar with the NAEYC Code of Ethical Conduct and are guided by its ideals and principles. This means honoring their responsibilities to uphold high standards of confidentiality, sensitivity, and respect for children, families, and colleagues. Candidates know how to use the Code to analyze and resolve professional ethical dilemmas and are able to give defensible justifications for their resolutions of those dilemmas. Well-prepared candidates also know and obey relevant laws such as those pertaining to child abuse, the rights of children with disabilities, and school attendance. Finally, candidates are familiar with relevant professional guidelines such as national, state, or local standards for content and child outcomes; position statements about, for example, early learning standards, linguistic and cultural diversity, early childhood mathematics, technology in early childhood, and prevention of child abuse; child care licensing requirements; and other professional standards affecting early childhood practice.

Continuous, collaborative learning to inform practice is a hallmark of a professional in any field. An attitude of inquiry is evident in well-prepared candidates' writing, discussion, and actions. Whether engaging in classroom-based research, investigating ways to improve their own practices, participating in conferences, or finding resources in libraries and Internet sites,

candidates demonstrate self-motivated, purposeful learning that directly influences the quality of their work with young children. Candidates—and professional preparation programs—view graduation or licensure not as the final demonstration of competence but as one milestone among many, including for-credit and not-for-credit experiences.

At its most powerful, learning is socially constructed, in interaction with others. Even as beginning teachers, early childhood candidates demonstrate involvement in collaborative learning communities with other candidates, higher education faculty, and experienced early childhood practitioners. By working together on common challenges, with lively exchanges of ideas, members of such communities benefit from one another's perspectives. Candidates also demonstrate understanding of and essential skills in interdisciplinary collaboration. Because many children with disabilities and other special needs are included in early childhood programs, every practitioner needs to understand the role of the other professionals who may be involved in young children's care and education (e.g., special educators, reading specialists, speech and hearing specialists, physical and occupational therapists, school psychologists). Candidates demonstrate that they have the essential communication skills and knowledge base to engage in interdisciplinary team meetings as informed partners and to fulfill their roles as part of IEP/ IFSP teams for children with developmental delays or disabilities.

As professionals prepared in four- and five-year higher education programs, early childhood candidates' decisions and advocacy efforts are grounded in multiple sources of knowledge and multiple perspectives. Even routine decisions about what materials to use for an activity, whether to intervene in a dispute between two children, how to organize nap time, what to say about curriculum in a newsletter, or what to tell families about new video games are informed by a professional context, research-based knowledge, and values. Well-prepared candidates' practice is influenced by **knowledgeable, reflective, and critical perspectives.** In their work with young children, candidates show that they make and justify decisions on the basis of their *knowledge* of the central issues, professional values and

Service-learning

Faculty find that service-learning contributes to candidates' growing professional knowledge base while developing dispositions related to justice and appreciation for diversity, which are prominent themes in our program's conceptual framework. Our faculty embraces this experiential pedagogy, which takes students out of the lecture hall and immerses them in the real world where young children are cared for and educated.

The power of these experiences can best be communicated in candidates' own words. Kathy was hopeful as she began the semester: "It feels nice to be needed. . . . Days like today remind me of how much I love children and am looking forward to making a difference in their lives." Wendy's final entry in her journal reflected the value of the service-learning project: "This experience reminded me that I am in the right place. . . . I am so excited to enter the teaching profession!"

—*Nancy Freeman*,
University of South Carolina

Impact of inquiry

For their final evaluations during the preschool student teaching semester, we ask candidates to identify a revelation they had about themselves. Many of them identify the inquiry projects as having the most impact on their practice:

"The inquiry presentation changed my way of looking at the child. . . . I focus on strengths."

"I was amazed at how children construct meaning and can learn on their own."

"I saw how different it is when you are the teacher; small changes make big differences in children's reactions."

—*Nancy Barbour*,
Kent State University

standards, and research findings in their field. They also show evidence of *reflective* approaches to their work, analyzing their own practices in a broader context, and using reflections to modify and improve their work with young children. Finally, well-prepared candidates display a *critical* stance, examining their own work, sources of professional knowledge, and the early childhood field with a questioning attitude. Their work demonstrates that they do not just accept a simplistic source of "truth"; instead, they recognize that while early childhood educators share the same core professional values, they do not agree on all of the field's central questions. Candidates demonstrate an understanding that through dialogue and attention to differences, early childhood professionals will continue to reach new levels of shared knowledge.

Finally, early childhood candidates demonstrate that they can engage in **informed advocacy for children and the profession.** They know about the central policy issues in the field, including professional compensation, financing of the early education system, and standards setting and assessment. They are aware of and engaged in examining ethical issues and societal concerns about program quality and provision of early childhood services and the implications of those issues for advocacy and policy change. Candidates have a basic understanding of how public policies are developed, and they demonstrate essential advocacy skills, including verbal and written communication and collaboration with others around common issues.

Key elements of Standard 5

5a: Identifying and involving oneself with the early childhood field

5b: Knowing about and upholding ethical standards and other professional guidelines

5c: Engaging in continuous, collaborative learning to inform practice

5d: Integrating knowledgeable, reflective, and critical perspectives on early education

5e: Engaging in informed advocacy for children and the profession

Rubrics for these key elements, outlining distinct levels of candidate performance and program evidence, appear in Appendix B.

References and Resources

Publications

[Numbers in brackets denote items pertinent to one or more of the five standards; "G" denotes items of *General* usefulness.]

Adams, M.J. 1994. *Beginning to read: Thinking and learning about print.* Cambridge, MA: Bradford Books. [4]

August, D., & K. Hakuta, eds. 1998. *Educating language-minority children.* Washington, DC: National Academy Press. [1,4]

Barnett, W.S., & S.S. Boocock. 1998. *Early care and education for children in poverty: Promises, programs, and long-term results.* Albany, NY: State University of New York Press. [G]

Barnett, W.S., J.W. Young, & L.J. Schweinhart. 1998. How preschool education influences long-term cognitive development and school success. In *Early care and education for children in poverty,* eds. W.S. Barnett & S.S. Boocock, 167–84. Albany, NY: State University of New York Press. [G]

Barrera, I. 1996. Thoughts on the assessment of young children whose sociocultural background is unfamiliar to the assessor. In *New visions for the developmental assessment of infants and young children,* eds. S.J. Meisels & E. Fenichel, 69–84. Washington, DC: ZERO TO THREE/ National Center for Infants, Toddlers, and Families. [3]

Beckman, P.J. 1996. *Strategies for working with families of young children with disabilities.* Baltimore, MD: Brookes. [2]

Bentzen, W.R. 1997. *Seeing young children: A guide to observing and recording behavior.* Albany, NY: Delmar. [1]

Bergen, D., R. Reid, & L. Torelli. 2001. *Educating and caring for very young children: The infant/toddler curriculum.* New York: Teachers College Press. [4]

Berk, L.E., & A. Winsler. 1995. *Scaffolding children's learning: Vygotsky and early childhood education.* Washington, DC: NAEYC. [1]

Bodrova, E., & D.J. Leong. 1996. *Tools of the mind: The Vygotskian approach to early childhood education.* Upper Saddle River, NJ: Prentice Hall. [4]

Bredekamp, S., & C. Copple, eds. 1997. *Developmentally appropriate practice in early childhood programs.* Rev. ed. Washington, DC: NAEYC. [G]

Bredekamp, S., & T. Rosegrant, series & vol. eds. 1992. *Reaching potentials. Vol.1: Appropriate curriculum and assessment for young children.* Washington, DC: NAEYC. [3,4]

Bredekamp, S., & T. Rosegrant, series & vol. eds. 1995. *Reaching potentials. Vol. 2: Transforming early childhood curriculum and assessment.* Washington, DC: NAEYC. [3,4]

Burns, M.S., P. Griffin, & C.E. Snow, eds. 1999. *Starting out right: A guide to promoting children's reading success.* Washington, DC: National Academy Press. [4]

Campbell, F.A., C.T. Ramey, E. Pungello, J. Sparling, & S. Miller-Johnson. 2002. Early childhood education: Young adult outcomes from the Abecedarian Project. *Applied Developmental Science* 6(1): 42–57.

Campbell, F.A., R. Harms, J.J. Sparling, & C.T. Ramey. 1998. Early childhood programs and success in school: The Abecedarian study. In *Early care and education for children in poverty,* eds. W.S. Barnett & S.S. Boocock, pp. 145–66. Albany, NY: State University of New York Press. [G]

Campbell, P.S., & C. Scott-Kassner, eds. 1995. *Music in childhood, from preschool through the early grades.* Belmont, CA: Wadsworth. [4]

Chafel, J., ed. 1997. *Families and early childhood education.* Advances in Early Education and Day Care, vol. 9. Stamford, CT: JAI Press. [2]

Chang, H.N., A. Muckelroy, & D. Pulido-Tobiassen. 1996. *Looking in, looking out: Redefining child care and early education in a diverse society.* San Francisco, CA: California Tomorrow. [G]

Chang, H.N., J.O. Edwards, C. Alvarado, D. Pulido-Tobiassen, & C.L. Morgan. 1999. *Transforming curriculum, empowering faculty: Deepening teachers' understanding of race, class, culture, and language.* San Francisco, CA: California Tomorrow. [G]

Child Mental Health Foundations and Agencies Network. 2000. *A good beginning: Sending America's children to school with the social and emotional competence they need to succeed.* Bethesda, MD: National Institute of Mental Health, Office of Communications and Public Liaison. [4]

Clements, D.H. 2001. Mathematics in the preschool. *Teaching Children Mathematics* 7: 270–75. [4]

Clements, D.H., & J. Sarama. 2000. Standards for preschoolers. *Teaching Children Mathematics* 7: 38–41. [4]

Clements, D.H., J. Sarama, & A.M. DiBiase, eds. In press. *Engaging young children in mathematics: Findings of the National 2000 Conference on Standards for Preschool and Kindergarten Mathematics Education.* Hillsdale, NJ: Erlbaum. [4]

Cohen, D.H., V. Stern, & N. Balaban. 1997. *Observing and recording the behavior of young children.* 4th ed. New York: Teachers College Press. [1]

Copley, J.V. 2000. *The young child and mathematics.* Washington, DC: NAEYC. [4]

Copley, J.V., ed. 1999. *Mathematics in the early years.* Reston, VA: National Council of Teachers of Mathematics; and Washington, DC: NAEYC. [4]

Darling-Hammond, L., J. Ancess, & B. Falk. 1993. *Authentic assessment in action: Studies of schools and students at work.* New York, NY: Teachers College Press. [3]

Darling-Hammond, L., L. Einbender, F. Frelow, & J. Ley-King. 1993. *Authentic assessment in practice: A collection of portfolios, performance tasks, exhibitions, and documentation.* New York: National Center for Restructuring Education, Schools, and Teaching (NCREST). [3]

Dunst, C.J., C.M. Trivette, & A.G. Deal. 1994. *Supporting and strengthening families: Methods, strategies, and practices.* Vol. 1. Cambridge, MA: Brookline Books. [2]

Edwards, P.A., H.M. Pleasants, & S.H. Franklin. 1999. *A path to follow: Learning to listen to parents.* Portsmouth, NH: Heinemann. [2]

Elkind, D. 1994. *A sympathetic understanding of the child: Birth to sixteen,* 3d ed. Boston: Allyn & Bacon.

Epstein, J.L., M.G. Sanders, & L.A. Clark. 1999. *Preparing educators for school-family-community partnerships: Results of a national survey of colleges and universities.* Baltimore, MD: Center for Research on the Education of Students Placed at Risk. [2]

Falk, B. 2000. *The heart of the matter: Using standards and assessment to learn.* Portsmouth, NH: Heinemann. [3]

Feeney, S., & N.K. Freeman. 1999. *Ethics and the early childhood educator: Using the NAEYC code.* Washington, DC: NAEYC. [5]

Feeney, S., N.K. Freeman, & E. Moravcik. 2000. *Teaching the NAEYC code of ethical conduct.* Washington, DC: NAEYC. [5]

Fillmore, L.W., & C.E. Snow. 2000. *What teachers need to know about language.* Washington, DC: Office of Educational Research and Improvement. [4]

Forman, G., & B. Fyfe. 1998. Negotiated learning through design, documentation, and discourse. In *The hundred languages of children: The Reggio Emilia approach—Advanced reflections,* 2d ed., eds. C. Edwards, L. Gandini, & G. Forman, 239–60. Greenwich, CT: Ablex. [4]

Gandini, L., & C.P. Edwards. 2001. *Bambini: The Italian approach to infant/toddler care.* New York: Teachers College Press. [4]

Gardner, H. 1993. *Frames of mind: The theory of multiple intelligences.* New York: Basic Books. [1]

Gregory, E., ed. 1997. *One child, many worlds: Early learning in multicultural communities.* New York: Teachers College Press. [2]

Guralnick, M.J., ed. 2001. *Early childhood inclusion: Focus on change.* Baltimore, MD: Brookes. [G]

Harbin, G.L., R.A. McWilliam, & J.J. Gallagher. 2000. Services for young children with disabilities and their families. In *Handbook of early childhood intervention,* 2d ed., eds. J.P. Shonkoff & S.J. Meisels, 387–415. New York: Cambridge University Press. [G]

Hart, B., & T.R. Risley. 1995. *Meaningful differences in everyday experience of young American children.* Baltimore, MD: Brookes. [4]

Heath, S.B. 1983. *Ways with words: Language, life, and work in communities and classrooms.* New York: Cambridge University Press. [4]

Helm, J.H., S. Beneke, & K. Steinheimer. 1998. *Windows on learning: Documenting young children's work.* New York: Teachers College Press. [3]

Heubert, J.P., & R.M. Hauser. 1999. *High stakes: Testing for tracking, promotion, and graduation.* Washington, DC: National Academy Press. [3]

Hodgkinson, H.L. 1992. *A demographic look at tomorrow.* Washington, DC: Institute for Educational Leadership. [G]

Hodgkinson, H.L. 2003. *Leaving too many children behind: A demographer's view on the neglect of America's youngest children.* Washington, DC: Institute for Educational Leadership. [G]

Johnson, J., & J.B. McCracken, eds. 1994. *The early childhood career lattice: Perspectives on professional development.* Washington, DC: NAEYC. [5]

Johnson, L.J., M.J. LaMontagne, P.M. Elgas, & A.M. Bauer. 1998. *Early childhood education: Blending theory, blending practice.* Baltimore, MD: Brookes. [G]

Kaiser, B., & J.S. Rasminsky. 1999. *Meeting the challenge: Effective strategies for challenging behaviors in early childhood environments.* Ottawa, Canada: Canadian Child Care Federation. [4]

Katz, L.G., & S.C. Chard. 2000. *Engaging children's minds: The project approach.* 2d ed. Greenwich, CT: Ablex. [4]

Kohn, A. 1999. *The schools our children deserve: Moving beyond traditional classrooms and "tougher standards."* Boston, MA: Houghton Mifflin. [5]

Ladson-Billings, G. 2001. *Crossing over to Canaan: The journey of new teachers in diverse classrooms.* San Francisco: Jossey-Bass. [5]

Lally, J.R. 1995. *Caring for infants and toddlers in groups: Developmentally appropriate practice.* Arlington, VA: ZERO TO THREE/National Center for Clinical Infant Programs. [4]

Lamb, M., ed. 1999. *Parenting and child development in "nontraditional" families.* Mahwah, NJ: Erlbaum. [2]

Lee, E., D. Menkart, & M. Okazawa-Rey, eds. 1998. *Beyond heroes and holidays: A practical guide to K–12 anti-racist, multicultural education and staff development.* Washington, DC: Network of Educators on the Americas. [4]

Losardo, A., & A. Notari-Syverson. 2001. *Alternative approaches to assessing young children.* Baltimore, MD: Brookes. [3]

Lynch, E.W., & M.J. Hanson. 1998. *Developing cross-cultural competence: A guide for working with children and their families.* 2d ed. Baltimore, MD: Brookes. [1,2]

McCabe, A. 1995. *Chameleon readers: Teaching children to appreciate all kinds of good stories.* Columbus, OH: McGraw-Hill Higher Education. [4]

McCarthy, J., J. Cruz, & N. Ratcliff. 1999. *Early childhood teacher education licensure patterns and curriculum guidelines: A state by state analysis.* Washington, DC: Council for Professional Recognition. [G]

McWilliam, P.J., P.J. Winton, & E.R. Crais. 1996. *Practical strategies for family-centered intervention.* San Diego, CA: Singular Publishing Group. [2]

Mussen, P., ed. 1997. *Handbook of child psychology.* 5th ed. New York: Wiley. [1]

NAEYC. 1996a. *Guidelines for preparation of early childhood professionals.* Washington, DC: Author. [G]

NAEYC. 1996b. *Technology and young children: Ages 3 through 8.* Position Statement. Washington, DC: Author. [G]

NAEYC. 1997. *Code of ethical conduct and statement of commitment.* Position Statement. Washington, DC: Author. [G]

NAEYC. 1997. *Licensing and public regulation of early childhood programs.* Position Statement. Washington, DC: Author. [5]

NAEYC. 1998. *Accreditation criteria and procedures of the National Academy of Early Childhood Programs.* Position Statement. Washington, DC: Author. [G]

NAEYC & National Association of Early Childhood Specialists in State Departments of Education (NAECS/SDE). 2002. *Early learning standards: Creating the conditions for success.* Joint Position Statement. Washington, DC: NAEYC. [G]

NAEYC & National Council of Teachers of Mathematics (NCTM). 2002. *Early childhood mathematics: Promoting good beginnings.* Joint Position Statement. Washington, DC: NAEYC. [4]

National Commission on Teaching and America's Future. 1996. *What matters most: Teaching for America's future.* New York: Author. [G]

National Council of Teachers of Mathematics (NCTM). 2000. *Principles and standards for school mathematics.* Reston, VA: Author. [4]

National Institute of Child Health and Human Development. 2000. *Report of the National Reading Panel. Teaching children to read: An evidence-based assessment of the scientific research literature on reading and its implications for reading instruction.* NIH Publication No. 00-4769. Washington, DC: U.S. Government Printing Office. [4]

National Institute on Early Childhood Development and Education, U.S. Department of Education. 2000. *New teachers for a new century: The future of early childhood professional preparation.* Jessup, MD: U.S. Department of Education, ED Publishing. [G]

National Research Council. 1998. *Preventing reading difficulties in young children,* eds. C.E. Snow, M.S. Burns, & P. Griffin. Committee on the Prevention of Reading Difficulties in Young Children, Commission on Behavioral and Social Sciences and Education. Washington, DC: National Academy Press. [4]

National Research Council. 1999. *How people learn: Brain, mind, experience, and school*, eds. J.D. Bransford, A.L. Brown, & R.R. Cocking. Committee on Developments in the Science of Learning, Commission on Behavioral and Social Sciences and Education. Washington, DC: National Academy Press. [G]

National Research Council. 2001a. *Adding it up: Helping children learn mathematics*, eds. J. Kilpatrick, J. Swafford, & B. Findell. Mathematics Learning Study Committee, Center for Education, Division of Behavioral and Social Sciences and Education. Washington, DC: National Academy Press. [4]

National Research Council. 2001b. *Eager to learn: Educating our preschoolers*, eds. B.T. Bowman, M.S. Donovan, & M.S. Burns. Committee on Early Childhood Pedagogy, Commission on Behavioral and Social Sciences and Education. Washington, DC: National Academy Press. [G]

National Research Council and Institute of Medicine. 2000. *From neurons to neighborhoods: The science of early childhood development*, eds. J.P. Shonkoff & D.A. Phillips. Board on Children, Youth, and Families, Commission on Behavioral and Social Sciences and Education. Washington, DC: National Academy Press. [G]

Neelly, L.P. 2001. Developmentally appropriate music practice: Children learn what they live. *Young Children* 56 (3): 32–43. [4]

Neuman, S.B., & D.K. Dickinson. 2001. *Handbook of early literacy research*. New York: Guilford. [4]

Neuman, S.B., C. Copple, & S. Bredekamp. 1999. *Learning to read and write: Developmentally appropriate practices for young children*. Washington, DC: NAEYC. [4]

New Standards/Speaking and Listening Committee. 2001. *Speaking and listening for preschool through third grade*. Washington, DC: National Center on Education and the Economy. [4]

Peisner-Feinberg, E.S., M.R. Burchinal, R.M. Clifford, M.L. Culkin, C. Howes, S.L. Kagan, N. Yazejian, P. Byler, J. Rustici, & J. Zelazo. 1999. *The children of the Cost, Quality, and Outcomes Study go to school*. Chapel Hill: University of North Carolina at Chapel Hill, Frank Porter Graham Child Development Center. [G]

Reynolds, A.J., J.A. Temple, D.L. Robertson, & E.A. Mann. 2001. Long-term effects of an early childhood intervention on educational achievement and juvenile arrest: A 15-year follow-up of low-income children in public schools. *Journal of the American Medical Association* 285 (18): 2339–46. [G]

Rosin, P., A.D. Whitehead, L.I. Tuchman, G.S. Jesien, A.L. Begun, & L. Irwin. 1996. *Partnerships in family-centered care: A guide to collaborative early intervention*. Baltimore, MD: Brookes. [2]

Sandall, S., M. McLean, & B. Smith. 2000. *DEC recommended practices in early intervention/early childhood special education*. Longmont, CO: Sopris West Educational Services. [G]

Seefeldt, C. 1995. Transforming curriculum in social studies. In *Reaching potentials. Vol. 2: Transforming early childhood curriculum and assessment*, eds. S. Bredekamp & T. Rosegrant, 145–66. Washington, DC: NAEYC. [4]

Seefeldt, C. 2001. *Social studies for the preschool/primary child*. 6th ed. Upper Saddle River, NJ: Prentice Hall/Merrill. [4]

Seefeldt, C., & A. Galper. 2000. *Active experiences for active children: Social studies*. Upper Saddle River, NJ: Prentice Hall/Merrill. [4]

Shartrand, A.M., H.B. Weiss, H.M. Kreider, & M.E. Lopez. 1997. *New skills for new schools*. Washington, DC: U.S. Department of Education. [2]

Shore, R. 1997. *Rethinking the brain: New insights into early development*. New York: Families and Work Institute. [G]

Sims, W.L. ed.; J. Cassidy, A. Freshwater, & C.D. Mack, assoc. eds. 1995. *Strategies for teaching: Prekindergarten music*. Reston, VA: National Association for Music Education (MENC). [4]

Snell, M.E., & R. Janney. 2000. *Teachers' guides to inclusive practices: Collaborative teaming*. Baltimore, MD: Brookes. [G]

Stauffer, S.L., & J. Davidson, eds. 1996. *Strategies for teaching: K-4 general music*. Reston, VA: National Association for Music Education (MENC). [4]

Tabors, P.O. 1997. *One child, two languages: A guide for preschool educators of children learning English as a second language*. Baltimore, MD: Brookes. [4]

Tabors, P.O. 1998. What early childhood educators need to know: Developing effective programs for linguistically and culturally diverse children and families. *Young Children* 53 (6): 20–26. [1,4]

Tabors, P.O., & C.E. Snow. 2001. Young bilingual children and early literacy development. In *Handbook of early literacy research*, eds. S.B. Neuman & D.K. Dickinson, 159–78. New York: Guilford. [4]

Teaching Children Mathematics. 2001. Focus issue: Mathematics and culture, 7 (6). [4]

Tertell, E.A., S.M. Klein, & J.L. Jewett, eds. 1998. *When teachers reflect: Journeys toward effective, inclusive practice*. Washington, DC: NAEYC. [5]

Turnbull, A.P., & H.R. Turnbull. 1997. *Families, professionals, and exceptionality: A special partnership*. 3d ed. Columbus, OH: Merrill. [2]

Van Scoter, J., E. Ellis, & J. Railsback. 2001. *Technology in early childhood education: Finding a balance*. Portland, OR: Northwest Regional Education Laboratory. [4]

Von Blackensee, L. 1999. *Technology tools for young learners*. Larchmont, NY: Eye on Education. [4]

Vygotsky, L.S. 1978. *Mind in society: The development of higher psychological processes*. Cambridge, MA: Harvard University Press. [1]

Whitebook, M., C. Howes, & D. Phillips. 1998. *Worthy work, unlivable wages: The National Child Care Staffing Study, 1988-97*. Washington, DC: National Center for the Early Childhood Work Force. [5]

Winton, P.J., J. McCollum, & C. Catlett, eds. 1997. *Reforming personnel preparation in early intervention: Issues, models, and practical strategies*. Baltimore, MD: Brookes. [G]

Wolery, M., & J.S. Wilbers, eds. 1994. *Including children with special needs in early childhood programs*. Washington, DC: NAEYC. [G]

Wozniak, R.H., & K.W. Fischer, eds. 1993. Development in context: Acting and thinking in specific environments, 3–44. Mahwah, NJ: Erlbaum. [1]

Yelland, N.J., ed. 2000. *Promoting meaningful learning: Innovations in educating early childhood professionals*. Washington, DC: NAEYC. [5]

Websites

American Associate Degree Early Childhood Educators, www.accessece.org

American Association of Colleges for Teacher Education, www.aacte.org

American Alliance for Health, Physical Education, Recreation, and Dance, www.aahperd.org

Center for the Improvement of Early Reading Achievement, www.ciera.org

CEO Forum on Education and Technology, Self-Assessment for Teacher Preparation, www.ceoforum.org

Children and Computers, www.childrenandcomputers.com

Council for Exceptional Children, www.cec.sped.org

Division for Early Childhood, www.dec-sped.org

ERIC Clearinghouse on Assessment and Evaluation, http://ericae.net

International Reading Association, www.reading.org

MENC: National Association for Music Education, www.menc.org

MuSICA: Music and Science Information Computer Archive, www.musica.uci.edu

National Association for Bilingual Education, www.nabe.org

National Association for Early Childhood Teacher Educators, www.naecte.org

National Association for the Education of Young Children, www.naeyc.org

National Center for Research on Evaluation, Standards, and Student Testing, http://cresst96.cse.ucla.edu

National Center on Education and the Economy, www.ncee.org

National Clearinghouse for English Language Acquisition and Language Instruction Educational Programs, www.ncela.gwu.edu

National Council of Teachers of Mathematics, www.nctm.org

National Early Childhood Technical Assistance Center, www.nectac.org

National Education Goals Panel, www.negp.gov

National Educational Technology Standards Projects, http://cnets.iste.org

National Geographic Society, National Standards for Geography, www.nationalgeographic.com/xpeditions/standards/

National Institute for Early Education Research, http://nieer.org/

Program for Infant/Toddler Caregivers, www.pitc.org

Technology & Young Children (NAEYC Technology & Young Children Interest Forum), http://techandyoungchildren.org/index.shtml

ZERO TO THREE, www.zerotothree.org

Appendix A

Comparison of INTASC principles with related sections of NAEYC Initial Licensure Standards

INTASC Principles

NAEYC Initial Licensure Standards	1. Subject Matter	2. Student Learning	3. Diverse Learners	4. Instructional Strategies	5. Learning Environment	6. Communication	7. Planning Instruction	8. Assessment	9. Reflection & Professional Development	10. Collaboration, Ethics, & Relationships
1. Promoting Child Development and Learning		X	X		X		X			
2. Building Family and Community Relationships			X				X			X
3. Observing, Documenting, and Assessing to Support Young Children and Families						X	X	X		
4. Teaching and Learning 4a. Connecting with children and families						X	X			X
4b. Using developmentally effective approaches	X	X	X	X	X	X	X			
4c. Understanding content knowledge in early education	X									
4d. Building meaningful curriculum	X	X		X	X		X			
5. Becoming a Professional									X	X

Appendix B

Rubrics, aligned with NAEYC's 2001 Initial Licensure Standards

Introduction

As part of the process of standards revision, NCATE requires all specialty organizations to construct rubrics that are linked to the new standards. This document contains such rubrics, aligned with NAEYC's standards for initial licensure 4- and 5-year programs. These rubrics were used by NAEYC in its Spring 2002 reviews of programs that chose to respond to the new standards. However, the rubrics will continue to be refined in light of feedback from programs and reviewers.

In reading the rubrics, please keep these considerations in mind:

• NCATE defines "**rubrics**" as "written and shared criteria for judging performance that indicate the qualities by which levels of performance can be differentiated, and that anchor judgments about the degree of success on a candidate assessment" (*NCATE Professional Standards* 2001, 56). Some use the term "**criteria**," but NAEYC is aligning its language with that of NCATE at the unit level.

• Please note that the language of the rubrics is intentionally drawn from the key elements and supporting explanations of the new NAEYC standards. The purpose is to align these components as closely as possible.

• The rubrics are intended to be used by programs and by NAEYC reviewers of early childhood Program Reports. Again, note that the rubrics are tied to key elements *within* each of the five standards. Reviewers will be making a global judgment about whether evidence shows that each standard is met *as a whole*—not element by element. Thus, reviewers will use the rubrics as guides to help them focus on the quality of evidence in each area, but they will not use them as a scoring system.

• The rubrics describe rather broad levels of performance as judged by evidence submitted by programs. Thus, these rubrics may serve as guides for programs in devising systems to collect and summarize evidence about candidate performance; however, programs will still need to develop their own, program-level rubrics by which they may judge, for example, candidates' portfolios or performance required for admission to student teaching.

• In constructing these rubrics, we tried to be as clear, concise, and concrete as possible. However, we also want to emphasize that there are multiple ways for faculty to interpret and apply the standards and rubrics as they develop programs.

• Although the standards and accompanying rubrics may be implemented flexibly, specific values are threaded throughout the materials that characterize NAEYC's vision of early childhood professionals: for example, knowledge of child development; the importance of family partnerships; respect for diversity of culture, ability, and economic means; a view of children and families as the center of multiple, interrelated systems; and the importance of relationships in all settings that serve young children.

• The term "**candidates' work**" frequently occurs in the rubrics. "**Work**" refers to many sources of evidence, including direct observations, examinations, simulations, ratings by supervisors, evaluations of portfolio material, and so on. Attention should be given to documenting candidates' *knowledge, skills, dispositions*, and *positive effects* on young children, although different standards and key elements place greater or lesser emphasis on certain dimensions.

• NAEYC uses the following terminology to describe levels of performance:

DOES NOT YET MEET EXPECTATIONS: Program evidence does not show that candidates' performance meets the expectations described for the standard or key element.

MEETS EXPECTATIONS: Program evidence shows that, in general, candidates' performance meets the expectations described for the standard or key element.

EXCEEDS EXPECTATIONS: Program evidence shows that, in general, candidates' performance exceeds the expectations described for the standard or key element.

Standard 1. Promoting Child Development and Learning

Candidates use their understanding of young children's characteristics and needs, and of multiple interacting influences on children's development and learning, to create environments that are healthy, respectful, supportive, and challenging for all children.

1a: Knowing and understanding young children's characteristics and needs

DOES NOT YET MEET EXPECTATIONS: Program evidence does not show that candidates are provided with adequate opportunities to gain essential understanding of young children's characteristics and needs. Candidates' work displays a limited knowledge base, insufficiently grounded in theory and research.

MEETS EXPECTATIONS: Program evidence shows that candidates are provided with multiple, developmental opportunities to gain essential understanding of young children's characteristics and needs. As a result, candidates' work reflects current, research-based knowledge in most respects; candidates are knowledgeable about development in all areas and can give examples of interrelationships among developmental areas.

EXCEEDS EXPECTATIONS: Program evidence shows that candidates are provided with extensive, developmental opportunities to gain in-depth understanding of young children's characteristics and needs. As a result, candidates' work shows a thorough grounding in theories and current research in all areas of child development and learning. Candidates' work shows that they understand interrelationships among developmental areas, as seen in their rich examples of these interrelationships. Candidates actively seek out new information about child development and learning using multiple sources, including technology.

1b: Knowing and understanding the multiple influences on development and learning

DOES NOT YET MEET EXPECTATIONS: Program evidence does not show that candidates are provided with adequate opportunities to gain essential understanding of the multiple influences on young children's development and

learning. As a result, candidates' work displays a limited knowledge base and may reflect a simplified view of influences on development. Candidates' work shows only a limited knowledge of early intervention.

MEETS EXPECTATIONS: Program evidence shows that candidates are provided with multiple, developmental opportunities to gain essential understanding of the multiple influences on young children's development and learning. As a result, candidates' work shows that they can describe the nature of these influences and understand that influences may interact in complex ways. Their work demonstrates familiarity with the most well known early intervention programs, and they can cite research about the influence of these programs on child outcomes.

EXCEEDS EXPECTATIONS: Program evidence shows that candidates are provided with extensive, developmental opportunities to gain in-depth understanding of the multiple influences on young children's development and learning. As a result, candidates' work shows that they not only know about the number and variety of these influences but they also have thorough knowledge of possible interactions among these influences and of relevant theory and research. Their understanding is demonstrated in their many research-based examples of how early intervention programs may influence outcomes for children.

1c: Using developmental knowledge to create healthy, respectful, supportive, and challenging learning environments

DOES NOT YET MEET EXPECTATIONS: Program evidence does not show that candidates are provided with adequate opportunities to apply child development knowledge in creating learning environments that are healthy, respectful, supportive, and challenging. As a result, candidates' work shows limited ability to describe the developmental research and principles that they are using as a basis for creating learning environments. There is insufficient evidence that the environments created by these candidates support children's health, respect their culture and individuality, promote positive development, and challenge children to gain new competencies.

MEETS EXPECTATIONS: Program evidence shows that candidates are provided with multiple, developmental opportunities to apply child development knowledge in creating learning environments that are healthy, respectful, supportive, and challenging. As a result of these experiences, candidates' work shows that they can describe the essentials of developmental research and the principles that they are using as a basis for creating effective learning environments. There is adequate evidence that the environments created by these candidates support children's health, respect their culture and individuality, promote positive development, and challenge children to gain new competencies.

EXCEEDS EXPECTATIONS: Program evidence shows that candidates are provided with extensive, developmental opportunities to apply child development knowledge in creating learning environments that are healthy, respectful, supportive, and challenging. As a result of these experiences, candidates' work shows their ability to describe, in-depth, the developmental research and principles that they are using as a basis for creating effective learning environments. Evidence is convincing that the environments created by candidates support children's health, respect their culture and individuality, promote positive development, and challenge children to gain new competencies.

Standard 2. Building Family and Community Relationships

Candidates know about, understand, and value the importance and complex characteristics of children's families and communities. They use this understanding to create respectful, reciprocal relationships that support and empower families, and to involve all families in their children's development and learning.

2a: Knowing about and understanding family and community characteristics

DOES NOT YET MEET EXPECTATIONS: Program evidence does not show that candidates are provided with adequate opportunities to gain essential understanding of family and community characteristics as they affect early childhood

practice. As a result, candidates' work shows limited or stereotyped knowledge of these characteristics.

MEETS EXPECTATIONS: Program evidence shows that candidates are provided with multiple, developmental opportunities to gain essential understanding of family and community characteristics as they affect early childhood practice. As a result, candidates' work shows general knowledge of family theory and research, and it shows that candidates can identify a variety of family and community factors as they impact young children's lives. Candidates demonstrate that they know the significant characteristics of the families and communities in which they are practicing.

EXCEEDS EXPECTATIONS: Program evidence shows that candidates are provided with extensive, developmental opportunities to gain in-depth understanding of family and community characteristics as they affect early childhood practice. As a result, candidates' work shows that they articulate and integrate family theory and research-based knowledge of multiple family and community factors that impact young children's lives. Candidates' descriptions of the characteristics of the families and communities in which they are practicing show in-depth understanding.

2b: Supporting and empowering families and communities through respectful, reciprocal relationships

DOES NOT YET MEET EXPECTATIONS: Program evidence does not show that candidates are provided with adequate opportunities to gain essential understanding of how respectful, reciprocal relationships can support and empower families. As a result, candidates' work shows limited knowledge of families' goals, language and culture, and individual characteristics; a limited repertoire of communication strategies; and limited knowledge of community resources to support families.

MEETS EXPECTATIONS: Program evidence shows that candidates are provided with multiple, developmental opportunities to gain essential understanding and skills in using respectful, reciprocal relationships to support and empower families. As a result, candidates' work shows that they can describe how to use knowledge of families' goals, language and culture, and individual characteristics to build these relationships. Candidates apply their knowledge in using varied family communication strategies including technology; in linking families with key community resources; and in accessing information about other resources as needed.

EXCEEDS EXPECTATIONS: Program evidence shows that candidates are provided with extensive, developmental opportunities to gain in-depth understanding and skills in using respectful, reciprocal relationships to support and empower families. As a result, candidates' work displays extensive knowledge of families' goals, language and culture, and individual characteristics as tools to build these relationships. Their work reflects skilled, varied family communication strategies including uses of technology. Evidence shows that candidates can link families with multiple community resources appropriate for specific purposes.

2c: Involving families and communities in their children's development and learning

DOES NOT YET MEET EXPECTATIONS: Program evidence does not show that candidates are provided with adequate opportunities to gain essential understanding and skills concerning family and community involvement. As a result, candidates' work shows limited knowledge of theory and research related to family and community involvement, and a limited repertoire of approaches to family and community involvement.

MEETS EXPECTATIONS: Program evidence shows that candidates are provided with multiple, developmental opportunities to gain essential understanding and skills concerning family and community involvement. As a result, candidates' work shows that they can articulate theory and research to support the concept that families are young children's primary teachers, and that family and community involvement are critical to successful early learning. Their knowledge is shown in their varied approaches to family and community involvement, and their modification of approaches when their first attempts are not successful.

EXCEEDS EXPECTATIONS: Program evidence shows that candidates are provided with exten-

sive, developmental opportunities to gain in-depth understanding and skills concerning family and community involvement. As a result, candidates' work shows that they articulate theory and research to support the concept that families are young children's primary teachers, and that family and community involvement are critical to successful early learning. Their knowledge is shown in their use of a wide range of approaches to family and community involvement, and their use of in-depth self-evaluation and modification of approaches when their first attempts are not successful.

Standard 3. Observing, Documenting, and Assessing to Support Young Children and Families

Candidates know about and understand the goals, benefits, and uses of assessment. They know about and use systematic observations, documentation, and other effective assessment strategies in a responsible way, in partnership with families and other professionals, to support children's development and learning.

3a: Understanding the goals, benefits, and uses of assessment

DOES NOT YET MEET EXPECTATIONS: Program evidence does not show that candidates are provided with adequate opportunities to gain in-depth understanding of the goals, benefits, and uses of assessment. As a result, candidates' work shows little evidence of knowledge of assessment's essential goals, positive uses, and potential risks.

MEETS EXPECTATIONS: Program evidence shows that candidates are provided with multiple, developmental opportunities to gain essential understanding of the goals, benefits, and uses of assessment. As a result, candidates' work shows knowledge of the important goals of early childhood assessment. Their work generally shows alignment between goals, curriculum, teaching strategies, and assessments. In their work, candidates explain how assessment may be used in positive ways, and they also explain how inappropriate assessment may harm children and families.

EXCEEDS EXPECTATIONS: Program evidence shows that candidates are provided with extensive, developmental opportunities to gain in-depth understanding of the goals, benefits, and uses of assessment. As a result, candidates' work shows in-depth knowledge, understanding, and articulate expression of the significance of assessment. Candidates' work shows knowledge of a wide range of assessment goals, and close alignment among goals, curriculum, teaching strategies, and assessments. In their work, candidates articulate and document positive uses of assessment in early childhood programs; and they articulate and document situations in which inappropriate assessment may harm children and families.

3b: Knowing about and using observation, documentation, and other appropriate assessment tools and approaches

DOES NOT YET MEET EXPECTATIONS: Program evidence does not show that candidates are provided with adequate opportunities to gain essential understanding and skills concerning appropriate assessment tools and approaches. As a result, candidates' work shows limited knowledge and competence in observation, documentation, and other assessment tools. Their work reflects a lack of essential knowledge of the most frequently used assessment tools and approaches, and they do not demonstrate essential skills in using assessments, interpreting assessment results, making referrals, and using assessment information to influence practice.

MEETS EXPECTATIONS: Program evidence shows that candidates are provided with multiple, developmental opportunities to gain essential understanding and skills concerning appropriate assessment tools and approaches. As a result of these opportunities, candidates' work shows research-based knowledge and basic competence in observation, documentation, and other assessment tools. Their work reflects essential knowledge of the characteristics, strengths, limitations, and appropriate uses of the most frequently used assessment tools and approaches, including approaches for children with disabilities and culturally and linguistically diverse children. Candidates demonstrate essential skills in using assessments, interpreting

assessment results, making referrals, and using assessment information to influence practice.

EXCEEDS EXPECTATIONS: Program evidence shows that candidates are provided with extensive, developmental opportunities to gain in-depth understanding and skills concerning appropriate assessment tools and approaches. As a result of these opportunities, candidates' work shows a high level of research-based knowledge and competence in observation, documentation, and multiple other assessment tools. Their work reflects in-depth knowledge of the characteristics, strengths, limitations, and appropriate uses of a wide range of assessment tools and approaches, including approaches for children with disabilities and culturally and linguistically diverse children. Candidates demonstrate a high level of skill in using assessments, interpreting assessment results, making referrals, and using assessment information to influence practice.

3c: Understanding and practicing responsible assessment

DOES NOT YET MEET EXPECTATIONS: Program evidence does not show that candidates are provided with adequate opportunities to gain essential understanding of responsible assessment. As a result, candidates' work shows insufficient knowledge of current educational, legal, and ethical issues with respect to assessment practices, and their practice shows limited application of principles of responsible assessment.

MEETS EXPECTATIONS: Program evidence shows that candidates are provided with multiple, developmental opportunities to gain essential understanding and skills concerning the concept of responsible assessment. As a result, candidates' work shows that they can identify current educational, legal, and ethical issues with respect to assessment practices. Candidates can provide examples of responsible as well as irresponsible assessment. In their practice, they apply responsible assessment practices when working with diverse children.

EXCEEDS EXPECTATIONS: Program evidence shows that candidates are provided with extensive, developmental opportunities to gain in-depth understanding and skills concerning the concept of responsible assessment. As a result, candidates' work shows that they are well versed in current educational, legal, and ethical issues with respect to assessment practices. Candidates can provide detailed multiple examples of responsible as well as irresponsible assessment. In their practice, they apply complex understandings of responsible assessment practices when working with diverse children.

3d: Knowing about assessment partnerships with families and other professionals

DOES NOT YET MEET EXPECTATIONS: Program evidence does not show that candidates are provided with adequate opportunities to gain essential understanding of assessment partnerships. As a result, candidates' work shows insufficient knowledge of the research and legal basis of these partnerships and shows limited skills in team building and communication with families and other professionals around assessment issues.

MEETS EXPECTATIONS: Program evidence shows that candidates are provided with multiple, developmental opportunities to gain essential understanding of assessment partnerships involving families and other professionals. As a result, candidates' work articulates the research and legal base that supports these partnerships. Candidates demonstrate core skills in team building and in communication with families and other professionals around assessment issues.

EXCEEDS EXPECTATIONS: Program evidence shows that candidates are provided with extensive, developmental opportunities to gain in-depth understanding of, and skills in, building assessment partnerships with families and other professionals. As a result, candidates' work articulates the research and legal basis for such partnerships and applies this knowledge in practice. Candidates demonstrate that they can contribute to partnerships with families and other professionals in designing, interpreting, communicating, and acting upon assessment information.

Standard 4. Teaching and Learning

Candidates integrate their understanding of and relationships with children and families; their understanding of developmentally effective approaches to teaching and learning; and their knowledge of academic disciplines, to design, implement, and evaluate experiences that promote positive development and learning for all children.

Sub-Standard 4a. Connecting with children and families

Candidates know, understand, and use positive relationships and supportive interactions as the foundation for their work with young children.

Sub-Standard 4b. Using developmentally effective approaches

Candidates know, understand, and use a wide array of appropriate, effective approaches and strategies to support young children's development and learning.

Sub-Standard 4c. Understanding content knowledge in early education

Candidates understand the importance of each content area in young children's learning. They know the essential concepts, inquiry tools, and structure of content areas including academic subjects and can identify resources to deepen their understanding.

Sub-Standard 4d. Building meaningful curriculum

Candidates use their own knowledge and other resources to design, implement, and evaluate meaningful, challenging curriculum that promotes comprehensive developmental and learning outcomes for all young children.

4a: Knowing, understanding, and using positive relationships and supportive interactions

DOES NOT YET MEET EXPECTATIONS: Program evidence does not show that candidates are provided with adequate opportunities to gain knowledge and skill in building positive relationships and supportive interactions. As a result, candidates' work shows minimal knowledge of theory and research underlying the early childhood field's focus on relationships and interactions. Their skills in relationship-building are evident to only a limited extent.

MEETS EXPECTATIONS: Program evidence shows that candidates are provided with multiple, developmental opportunities to gain knowledge and skill in building positive relationships and supportive interactions. As a result, candidates' work shows essential knowledge of theory and research underlying the early childhood field's focus on relationships and interactions. They know the importance of creating relationships with all children, as seen in their competent, beginning skills in relationship-building with diverse children and families.

EXCEEDS EXPECTATIONS: Program evidence shows that candidates are provided with extensive, developmental opportunities to gain knowledge and skill in building positive relationships and supportive interactions. As a result, candidates' work shows extensive understanding of the theories and research underlying the early childhood field's focus on relationships and interactions. This understanding is seen in candidates' sensitivity and skill in creating relationships with culturally and linguistically diverse children and families, varying approaches depending on children's ages and family and cultural practices.

4b: Knowing, understanding, and using appropriate, effective approaches and strategies for early education

DOES NOT YET MEET EXPECTATIONS: Program evidence does not show that candidates are provided with adequate opportunities to gain knowledge and skill in how to support development and learning through a wide range of approaches and strategies. As a result, candidates' work shows limited knowledge and skills, in at least some of the following areas: fostering oral language and communication; drawing from a continuum of teaching strategies; making the most of environments and routines; capitalizing on incidental teaching; focusing on children's

characteristics, needs, and interests; linking children's language and culture to the early childhood program; teaching through social interactions; creating support for play; addressing children's challenging behaviors; supporting learning through technology; and using integrative approaches to curriculum.

MEETS EXPECTATIONS: Program evidence shows that candidates are provided with multiple, developmental opportunities to gain knowledge and skill in how to support development and learning through a wide range of approaches and strategies. As a result, candidates' work demonstrates each of the following approaches and strategies with competence and with knowledge of the underlying theory and research: fostering oral language and communication; drawing from a continuum of teaching strategies; making the most of environments and routines; capitalizing on incidental teaching; focusing on children's characteristics, needs, and interests; linking children's language and culture to the early childhood program; teaching through social interactions; creating support for play; addressing children's challenging behaviors; supporting learning through technology; and using integrative approaches to curriculum.

EXCEEDS EXPECTATIONS: Program evidence shows that candidates are provided with extensive, developmental opportunities to gain knowledge and skill in how to support development and learning through a wide range of approaches and strategies. As a result, candidates' work demonstrates each of the following approaches and strategies with a high degree of competence and with in-depth knowledge of the underlying theory and research: fostering oral language and communication; drawing from a continuum of teaching strategies; making the most of environments and routines; capitalizing on incidental teaching; focusing on children's characteristics, needs, and interests; linking children's language and culture to the early childhood program; teaching through social interactions; creating support for play; addressing children's challenging behaviors; supporting learning through technology; and using integrative approaches to curriculum.

4c: Knowing and understanding the importance, central concepts, inquiry tools, and structures of content areas or academic disciplines

DOES NOT YET MEET EXPECTATIONS: Program evidence does not show that candidates are provided with adequate opportunities to gain essential knowledge and skill in each content area: language and literacy; the arts; mathematics; physical activity and physical education; science; and social studies, with special depth in the areas of language and literacy and mathematics. As a result, candidates' work shows that they lack knowledge of the theories and research underlying the early childhood field's focus on content, and that they have limited ability to articulate priorities and desired outcomes for high quality, meaningful experiences in each content area. Candidates have limited familiarity with authoritative resources to supplement their own content knowledge.

MEETS EXPECTATIONS: Program evidence shows that candidates are provided with multiple, developmental opportunities to gain essential knowledge and skill in each content area: language and literacy; the arts; mathematics; physical activity and physical education; science; and social studies, with special depth in the areas of language and literacy and mathematics. As a result, candidates' work shows knowledge of the theories and research underlying the early childhood field's focus on content, both in general and with respect to each content area, including academic subjects. Taking developmental and individual differences into account, candidates' work shows that they use this knowledge to articulate priorities for high quality, meaningful experiences in each content area, with desired outcomes for children that connect with professional standards and resources. Candidates are familiar with authoritative resources to supplement their own content knowledge.

EXCEEDS EXPECTATIONS: Program evidence shows that candidates are provided with extensive, developmental opportunities to gain in-depth knowledge and skill in each content area: language and literacy; the arts; mathematics; physical activity and physical education; science; and social studies, with special depth in the areas

of language and literacy and mathematics. As a result, candidates' work shows extensive understanding of the theories and research underlying the early childhood field's focus on content, both in general and with respect to each content area, including academic subjects. Taking developmental and individual differences into account, candidates' work shows that they use this knowledge to articulate priorities for high quality, meaningful experiences in each content area, with desired outcomes for children that connect with professional standards. Candidates readily access multiple, authoritative resources to supplement their own content knowledge.

4d: Using own knowledge and other resources to design, implement, and evaluate meaningful, challenging curriculum to promote positive outcomes

DOES NOT YET MEET EXPECTATIONS: Program evidence does not show that candidates are provided with adequate opportunities to gain essential skill in designing, implementing, and evaluating meaningful, challenging curriculum. As a result, candidates' work shows limited ability to integrate multiple areas of knowledge in curriculum design and limited success in promoting positive outcomes. Curriculum development takes insufficient account of children's developmental, individual, and cultural characteristics, and it makes insufficient use of evaluation. Candidates' curriculum development is inadequately informed by the use of high quality professional resources.

MEETS EXPECTATIONS: Program evidence shows that candidates are provided with multiple, developmental opportunities to gain essential skill in designing, implementing, and evaluating meaningful, challenging, curriculum. As a result, candidates' work shows ability to integrate multiple areas of knowledge in curriculum design, with successful focus on building security and self-regulation; problem-solving and thinking skills, and academic and social competence. Candidates' curriculum development takes into account children's developmental, individual, and cultural characteristics, and it makes use of reflective, ongoing evaluation. Candidates' curriculum development is characterized by use of high quality professional resources to supplement and inform their own understanding.

EXCEEDS EXPECTATIONS: Program evidence shows that candidates are provided with extensive, developmental opportunities to gain a high level of skill in designing, implementing, and evaluating meaningful, challenging, curriculum. As a result, candidates' work shows strong ability to integrate multiple areas of knowledge in curriculum design, with successful focus on building security and self-regulation; problem-solving and thinking skills, and academic and social competence. Candidates' curriculum development is notable for its complex attention to developmental, individual, and cultural characteristics, and for its use of highly reflective and continuous evaluation. Candidates' curriculum development is characterized by extensive use of high quality professional resources to supplement and inform their own understanding.

5. Becoming a Professional

Candidates identify and conduct themselves as members of the early childhood profession. They know and use ethical guidelines and other professional standards related to early childhood practice. They are continuous, collaborative learners who demonstrate knowledgeable, reflective, and critical perspectives on their work, making informed decisions that integrate knowledge from a variety of sources. They are informed advocates for sound educational practices and policies.

5a: Identifying and involving oneself with the early childhood field

DOES NOT YET MEET EXPECTATIONS: Program evidence does not show that candidates are provided with adequate opportunities to gain a beginning identification with and involvement in the early childhood field. As a result, candidates' work shows limited knowledge of the early childhood field as a distinctive profession, and there is little evidence that they have begun to involve themselves in the profession.

MEETS EXPECTATIONS: Program evidence shows that candidates are provided with multiple, developmental opportunities to gain a beginning identification with and involvement in the early childhood field. As a result, candidates' work shows an understanding of the early

childhood field as a distinctive profession and of the essentials of its history. In their work, candidates demonstrate understanding of their own emerging professional roles and the possibilities, opportunities, and challenges within the early childhood field. They show some evidence of active involvement in the profession.

EXCEEDS EXPECTATIONS: Program evidence shows that candidates are provided with extensive, developmental opportunities to gain a well-formed identification with and involvement in the early childhood field. As a result, candidates' work shows a clear sense of belonging to a distinctive profession with complex historical roots and links to other movements. In their work, candidates describe the multiple roles that early childhood professionals may assume and those they think will suit them best. They articulate well-developed perspectives on the challenges facing the profession. They are already involved in the profession in varied ways, as shown by membership in associations and other activities.

5b: Knowing about and upholding ethical standards and other professional guidelines

DOES NOT YET MEET EXPECTATIONS: Program evidence does not show that candidates are provided with adequate opportunities to learn about and practice upholding the field's ethical standards and other professional guidelines. As a result, candidates' work lacks essential knowledge of NAEYC's Code of Ethical Conduct and of other legal standards and professional guidelines.

MEETS EXPECTATIONS: Program evidence shows that candidates are provided with multiple, developmental opportunities to learn about and practice upholding the field's ethical standards and other professional guidelines. As a result, candidates' work shows essential knowledge of NAEYC's Code of Ethical Conduct, as seen in citations of examples of how the Code may be used to analyze and resolve ethical dilemmas. Candidates are familiar with relevant legal standards and other professional guidelines and can apply these in practice.

EXCEEDS EXPECTATIONS: Program evidence shows that candidates are provided with extensive, developmental opportunities to learn about and practice upholding the field's ethical standards and other professional guidelines. As a result, candidates' work shows in-depth knowledge of NAEYC's Code of Ethical Conduct, as seen in citations of multiple examples of how the Code may be used to analyze and resolve ethical dilemmas. Candidates also have detailed knowledge of, and ability to apply, legal standards and other relevant guidelines in multiple situations of early childhood practice.

5c: Engaging in continuous, collaborative learning to inform practice

DOES NOT YET MEET EXPECTATIONS: Program evidence does not show that candidates are provided with multiple, developmental opportunities to become continuous, collaborative learners. As a result, candidates' work lacks an orientation toward inquiry and self-motivation, and it shows only limited involvement and skill in collaborative learning, including collaboration across disciplines and in inclusive settings. Effects on candidates' practice and on children are absent.

MEETS EXPECTATIONS: Program evidence shows that candidates are provided with multiple, developmental opportunities to become continuous, collaborative learners. As a result, candidates' work shows evidence of an orientation toward inquiry and self-motivation, combined with involvement and beginning skills in collaborative learning, including collaboration across disciplines and in inclusive settings. Candidates' work shows positive effects of this learning orientation, in their practice and in effects on children.

EXCEEDS EXPECTATIONS: Program evidence shows that candidates are provided with extensive, developmental opportunities to become continuous, collaborative learners. As a result, candidates' work shows a strong orientation toward inquiry and self-motivation, combined with extensive involvement and skill in collaborative learning, including collaboration across disciplines and in inclusive settings. Candidates' work shows notable, positive effects of this learning orientation, in their practice and in effects on children.

5d: Integrating knowledgeable, reflective, and critical perspectives on early education

DOES NOT YET MEET EXPECTATIONS: Program evidence does not show that candidates are provided with multiple, developmental opportunities to construct and apply knowledgeable, reflective, and critical perspectives on their field. As a result, candidates' work lacks understanding of the field's central issues, standards, and research findings. Their reflection upon their practice shows limited insight and a limited level of critical thinking. Effects on candidates' practice and on children are absent.

MEETS EXPECTATIONS: Program evidence shows that candidates are provided with multiple, developmental opportunities to construct and apply knowledgeable, reflective, and critical perspectives on their field. As a result, candidates' work shows essential understanding of the field's central issues, standards, and research findings. In their work, candidates analyze and reflect upon their practice and demonstrate critical thinking about the issues in the field and an understanding of the value of dialogue in resolving differences. Candidates' work shows positive effects of these professional perspectives, in their practice and in effects on children.

EXCEEDS EXPECTATIONS: Program evidence shows that candidates are provided with extensive, developmental opportunities to construct and apply knowledgeable, reflective, and critical perspectives on their field. As a result, candidates' work shows in-depth, complex understanding of the field's central issues, standards, and research findings. In their work, candidates analyze and reflect upon their practice with notable insight and demonstrate a sophisticated level of critical reasoning about the issues in the field and an understanding of the value of dialogue in resolving differences. Candidates' work shows notable, positive effects of these professional perspectives, in their practice and in effects on children.

5e: Engaging in informed advocacy for children and the profession

DOES NOT YET MEET EXPECTATIONS: Program evidence does not show that candidates are provided with multiple, developmental opportunities to develop early childhood advocacy skills. As a result, candidates' work lacks essential knowledge of the central policy issues in the field, as seen in their limited ability to discuss ethical and societal issues in early education, and their limited ability to outline how public policies are developed at the state and federal levels. Evidence does not show that candidates possess beginning advocacy skills, including written and verbal communication and collaboration.

MEETS EXPECTATIONS: Program evidence shows that candidates are provided with multiple, developmental opportunities to develop early childhood advocacy skills. As a result, candidates' work shows essential knowledge of the central policy issues in the field, as seen in their discussions of ethical and societal issues in early education. In their work, candidates can

outline how public policies are developed at the state and federal levels. Candidates possess beginning advocacy skills, including written and verbal communication and collaboration.

EXCEEDS EXPECTATIONS: Program evidence shows that candidates are provided with extensive, developmental opportunities to develop early childhood advocacy skills. As a result, candidates' work shows in-depth knowledge of the central policy issues in the field, as reflected in their complex examination of ethical and societal issues in early education. In their work, candidates describe in detail how public policies are developed at the state and federal levels. Candidates possess strong advocacy skills, including written and verbal communication and collaboration.

Appendix C

Initial Licensure Standards Work Group

NAEYC gratefully acknowledges the expertise and commitment of the members of the Initial Licensure Standards Work Group:

Linda Hassan-Anderson, National Black Child Development Institute (NBCDI)–Atlanta Affiliate
Nancy Barbour, Kent State University
Josué Cruz Jr., University of South Florida
John Johnston, University of Memphis
Ann Marie Leonard, James Madison University

NAEYC Staff
Marilou Hyson, Associate Executive Director for Professional Development
Parker Anderson, Assistant Director for Professional Development

---

Institutional affiliations reflect those held by the members at the time the Work Group was convening.

Contents

Introduction 65

    Standards and leadership in early childhood education:
      The role of advanced professional preparation 65

    Essentials of high-quality advanced programs in professional education 65

    Early childhood advanced professional education:
      Special considerations from the field 66

    Gaining focus: Identifying areas of specialization in early childhood
      advanced professional programs 68

    NAEYC's process of standards revision for advanced programs 70

    NAEYC's revised standards: What is the same? 71

    And what has changed? 71

    How programs will document compliance with NAEYC's standards
      for advanced professional education 73

    Transition to NAEYC's new standards for advanced professional programs
      and documentation of performance 74

    The big picture in advanced professional education: Innovations and risks 74

Standards Summary 76

I. Core Standards 78

    Standard 1. Promoting Child Development and Learning 78

    Standard 2. Building Family and Community Relationships 79

    Standard 3. Observing, Documenting, and Assessing to Support
      Young Children and Families 80

    Standard 4. Teaching and Learning 81

    Standard 5. Growing as a Professional 83

II. Essential Professional Tools for All Candidates in Advanced Programs 84

    1. Cultural Competence 84

    2. Knowledge and Application of Ethical Principles 84

    3. Communication Skills 84

    4. Mastery of Relevant Theory and Research 85

    5. Skills in Identifying and Using Professional Resources 85

    6. Inquiry Skills and Knowledge of Research Methods 85

    7. Skills in Collaborating, Teaching, and Mentoring 86

    8. Advocacy Skills 86

    9. Leadership Skills 86

III. Additional Specialized Competencies 87

References and Resources 87

Appendix

    A: Alignment of NAEYC core standards for advanced programs and
      NBPTS Early Childhood/Generalist Standards 88

    B: Expectations for evidence, aligned with NAEYC's 2002 Advanced Standards 89

    C: Advanced Standards Work Group 91

NAEYC Standards for Early Childhood Professional Preparation

Advanced Programs

Approved by NAEYC Governing Board, July 2002

Approved by NCATE, October 2002

Introduction

Standards and leadership in early childhood education: The role of advanced professional preparation

The need for leadership in the early childhood field has never been greater. New research on the importance of early development and learning, and on the role of highly qualified teachers in promoting positive outcomes for children, makes it imperative to produce a new generation of professionals with outstanding preparation well beyond that provided in initial licensure programs. NAEYC and NCATE share a commitment to a continuum of professional development in which advanced master's and doctoral training play a critical role.

Like the field of education in general, the early childhood profession suffers from critical shortages at every level, from beginning practitioners through university faculty. Excellent programs at the advanced master's and doctoral levels are urgently needed to produce the accomplished teachers, administrators, state early childhood specialists, child and family advocates, professional development specialists, teacher educators, and researchers who will be the intellectual, programmatic, and public policy leaders of the future. Advanced study and advanced accomplishments are among the hallmarks of a profession. The urgency of the shortages in the early childhood field cannot obscure the need for high professional standards. Support must be pro-

vided so that current and future early childhood leaders have the opportunity to meet these standards.

Essentials of high-quality advanced programs in professional education

Graduate programs in all fields of professional education have come under scrutiny. In the context of reforms in teacher education, recommendations have been made for the improvement of graduate education. Greater depth, focus, and rigor are needed in the preparation of advanced master's and doctoral students. Advanced study requires greater relevance to candidates' professional roles. Recent publications describe a growing professional consensus about the desirable features of high-quality graduate programs in any field of professional education, including early childhood education (Blackwell & Diez 1998; Diez & Blackwell 2001). Those features include the following.

A common core

Even if they include varied specializations, all advanced programs need a consistent framework and common experiences that allow candidates to experience the program in a coherent way. Creating this coherence within a graduate program requires developing a shared conceptual framework and a common vocabulary and reference points—for example, theoretical perspectives on development, curriculum, and pedagogy. Vehicles for ensuring this common framework may include a set of core courses, a first-year or final-semester seminar, or other unifying experiences.

Depth and specialization

Beyond the common core, each candidate needs the opportunity to gain significant depth of theory, research, and professional competence in an area relevant to the candidate's current work and future goals. Later sections of this document elaborate on the importance of providing specialized focus in advanced programs.

A culture of participation in the graduate experience

High-quality advanced programs are communities of learning, sharing a commitment to improving teaching and learning and reaching out beyond the higher education institution to the larger community. Advanced program candidates, faculty, and others in the professional community are stakeholders who participate in program development and revision and critique existing practices in a collegial spirit.

Interactive learning processes with many opportunities for high-quality feedback and reflection

Studies of programs in professional education (Blackwell & Diez 1998; Glazer 1986) find that strong programs emphasize interactive teaching and learning, featuring critical dialogue, mentoring, individual instruction, and collaborative learning with faculty as well as peers. Course assignments, field supervision, and capstone experiences all promote the feedback and reflective stance needed for leadership in the education profession.

Immersion in one or more hands-on "learning situations"

Strong advanced programs also offer candidates intensive internships, field experiences, research opportunities, or other contexts in which to apply theoretical and research-based knowledge in a systematic, scholarly way and to develop advanced skills. Professional consensus and NCATE requirements call for every candi-

date in an advanced program to have such well-designed and professionally supervised experiences.

Capstone experiences to promote synthesis and reflection

Whatever the specialization or professional focus, advanced programs need some kind of well-designed and well-assessed capstone. Programs have successfully used experiences such as theses and dissertations, integrative examinations, portfolios, field projects, seminars with reflective papers, and many other approaches. At their best, these experiences become vehicles to support candidates' synthesis of and reflection upon their graduate education.

Early childhood advanced professional education: Special considerations from the field

The features just described are appropriate and relevant for *all* advanced master's and doctoral programs in professional education, including those that prepare early childhood candidates. But some special characteristics of the early childhood field are also important to consider when setting standards for and designing high-quality programs.

Early childhood as a strongly interdisciplinary, collaborative, and systems-oriented profession

Effective early childhood education and the promotion of positive development and learning in the early years call for a strongly interdisciplinary and systems-oriented approach. By its nature the early childhood field is, and historically has been, interdisciplinary. Effective early childhood professionals require deep and integrated knowledge of all aspects of development. Besides giving attention to content knowledge in academic disciplines, early intervention programs and other programs for young children draw on knowledge from other disciplines, including speech and language therapy, occupational therapy, special education, bilingual education, family dynamics, mental health, and multiple other approaches to the comprehensive well-being of young children and their families. Young children develop and learn not simply as individuals but as unique members of multiple interacting systems that include families, school or child care settings, communities, and cultures. An interdisciplinary, systems-oriented perspective is essential if professionals, especially at the advanced level, are to integrate multiple sources of knowledge into a coherent approach to their work. Finally, early childhood candidates prepared at the advanced level—whatever their specialization—must be ready to serve *all* children and *all* families as agents of change and as potential leaders who can address complex issues of access, diversity, and equity.

Depth of commitment to inclusion and diversity

Although all areas of professional education share this commitment, early childhood education has traditionally had a special concern with these issues. Much of the history of the field has been an effort to prevent later social, emotional, and academic difficulties through high-quality intervention, especially for those young children living in poverty or experiencing developmental challenges. Traditionally, but to a growing extent in recent years, equity and justice concerns, antibias approaches to early education, and cultural competence have influenced the early childhood field's position statements and standards. NAEYC's Governing Board has identified as its overarching priority the creation of a "high performing, inclusive organization" that draws from and attracts diverse perspectives and cultures to create excellence.

Diversity of early childhood professional settings and roles

Early childhood professionals work in a much greater variety of settings and professional roles than many other education professionals. Public school programs from state-funded preK to third grade, community child care programs, Head Start, resource-and-referral agencies, specialized infant/toddler programs, inclusive early childhood programs, state agencies, nonprofit organizations serving children and families, community colleges, university teacher education programs,

and many other settings are typical of the diversity of the early childhood world. Within those settings, professionals holding advanced degrees may be master teachers, program directors, trainers, faculty, early education specialists, advocates, agency administrators—or other professionals. A challenge for early childhood advanced programs is to acknowledge this diversity of settings and roles, preparing candidates for specialized and leadership positions while attending to the coherence and depth needed for high-quality advanced preparation. As will be seen later in this document, NAEYC's standards require programs to identify one or more areas of focus and to document how program candidates achieve depth while also gaining a broad understanding of the complexities of the early childhood field.

Diversity of pathways bringing candidates into advanced early childhood programs

Graduate students in early childhood programs enter these programs with especially diverse prior preparation and experience. Because of the diversity of the field itself, advanced program candidates may have relatively little in common as they begin their graduate work. Their work experiences may differ widely, and their undergraduate preparation may be equally varied. Although this diversity of prior experience has potential to enhance the learning community, early childhood advanced programs need to be especially vigilant to document that *all* candidates are competent in the areas addressed by NAEYC's Initial Licensure Standards. In cases in which prior study and experience have not provided a candidate with this competence, the graduate program must find other ways of building this base of knowledge, disposition, and skill *before* candidates embark on advanced study—for example, through noncredit professional seminars or directed readings. (Master's programs that lead to initial teacher certification/licensure for candidates who lack prior preparation in a closely related teacher education field are not considered "advanced" by NAEYC or NCATE, and such programs should be reviewed as "initial" programs.)

Continuous learning

I am still a work in progress. I continue to learn from my students as well as colleagues. I look forward to achieving more in the future, but for now it is a time to practice what I "preach."

—*Ginger Gregory*, NBCT®, first grade teacher

Advocacy dispositions

For most of our advanced master's students, developing a disposition for advocacy was as natural as falling off a log. As teachers and administrators in public schools, private schools, Head Start programs, child care centers, and preschools, they *live* these issues every day. In the graduate courses they acquire some of the tools to be effective advocates, share accurate information about the issues, and develop the confidence to speak out and act.

—*Edyth Wheeler*,
Towson University

Meeting multiple needs

In revising our program according to the new Advanced standards, we have created a program model that enables us to draw persons from multiple backgrounds. Candidates will complete a "stem" of core courses in advanced early childhood education, and then select a specialization: initial teacher certification, early intervention specialist, early childhood supervision, or early childhood curriculum specialist.

We also are introducing a bridge two-credit course, Seminar on Topics and Issues in Early Childhood, as a way to provide clusters of professional development seminars that address the needs of our varied constituencies.

—*Roberta Schomburg*,
Carlow College

Highly dynamic, developmental, and policy-relevant nature of the early childhood field

The field of early childhood development and education is receiving intensive attention from the academic and political communities. Perhaps more than at any time since the 1960s, research and public policies are directed at the early years. Rapid changes are occurring in the number of state-supported prekindergarten programs. Programs serving children living in poverty and children at developmental and educational risk are experiencing significant changes. Policies mandating higher qualifications for early childhood teachers are being implemented at the federal and state levels. State and federal agencies are developing new content and program standards. Controversies swirl around school readiness assessments and accountability.

For these reasons and more, early childhood graduate programs must be ready to prepare professionals for a dynamic and rapidly developing future. Whether leadership is exerted in a classroom role, at the program or agency level, or in two- or four-year institutions, advanced program candidates and advanced program faculty need a strong future orientation. While articulating the profession's traditions and core values, advanced program candidates must also be taught how to analyze trends, how to critically assess the field's emerging knowledge base, and how to use a variety of tools to find professional resources that will enable them to stay at the forefront of their field as lifelong learners. Finally, the nature of the early childhood field requires that all professionals, whatever their specific role, share a commitment to and skill in advocacy for young children, families, and their profession.

Gaining focus: Identifying areas of specialization in early childhood advanced professional programs

In moving toward greater focus and coherence—and therefore greater effectiveness—of advanced study in the early childhood field, NAEYC's Advanced Professional Preparation Standards ask each program to identify one or more areas of specialization or focus. NAEYC expects programs to interpret this requirement flexibly; it is *not* intended to prescribe a narrow set of courses or to limit programs' and candidates' innovation. Depending on the prior experience and future goals of the candidates they serve, programs may offer a relatively extensive common core of courses to introduce candidates to a variety of specializations, helping them identify a focus for the latter part of their study. Other programs may primarily serve candidates who enter with a clear area of focus consistent with the program's strengths—program administration, for example, or early literacy.

Although the program may set forth the general features, these specializations may be further refined and individualized as candidates develop their own professional goals and their plans to reach those goals. Programs with several possible options or areas of focus will frequently find candidates with different interests enrolled in the same courses; depth and focus can still be provided through differentiated assignments and other individualized experiences.

As described in NAEYC's Early Childhood Advanced Professional Preparation Program Report Outline (available at www.naeyc.org), programs may **select one or more of the following areas** of focus (with or without the names used here), or they may **modify these areas** to be consistent with their unique features, or they may **identify other areas** consistent with the intentions of this requirement:

Examples (not exhaustive) of areas of focus

Early childhood accomplished teacher

This focus provides in-depth advanced study for experienced teachers. Within this focus may be preparation for specialized teaching roles such as infant/toddler specialists, early literacy specialists, etc. In all cases candidates will have already successfully demonstrated competence in relation to NAEYC's Initial Licensure Standards—i.e., this focus is not for initial licensure. NAEYC's Early Childhood Accomplished Teacher specialization is intended to align with and support the Early Childhood/Generalist Standards of the National Board for Professional Teaching Standards (NBPTS). Appendix A displays a matrix showing this alignment. In its Program Report Outline, NAEYC asks programs to show how this focus

area links to the NBPTS early childhood expectations (National Board for Professional Teaching Standards 2001).

Early childhood administrator

This focus provides in-depth study for those seeking to become or enhance their credentials as early childhood administrators. These roles might include child care program director, state preK coordinator, Head Start coordinator, or other administrative positions within an early childhood education system. Although many administrators are not required to have advanced degrees, this program focus allows experienced teachers to add administrative depth and management specialization to their repertoire. The specialization assumes candidates already possess background and competence consistent with initial licensure in early childhood education. A primary focus in this specialization is to acquire additional specialized competencies—for example, in personnel management or budgeting—but with specific application to early childhood contexts. In addition, this focus reflects NAEYC's recognition of the value of advanced study for those in early childhood administrative roles.

Early childhood public policy and advocacy specialist

As seen in the description of essential professional tools later in this document, NAEYC believes that *all* early childhood professionals should have knowledge and skills in advocacy and that advanced programs should enhance all candidates' competence in this area. However, this program focus provides in-depth study and experience for those who have or aspire to professional careers in early childhood public policy and advocacy. Building on existing competence in the core areas described in NAEYC's Initial Licensure Standards, candidates gain understanding and skill in translating that competence into building coalitions and designing effective public policies or advocacy initiatives.

Early childhood teacher educator/researcher

This focus provides in-depth study for those whose professional roles emphasize the preparation of future early childhood practitioners in two- and four-year preparation programs as well as through community training, technical

Inquiry and research

As a result of undertaking the self-study process, we determined that our program needs a stronger focus on developing inquiry and research. For example, we found a particular shortcoming in the area of documenting literacy and numeracy abilities.

Candidates now begin gathering data about children's development and abilities in their very first courses. We are discovering that by having candidates conduct field research for each of the classes, we have a wealth of information that can lead to further inquiry.

—*Roberta Schomburg,*
Carlow College

Essential tools

For our advanced master's program, the essential professional tools are a welcome component of the new standards document. These tools are elements we have always tried to emphasize, and their explicit inclusion in the new Advanced Standards validates our efforts.

—*Edyth Wheeler,*
Towson University

Leadership

The focus on leadership in the revised Advanced Standards resonates with our faculty members and candidates. Particularly appealing are the various tracks to leadership. Rather than equate leadership with positions, such as program director, school principal, or early childhood supervisor, the standards present a broader view of leadership ... with dimensions related to teacher leaders and others who lead from where they are (typically in the classroom). We can't afford to lose seasoned teachers to administrative positions, so we use this opportunity to encourage candidates to talk about the role of nonpositional leadership as they develop skills in collaboration, conflict resolution, negotiation, mentoring, and coaching. We include dimensions of nonpositional leadership across the program. Under performance-based assessments, candidates are beginning to see the effects of their leadership in ways they did not previously recognize.

—*Roberta Schomburg,*
Carlow College

assistance, and CDA training. This specialization requires a focus both on content and on pedagogy, including adult learning principles and skills in working with diverse students or trainees. The specialization also emphasizes skills in generating new knowledge through research, most strongly at the doctoral level.

Other early childhood leadership roles

Once again, the examples above are simply examples. Programs may modify or rename those suggested, propose other areas of focus, or combine those outlined above in ways that fit programs' unique mission, strengths, and community needs.

NAEYC's process of standards revision for advanced programs

Before approving new Initial Licensure Standards in 2001, NAEYC spent two years revising its existing Guidelines (last approved in 1994) and creating new performance assessment and review procedures, which received the field's widespread support. As a result, its processes for seeking input and consensus on revision of the Advanced Standards could be more targeted and streamlined.

Feedback on the Advanced Standards from the early childhood professional community and other stakeholders was obtained through

• establishing an 11-member Advanced Standards Work Group of national leaders in early childhood graduate education and related fields

• seeking views on the 1994 Guidelines through announcements on the Web and in NAEYC's journal *Young Children* and through consultation with NAEYC's Professional Development Panel members

• posting drafts of the revision on NAEYC's Website, with an electronic feedback option

• sending drafts with invitations for feedback to numerous stakeholders in related groups and organizations

• holding a facilitated discussion of the revised, draft Advanced Standards at NAEYC's National Institute for Early Childhood Professional Development in June 2002.

NAEYC's Governing Board reviewed a final draft of the Advanced Professional Preparation Standards document and voted its approval of the substance of the document on July 29, 2002. NCATE's Specialty Area Studies Board approved the standards in October 2002.

NAEYC's revised standards: What is the same?

Although this standards document and its predecessor (see NAEYC 1996) may look very different, it is important to highlight the consistencies between these new standards and NAEYC's former Guidelines for advanced programs.

Like those former Guidelines and the Initial Licensure Standards approved in 2001, the standards for advanced programs described here continue to encompass the birth-through-8 age range. They also affirm and emphasize the diversity of professional settings in which early childhood professionals work. Likewise, the standards' core values remain, as articulated both in the "core principles" of the 1994 Guidelines and in the 2001 Initial Licensure Standards.

And what has changed?

Core standards identical for initial licensure and advanced programs

As described above, the standards for advanced programs in this document explicitly build on the 2001 Initial Licensure Standards. Indeed, the core standards in the two documents are themselves identical, just the degree of specialization and the nature and level of competence expected from the advanced candidate are different. Thus, administrators and faculty who are developing advanced graduate programs or are preparing for review of those programs need to be thoroughly familiar with the rationales (called "supporting explanations") for each of NAEYC's Initial Licensure Standards. Those explanations and the related references provide the foundation for the advanced program level.

Enhanced attention to high-priority areas (same as Initial)

As seen in the 2001 Initial Licensure Standards document, as compared with earlier versions NAEYC's Advanced Standards now give increased attention to a number of areas in the preparation of early childhood professionals: linguistic and cultural diversity; inclusion; subject matter or content knowledge in early childhood curriculum; community contexts for children's development and education; the complexities of early childhood assessment; use of a continuum of varied, effective teaching strategies; and attention to field experiences integrated throughout the standards. These emphases are equally relevant to advanced programs, although the way they are used will differ depending on the specialization, and the nature and level of competence expected will be higher.

"Essential professional tools" for all advanced program candidates, and additional competencies for some specializations

Two other features are also new in these Advanced Standards: a set of "essential professional tools" for all advanced program candidates (see below) and—where relevant—additional competencies that are essential for a particular specialization (such as skills in personnel management or business practices for the Early Childhood Administrator specialization or detailed knowledge of the legislative process for Early Childhood Public Policy and Advocacy Specialists).

Changes in terminology and format

This Advanced Professional Preparation Standards document includes a number of major changes in terminology and format. Many, but not all, of these are identical to changes in the Initial Licensure Standards as approved by NAEYC and NCATE in 2001.

Expectations for advanced program candidates are worded in more strongly "performance-based" language. What should competent early childhood professionals at the advanced level know and be able to do? In the former guidelines and the 2001 Initial Licensure Standards, NAEYC had already moved toward using performance language. The revisions in this document adopt and extend that language.

"Essential professional tools" for all candidates in advanced programs are identified. All advanced program candidates are expected to demonstrate mastery of a set of professional tools essential to effective leadership in early childhood education. In their Program Report, programs will document candidates' competence in using each of the essential professional tools as well as in the five core standards areas and—if relevant—mastery of additional specialized competencies.

Each core standard is followed by a "supporting explanation" focused on advanced preparation. In this document, NAEYC attempts to help readers understand the rationale behind each core standard as it applies to advanced program candidates. The Initial Licensure Standards also include extended discussions—there also called "supporting explanations"—of the knowledge base and professional values that support each Initial standard. Advanced programs should incorporate and build on that material; in this Advanced Standards document, the supporting explanations describe what is *added* to those Initial foundations for all advanced program candidates and for candidates specializing in various areas.

Supporting explanations for each core standard are followed by "key elements" of that standard. This document identifies the "key elements" of each core standard and of each standard's supporting explanation. The elements are presented as concise, bulleted points that identify the standard's critical components as represented in the standard itself. Again, because the Initial Licensure and Advanced core standards are the same, the Initial and Advanced key elements are also the same.

"Expectations for evidence" of candidates' competence are described for each component of advanced early childhood programs. These expectations describe the kinds of evidence

needed to make a convincing case that—within the advanced program's self-described area(s) of focus—candidates demonstrate appropriate mastery of the core standards, the essential professional tools, and any additional specialized competencies. The expectations are provided in Appendix B.

In its Initial Licensure Standards document, NAEYC developed rubrics detailing three levels of candidate performance on each key element: "Does Not Yet Meet Expectations," "Meets Expectations," and "Exceeds Expectations." The Advanced Standards take a different approach. Instead, programs need to provide for each of the core standards, for the essential professional tools, and for any additional specialized competencies convincing evidence of (1) "Opportunities," (2) "Assessments," and (3) "Outcomes," as described in that Expectations for Evidence document.

References and resources for advanced programs accompany the standards. The Initial Licensure Standards document includes key references to standards documents written by other professional groups, syntheses of relevant research, significant work on early childhood pedagogy, valuable Websites, and other resources intended to help programs find relevant information. This Advanced Standards document assumes that programs are using those Initial references as guides, then adds other references specific to graduate education in general and to early childhood specializations in particular.

Some notes on the terminology used in this document

"Candidates" refers to those who are preparing for professional positions serving young children and their families. In this Advanced Standards document, candidates are assumed to be building on prior professional preparation and preparing for *deepened* or *new* professional roles in early childhood education, through a master's or doctoral program.

Important: Programs preparing candidates who lack prior licensure in early childhood or a closely related field for their "initial" early childhood licensure, even if in a master's program, should not respond to NAEYC's Advanced Standards; rather, they should respond to NAEYC's Initial Licensure Standards.

"**Know**" refers to candidates' possession of key information; "**understand**" includes analysis and reflection; "**use**" refers to application in practice, always soundly based on professional knowledge.

"**All children**" means *all*: children with developmental delays or disabilities, children who are gifted and talented, children whose families are culturally and linguistically diverse, children from diverse socioeconomic groups, and other children with individual learning styles, strengths, and needs. Note that NAEYC uses the term *children*, rather than *students*, to reflect the focus on all aspects of development and learning and to remind ourselves that children have identities outside of their classroom roles.

The term "**field experiences**" includes observations, field work, practica, and student teaching or other "clinical" experiences such as home visiting.

The term "**culture**" includes ethnicity, racial identity, economic class, family structure, language, and religious and political beliefs, which profoundly influence each child's development and relationship to the world.

How programs will document compliance with NAEYC's standards for advanced professional education

A higher education institution that is applying for NCATE accreditation must submit documentation about its compliance with national standards for the institution overall and for all specialty programs in which it prepares education professionals. NAEYC is the NCATE specialty professional association (SPA) for early childhood programs. Thus, if an NCATE-affiliated institution has an early childhood professional preparation program, it must submit materials for review by NAEYC (unless the institution has a state partnership approved by NCATE and NAEYC allowing state-level review of the early childhood program).

Both at the institutional and the specialty program levels, the kinds of evidence that will be required under NCATE's new performance-based assessment system differ in substantial ways from the documentation that was previously required. The details of this process at the institutional level may be found on NCATE's Website (www.ncate.org). To align with but not duplicate that documentation, the specialty organizations (e.g., NAEYC, Council for Exceptional Children, National Council of Teachers of Mathematics) have drafted guidance for institutions concerning evidence required under the specialty organizations' standards. That information may be found on NCATE's Website at www.ncate.org/standard/interimsasbstand.pdf; see the attachment to that document, pp. 16–17.

In brief, however, the documentation required to show compliance with the early childhood education standards is similar at the initial licensure and advanced professional levels. Like NCATE, NAEYC expects institutions to provide documentation that includes:

• a description of the institutional and professional context within which the program operates

• an organized system by which the program tracks candidate performance across time, including positive effects on children

• a description of the kinds of evidence that the program collects to document candidate performance in relation to the standards, with emphasis on multiple assessments in authentic contexts such as field experiences

• summarized evidence of candidates' performance using these assessments, with samples of candidate work at varying levels of performance

• evidence that this information is used for continuous program improvement.

Further details about **what NAEYC requires advanced professional preparation programs to submit** may be found in NAEYC's Early Childhood Advanced Professional Preparation Program Report Outline, available online at www.naeyc.org.

Starting early

We include copies of the core standards and essential professional tools, along with a goals statement, with our acceptance letters to newly admitted students in our advanced master's program. The goals statement helps candidates plan their Area of Focus in order to meet their own professional and academic goals.

—Edyth Wheeler,
Towson University

Linking theory and application

While earning my master's degree I made lasting connections between the theory I had studied for National Board and the application of theory in developing my National Board portfolio. I wrestled with the big ideas of school change and standards. I was intrigued by the various philosophies of education. My love of learning and quest for answers brought me into the realm of higher education. My professor and advisor opened the doors for me to explore teaching as an adjunct professor. Teaching adults and working with colleagues is an exciting yet challenging experience. It gives me the chance to develop my own understanding. It furthers my education and ability to reflect and know myself. I have also served as chair of our school improvement committee for the past three years.

—Ginger Gregory, NBCT®,
first grade teacher

Transition to NAEYC's new standards for advanced professional programs and documentation of performance

The Advanced Professional Preparation Standards described in this document were approved by NAEYC's Governing Board in July 2002 and by NCATE in October 2002. Advanced graduate programs now may begin a transition to the new standards and performance assessment system. By Spring 2004, all institutions submitting Program Reports will be expected to respond to these 2002 standards; until then, programs may respond either to the former (1994) Advanced Guidelines or to the 2002 Advanced Standards in this document.

NCATE and the SPAs, including NAEYC, have also adopted a timeline for the transition to performance-based program review, with all NCATE institutions to have fully functioning assessment systems by 2006. The use of candidate performance evidence by NAEYC is also being phased in over time, as institutions develop their own capacity. Transition timelines for initial licensure and advanced program evidence review are available online at www.naeyc.org.

The big picture in advanced professional education: Innovations and risks

There are many differences between undergraduate/initial licensure preparation and the approaches to advanced study supported by the profession and in this document. Advanced early childhood programs are, by design, more specialized and more diverse than is initial licensure preparation, which focuses on one (or variations on one) professional role—a teacher in a classroom or other group program for children birth through age 8. Except in a few cases, advanced graduate programs in early childhood education are not linked to state licensure, and thus have latitude for more varied approaches to program design.

Thus, advanced programs in early childhood have a greater opportunity for innovation and creativity. The risk that goes along with this opportunity is that programs can become a smorgasbord of interesting-sounding courses without real coherence or depth and without preparing candidates for future professional leadership at either the master's or doctoral level.

NAEYC is eager to work with programs in trying to meet the challenges of advanced study for the early childhood field. We hope that the framework NAEYC adopted in its Advanced Professional Standards—their connection with the Initial Licensure Standards, their focus on candidates' performance, their encouragement of focus and specialization, their identification of essential professional tools for advanced program candidates, and their invitation to programs to add specialized competencies—will not restrict programs' innovation but rather will support it.

Standards Summary

I. CORE STANDARDS

The Advanced Professional Preparation core standards are identical to NAEYC's Initial Licensure core standards for early childhood programs; but at the advanced level, candidates demonstrate competence at a higher level and with greater depth and specialization. Candidates in advanced programs are also expected to hold an initial license in early childhood education or a closely related field.

Standard 1. Promoting Child Development and Learning

Candidates use their understanding of young children's characteristics and needs, and of multiple interacting influences on children's development and learning, to create environments that are healthy, respectful, supportive, and challenging for all children.

Standard 2. Building Family and Community Relationships

Candidates know about, understand, and value the importance and complex characteristics of children's families and communities. They use this understanding to create respectful, reciprocal relationships that support and empower families, and to involve all families in their children's development and learning.

Standard 3. Observing, Documenting, and Assessing to Support Young Children and Families

Candidates know about and understand the goals, benefits, and uses of assessment. They know about and use systematic observations, documentation, and other effective assessment strategies in a responsible way, in partnership with families and other professionals, to positively influence children's development and learning.

Standard 4. Teaching and Learning

Candidates integrate their understanding of and relationships with children and families; their understanding of developmentally effective approaches to teaching and learning; and their knowledge of academic disciplines to design, implement, and evaluate experiences that promote positive development and learning for all children.

Sub-Standard 4a. Connecting with children and families

Candidates know, understand, and use positive relationships and supportive interactions as the foundation for their work with young children.

Sub-Standard 4b. Using developmentally effective approaches

Candidates know, understand, and use a wide array of effective approaches, strategies, and tools to positively influence young children's development and learning.

Sub-Standard 4c. Understanding content knowledge in early education

Candidates understand the importance of each content area in young children's learning. They know the essential concepts, inquiry tools, and structure of content areas including academic subjects and can identify resources to deepen their understanding.

Sub-Standard 4d. Building meaningful curriculum

Candidates use their own knowledge and other resources to design, implement, and evaluate meaningful, challenging curriculum that promotes comprehensive developmental and learning outcomes for all young children.

Standard 5. Growing as a Professional

Candidates identify and conduct themselves as members of the early childhood profession. They know and use ethical guidelines and other professional standards related to early childhood practice. They are continuous, collaborative learners who demonstrate knowledgeable, reflective, and critical perspectives on their work, making informed decisions that integrate knowledge from a variety of sources. They are informed advocates for sound educational practices and policies.

II. Essential professional tools for all candidates in advanced programs

Candidates in advanced programs are also expected to demonstrate competence in using each of the following professional tools, as these tools apply to their areas of specialization and professional roles.

1. Cultural Competence

Advanced program candidates demonstrate a high level of competence in understanding and responding to diversity of culture, language, and ethnicity.

2. Knowledge and Application of Ethical Principles

Advanced program candidates demonstrate in-depth knowledge and thoughtful application of NAEYC's Code of Ethical Conduct and other guidelines relevant to their professional role.

3. Communication Skills

Advanced program candidates possess a high level of oral, written, and technological communication skills, with specialization for the specific professional role(s) emphasized in the program.

4. Mastery of Relevant Theory and Research

Advanced program candidates demonstrate in-depth, critical knowledge of the theory and research relevant to the professional role(s) and focus area(s) emphasized in the program.

5. Skills in Identifying and Using Professional Resources

Advanced program candidates demonstrate a high level of skill in identifying and using the human, material, and technological resources needed to perform their professional roles and to keep abreast of the field's changing knowledge base.

6. Inquiry Skills and Knowledge of Research Methods

Using systematic and professionally accepted approaches, Advanced program candidates demonstrate inquiry skills, showing their ability to investigate questions relevant to their practice and professional goals.

7. Skills in Collaborating, Teaching, and Mentoring

Advanced program candidates demonstrate the flexible, varied skills needed to work collaboratively and effectively with other adults in professional roles.

8. Advocacy Skills

Advanced program candidates demonstrate competence in articulating and advocating for sound professional practices and public policies for the positive development and learning of all young children.

9. Leadership Skills

Advanced program candidates reflect on and use their abilities and opportunities to think strategically, build consensus, create change, and influence better outcomes for children, families, and the profession.

III. Additional specialized competencies

Beyond the core standards and essential professional tools, programs may identify additional competencies essential to particular focus areas or specializations. Examples might be knowledge of the legislative process for candidates specializing in public policy and advocacy, or skills in personnel and fiscal management for candidates in an early childhood administration program. Programs with such additional competencies should identify them in clear performance language and include criteria by which the program assesses these competencies.

In their Program Report, programs should (if relevant) insert these additional competencies where noted, providing documentation of learning opportunities and candidate performance in the same way as requested for the core standards and essential professional tools.

I. Core Standards

The following core standards are identical to the Initial Licensure core standards. In its position statements and publications about the continuum of early childhood professional preparation, and in the core competencies outlined in many state early childhood career development systems, NAEYC affirms the value of having a common set of outcomes shared by all in the profession, whatever their preparation or professional role.

As described earlier in this document, however, advanced programs distinguish themselves from initial licensure programs in (1) the focus or specialization offered to candidates, (2) the essential professional tools that advanced program candidates must possess, (3) the additional specialized competencies needed for certain professional roles, and (4) the level of performance expected of candidates in advanced programs.

Standard 1. Promoting Child Development and Learning

Candidates use their understanding of young children's characteristics and needs, and of multiple interacting influences on children's development and learning, to create environments that are healthy, respectful, supportive, and challenging for all children.

Supporting explanation: All advanced program candidates

All candidates in advanced programs base their practice on a sound foundation of child development knowledge. Those foundation is first acquired in initial licensure programs (or the equivalent) and its characteristics are described in NAEYC's Initial Licensure Standards document. This knowledge and skills, and related dispositions, are then given greater depth, complexity, and applicability to professional contexts through graduate education. As in other standards domains, the ways in which this occurs, and the expectations for how candidates will demonstrate their competence, vary according to the specialization.

Early childhood accomplished teacher

Both NAEYC and the National Board for Professional Teaching Standards (NBPTS) see child development knowledge as the foundation of accomplished early childhood practice. Candidates who are classroom teachers have some of the most direct opportunities to use child development knowledge in their work with young children and families. The differences between initial and advanced program candidates lie in the extent of developmental knowledge, the specificity of research-based understanding, and in some cases, the decision to focus in greater depth on one or more aspects of early development and learning. For example, candidates in some programs (or in a specialization within a program) might demonstrate in-depth understanding and application of child development research on risk and resilience, on language development, or on developmental issues in children's use of technology.

Early childhood administrator

Administrators, too, promote young children's development and learning, but their competence is demonstrated in different ways. Depending on the specifics of their roles, well-prepared candidates in advanced programs may apply current knowledge in designing programs, supporting staff, or developing state-level requirements related to the application of child development concepts. They evaluate their own and others' programs and staff interactions in light of knowledge about child development and learning. Because agencies and programs are so embedded in communities, these candidates need to show awareness of and responsiveness to variations in beliefs about, and evidence of, children's development and behavioral norms as a function of community and cultural contexts.

Early childhood public policy and advocacy specialist

Candidates focused on public policy and advocacy demonstrate their child development knowledge and skills through developing or identifying public policies that support development and learning in ways consistent with research and professional practices. They also should be able to critique policies that fail to support development and learning, using research to back up their views. They show ability to advocate for growth-promoting environments for all young children.

Early childhood teacher educator/researcher

These candidates are the furthest from having direct impact on individual children's development and yet have great potential to affect these outcomes. Demonstrations of competence may include using effective methodologies to generate new knowledge about development and the conditions that promote it, as well as using effective teaching strategies to make current child development knowledge meaningful and powerful for future teachers or other community practitioners.

Key elements of Standard 1

1a: Knowing and understanding young children's characteristics and needs

1b: Knowing and understanding the multiple influences on development and learning

1c: Using developmental knowledge to create healthy, respectful, supportive, and challenging learning environments

Standard 2. Building Family and Community Relationships

Candidates know about, understand, and value the importance and complex characteristics of children's families and communities. They use this understanding to create respectful, reciprocal relationships that support and empower families and to involve all families in their children's development and learning.

Supporting explanation: All advanced program candidates

Again, research-based, in-depth knowledge is vital to all candidates in advanced programs. Family and community contexts must be well understood and valued by advanced program candidates, whatever their professional role. Gaining deeper insight into the concept of reciprocal relationships with families is essential for accomplished teachers but also for administrators, policy makers and advocates, researchers, and teacher educators. As in other standards domains, the ways in which this occurs, and the expectations for how candidates will demonstrate their competence, vary according to the specialization.

Early childhood accomplished teacher

Those working directly with young children use their advanced preparation to gain greater currency and skill in understanding family dynamics and relationships, increasing their skill in building relationships with all families, and using effective teaching strategies that build on family and community norms and values. Some candidates may identify specific aspects of family and community in which to obtain even greater insight—for example, working with families in specific cultures, gaining more extensive skills in supporting families of children with disabilities, or developing family-centered assessments. As emphasized in the NBPTS Early Childhood/Generalist Standards, partnerships and engagement with families are hallmarks of the accomplished practitioner.

Early childhood administrator

Administrators often have great responsibility for linking with young children's families, enrolling families in programs, helping staff work on challenging family situations, or creating new state initiatives for involving families of prekindergarten children. Competencies for candidates specializing in administration may include the ability to identify appropriate roles for administrators and teachers in various aspects of family interaction; skills in linking families with agencies or helping teachers do so; and skills in developing program- or agency-wide approaches to strengthening families' bonds with the program and enhancing families' ability to support their children's learning. Finally, administrators must show competence in helping staff or other colleagues become more effective in communicating with families and assessing families' strengths and needs as they relate to young children's development.

Early childhood public policy and advocacy specialist

Candidates focused on public policy and advocacy also require in-depth understanding of family and community characteristics, including state and national trends, demographics, and other information relevant to public policy and advocacy work. Rather than directly supporting, empowering, or involving families, these candidates show competence in creating or advocating for conditions that allow these outcomes to occur. Candidates understand local, state, and federal policies relevant to families of young children and show skills in working effectively at these various levels.

Early childhood teacher educator/researcher

Depending on the specific emphases within their programs, these candidates show skill in using sound methodologies to generate new knowledge about families of young children, or they may devise more effective ways to help future teachers and community practitioners understand, engage, and support families.

Key elements of Standard 2

2a: Knowing about and understanding family and community characteristics

2b: Supporting and empowering families and communities through respectful, reciprocal relationships

2c: Involving families and communities in their children's development and learning

Standard 3. Observing, Documenting, and Assessing to Support Young Children and Families

Candidates know about and understand the goals, benefits, and uses of assessment. They know about and use systematic observations, documentation, and other effective assessment strategies in a responsible way, in partnership with families and other professionals, to positively influence children's development and learning.

Supporting explanation: All advanced program candidates

Assessment issues are relevant and challenging for all candidates in advanced programs. Future early childhood leaders should be at the forefront of research, policy, and best practices in the assessment of young children and in program evaluation. Advanced program candidates build on the competencies described in NAEYC's Initial Licensure Standards document, gaining greater depth and specialization related to their current or intended professional role.

Early childhood accomplished teacher

These candidates have great opportunities to articulate and use in-depth knowledge and skills in early childhood assessment and to link assessment to curriculum planning in increasingly skillful ways. Beyond the Initial competencies, candidates must show enhanced skills in analyzing, understanding, and using a variety of sound assessment practices. For all candidates—but to a greater or lesser extent depending on their focus—expertise and interdisciplinary teamwork in assessing culturally and linguistically diverse children, and children with developmental delays, disabilities, or other special needs, are critical. Consistent with National Board standards, candidates also show competence in working with other professionals on assessment issues, and a high level of skill in engaging families in assessment. In addition, advanced program candidates show skills in articulating issues around assessment and advocating within and beyond their workplace for ethical, effective assessment policies and practices.

Early childhood administrator

Assessment decisions (for example, selection of tools, development of assessment guidelines, training of evaluators, interpretation to families) are often in the hands of early childhood administrators. They often are responsible for monitoring others' use and skill in observation, documentation, and other forms of assessment. In addition, administrators are responsible for program or agency evaluation either in response to accountability requirements or simply for continuous program improvement. Thus, learning opportunities and demonstrated competencies in all these areas are essential for the well-prepared administrator in an advanced program.

Early childhood public policy and advocacy specialist

Candidates focused on public policy and advocacy have many opportunities to demonstrate mastery of assessment-related knowledge and skills. While not involved in direct assessment, they must have research-based understanding of assessment issues and assessment policies at the local, state, and federal levels—whether in child care, Head Start, or public school contexts. Advanced programs prepare candidates to analyze the implications of public policies for appropriate child and program-level assessment and to advocate for policies and resources that support beneficial approaches to assessment.

Early childhood teacher educator/researcher

Major gaps exist in the development and validation of assessment tools and in the analysis of the effects of various assessment approaches in improving child and program outcomes. Such research areas may be the focus of advanced program candidates in this specialization. Those emphasizing teacher education have challenges, too, as many future teachers and community practitioners lack knowledge and skills in assessment. Advanced programs nurture and evaluate candidates' knowledge, skills, and professional dispositions related to the study and promotion of sound assessment practices.

Key elements of Standard 3

3a: Understanding the goals, benefits, and uses of assessment

3b: Knowing about and using observation, documentation, and other appropriate assessment tools and approaches

3c: Understanding and practicing responsible assessment

3d: Knowing about assessment partnerships with families and other professionals

Standard 4. Teaching and Learning

Candidates integrate their understanding of and relationships with children and families; their understanding of developmentally effective approaches to teaching and learning; and their knowledge of academic disciplines to design, implement, and evaluate experiences that promote positive development and learning for all young children.

Sub-Standard 4a. Connecting with children and families

Candidates know, understand, and use positive relationships and supportive interactions as the foundation for their work with young children.

Sub-Standard 4b. Using developmentally effective approaches

Candidates know, understand, and use a wide array of effective approaches, strategies, and tools to positively influence young children's development and learning.

Sub-Standard 4c. Understanding content knowledge in early education

Candidates understand the importance of each content area in young children's learning. They know the essential concepts, inquiry tools, and structure of content areas, including academic subjects, and can identify resources to deepen their understanding.

Sub-Standard 4d. Building meaningful curriculum

Candidates use their own knowledge and other resources to design, implement, and evaluate meaningful, challenging curriculum that promotes comprehensive developmental and learning outcomes for all young children.

Supporting explanation: All advanced program candidates

In the Initial Licensure Standards document, Standard 4 is the most complex, having four sub-standards, each with a detailed supporting explanation. It is important for advanced programs and all advanced program candidates to share that foundation of knowledge and skills. For example, because all advanced candidates should understand the critical role of language and literacy in early childhood development, that understanding should be evident in their work within each specialization. In addition, the Accomplished Teacher specialization pays detailed attention to all elements of this standard, as these elements—aligned with and complementing the NBPTS Early Childhood/Generalist Standards—are the bases of accomplished early childhood practice. Reading Standard 4, it is clear that other specializations make more flexible use of the competencies suggested in the standard, adapting them and selecting specific aspects for greater depth and focused attention.

Early childhood accomplished teacher

These candidates have the most direct opportunities to apply advanced knowledge and skills in the areas of "Teaching and Learning" in their daily work with young children. Programs should refer to and be guided by the Early Childhood/Generalist Standards of the National Board for Professional Teaching Standards (see pp. 147–158 of this volume, or visit http://new.nbpts.org/standards/complete/ec_gen_2ed.pdf) for detailed expectations in this and other areas of accomplished classroom practice. In most cases, advanced program candidates will identify one or more of the key elements (or even more specific aspects of those elements) in which to document genuine expertise. For example, some programs and candidates might place special emphasis on uses of technology in early childhood environments, especially for young children living in poverty or children whose language and literacy skills are problematic. Other candidates (or other program specializations) might focus on early childhood mathematics, developing in-depth knowledge and application of recent research on children's mathematical competence. Still others might organize their graduate study around issues in teacher-child or teacher-family relationships, using inquiry skills to develop action research projects.

Early childhood administrator

Effective administrators ensure that teaching and learning takes place at a high level of quality in their programs or agencies. Candidates in the Administrator specialization learn about and document their competence in taking current research and best practices in relationships, curriculum, and pedagogy and translating those into program-, state-, or agency-level actions. Candidates might develop resources for program staff, design criteria for programs applying for a new state prekindergarten initiative, research innovative approaches to physical space for an inclusive program—there are many possibilities.

Early childhood public policy and advocacy specialist

Candidates focused on policy and advocacy will demonstrate mastery of the "Teaching and Learning" domain by developing or identifying public policies that support high-quality teaching and learning in ways consistent with research and professional practices. As in the other advanced specializations, they may take one or more of the subtopics for in-depth study. They are able to critique policies that fail to support high-quality teaching and learning, using research to back up their views. They show an ability to advocate for classroom practices, curriculum, and relationship-building opportunities that support the learning and positive development of all young children.

Early childhood teacher educator/researcher

The "Teaching and Learning" standard offers rich opportunities for these candidates to gain and document their expertise. Every subtopic within this standard suggests multiple research questions that can be addressed through quantitative or qualitative methods. Candidates should identify significant research questions, critique current research, and design worthwhile studies. Those candidates who will be preparing future teachers in higher education or community programs learn and demonstrate research-based approaches to building others' skills in curriculum development and teaching strategies.

Key elements of Standard 4

4a: Knowing, understanding, and using positive relationships and supportive interactions

4b: Knowing, understanding, and using effective approaches, strategies, and tools for early education

4c: Knowing and understanding the importance, central concepts, inquiry tools, and structures of content areas or academic disciplines

4d: Using own knowledge and other resources to design, implement, and evaluate meaningful, challenging curriculum to promote positive outcomes

Standard 5. Growing as a Professional [1]

Candidates identify and conduct themselves as members of the early childhood profession. They know and use ethical guidelines and other professional standards related to early childhood practice. They are continuous, collaborative learners who demonstrate knowledgeable, reflective, and critical perspectives on their work, making informed decisions that integrate knowledge from a variety of sources. They are informed advocates for sound educational practices and policies.

Supporting explanation: All advanced program candidates

Candidates who have chosen to engage in graduate education have taken charge of their own professional development and have made a deep commitment to their profession. Their mastery of the essential professional tools for advanced program candidates, and their demonstration of specialized knowledge and skills, document their continuing professional development. As future leaders (and many present leaders), candidates in advanced programs should demonstrate in-depth knowledge of the early childhood profession. They build on the competencies outlined in NAEYC's Initial Licensure Standards document but now are more engaged in the work of the profession and committed to collaboration across multiple and often complex communities. Similarly, candidates show a high level of awareness and application of ethical standards, focusing on ethical issues typical of their current or future role.

Early childhood accomplished teacher

These candidates have chosen to move forward within teaching to gain greater depth, specialization, and sophistication in their practice. Well-prepared candidates demonstrate notable ability to reflect on their practice, to articulate the complex professional bases for their teaching decisions, and to use others—including colleagues from other disciplines—as resources to improve their practice. Engagement in National Board certification gives many candidates the most direct opportunity to demonstrate professional skill and disposition. Finally, candidates in this specialization show that they connect in productive ways with teachers and other professionals within and across disciplines, using learning communities for continuous growth and reflection.

Early childhood administrator

Every aspect of professionalism becomes a part of the advanced preparation of early childhood administrators. Programs offer opportunities for candidates to develop competence in helping agency staff or other personnel to gain professional dispositions and skills. Candidates show ability to identify and address ethical dilemmas common in program administration. They also nurture professional networks as administrators, learning with and from other professionals.

Early childhood public policy and advocacy specialist

Almost every aspect of public policy is relevant to the status of the early childhood profession. Specialization in this area strengthens candidates' ability to identify, research, and develop policies that support a well-compensated, stable early childhood work force and a well-financed system of early education. Candidates will demonstrate the ability to address other critical professional issues, both for early childhood educators and for the children and families they serve. Skill in building coalitions around core professional issues is essential.

Early childhood teacher educator/researcher

Teacher educators are key to the socialization of new professionals into the field. Advanced programs provide them with opportunities to help newer professionals learn about the scope, mission, and critical issues in the field. Candidates in this specialization should know and use effective, sound methodology to develop and conduct studies of the profession—whether of the effectiveness of various forms of preparation, of practitioners' understanding of ethical issues, or of other professional issues. To be effective, their work requires them to engage collaboratively with others both within and outside academia. And researcher candidates require

---

[1]While the text of Standard 5 is the same in both the Initial Licensure and this Advanced Standards documents, the title given to Standard 5 in the two documents differs. In the Initial document, the title is "Becoming a Professional"; for the Advanced document it was changed intentionally to highlight the further growth in this dimension expected from candidates in advanced programs.

special competence in understanding and using ethical guidelines for the protection of human subjects, especially when those research subjects are vulnerable young children.

Key elements of Standard 5

5a: Identifying and involving oneself with the early childhood field

5b: Knowing about and upholding ethical standards and other professional guidelines

5c: Engaging in continuous, collaborative learning to inform practice

5d: Integrating knowledgeable, reflective, and critical perspectives on early education

5e: Engaging in informed advocacy for children and the profession

II. Essential Professional Tools for All Candidates in Advanced Programs

Although advanced programs and candidates may differ according to their focus or specialization, certain professional tools or competencies are essential. At the advanced level, these tools are essential components of each specialization and of each of the five NAEYC standards: (1) Promoting Child Development and Learning; (2) Building Family and Community Relationships; (3) Observing, Documenting, and Assessing to Support Young Children and Families; (4) Teaching and Learning; and (5) Growing as a Professional.

As described in the Program Report Outline (see www.naeyc.org), advanced programs must provide evidence that their candidates have achieved competence in each of these areas:

1. Cultural Competence

Advanced program candidates demonstrate a high level of competence in understanding and responding to diversity of culture, language, and ethnicity.

Across all core standards and specializations, all candidates' work demonstrates application of knowledge about the cultural contexts for early childhood education. For example, if candidates

are becoming specialists in technology and early childhood, their competence is reflected in the criteria they use to select and evaluate software. Candidates focusing on administration address cultural issues in personnel practices, program design, family engagement strategies, and other areas. Whatever the focus, strong evidence should be present to document candidates' cultural competence.

2. Knowledge and Application of Ethical Principles

Advanced program candidates demonstrate in-depth knowledge and thoughtful application of NAEYC's Code of Ethical Conduct and other guidelines relevant to their professional role.

NAEYC's Initial Licensure Standards address ethical issues in Standard 5; however, advanced program candidates require even broader, more sophisticated understanding and use of ethical principles. The nature of the ethical dilemmas differs depending on the professional role. For example, Early Childhood Accomplished Teacher candidates can apply ethical guidelines when considering high-stakes assessments that potentially exclude children from services. Those specializing in public policy and advocacy can analyze ethical dimensions of legislation. More broadly, programs should provide advanced candidates with extensive opportunities to consider and apply ethical values of caring, justice, and equity.

3. Communication Skills

Advanced program candidates possess a high level of oral, written, and technological communication skills, with specialization for the specific professional role(s) emphasized in the program.

For example, if candidates are learning to design and conduct training for early childhood practitioners, their communication skills include effective presentation techniques. Those candidates emphasizing public policy and advocacy are skilled in writing concise policy briefs. Candidates preparing for research careers demonstrate competence in writing for peer-reviewed journals. All candidates demonstrate skills in the use of technology needed for their professional role, including use of word processing and editing tools, databases, search engines and other Internet tools, and presentation software.

4. Mastery of Relevant Theory and Research

Advanced program candidates demonstrate in-depth, critical knowledge of the theory and research relevant to the professional role(s) and focus area(s) emphasized in the program.

For example, candidates preparing for work in Head Start have in-depth understanding of current research about the effectiveness of Head Start and other interventions and about the gaps in current knowledge. All candidates, regardless of specialization, apply critical perspectives as they read and evaluate scholarly writing and research in their field.

5. Skills in Identifying and Using Professional Resources

Advanced program candidates demonstrate a high level of skill in identifying and using the human, material, and technological resources needed to perform their professional roles and to keep abreast of the field's changing knowledge base.

All candidates demonstrate familiarity and skill in using relevant library and Internet resources as well as community resources, networks of colleagues, and other sources of knowledge and professional growth.

6. Inquiry Skills and Knowledge of Research Methods

Using systematic and professionally accepted approaches, advanced program candidates demonstrate inquiry skills, showing their ability to investigate questions relevant to their practice and professional goals.

All candidates also demonstrate essential knowledge of the strengths and limitations of various research methods, with emphasis on the professional role(s) and focus area(s) emphasized

Action research

When I began my action research project I was very insecure about conducting research in my own classroom. I thought it wouldn't work because much of the research we read about is based on what I call the "ideal classroom"—middle-class children from two-parent homes, with parents very involved in their children's education. The children in my class are almost the complete opposite of that. In spite of my doubts I read the professional literature and found research, standards, and best practices related to my goals. So I made a plan.

When I implemented the new teaching strategies in my classroom I saw positive results, and my skepticism faded. Now I have documented evidence that children's attitudes can be affected positively by the teacher's attitude. Now I know that *how* I present activities is as important as the content. Now I know that I can make positive changes if I use new professional knowledge to make a plan, and I can gather evidence to document my actions and the actions of the children in my class.

—*master's student,* University of Memphis

Technology vs. people

Our goal—to integrate technology across the program—requires candidates to demonstrate their technological proficiency. One term I set up a group project to be carried out through chat rooms on the Website. After my elaborate planning, organization, and coordination of schedules, some older graduate students approached me. "Can't we just get together with our groups at a local coffee shop to work on our projects?"

Lesson learned: Technology is just a tool, not an end in itself. We have to be careful not to create barriers or substitute impersonal ways of connecting in a field where personal collaboration, nonverbal communication, and rich personal interactions are necessary competencies.

—*Roberta Schomburg,* Carlow College

Advocacy skills

Being an advocate is a continuing theme across required and elective courses in the early childhood graduate courses:

• In the course Growth and Development of Young Children, candidates write a position statement paper and present their issues in roundtables. They also develop their "elevator speech": You are in an elevator with a policy maker and need to get your point across quickly but effectively. Each class member distributes to the others a "talking points" handout on her/his topic to extend students' repertoires of issues.

• In the course Teacher as Researcher, students learn how to use research as an advocacy tool, to read and understand research findings, and to speak with authority on current issues.

• The culminating assignment in Learner Diversity and Inclusion is a "plan for commitment and action."

• The course Assessment, Observation, and Evaluation has students developing positions and action on issues of high-stakes testing as well as appropriate alternatives. Exploring position statements on this topic from several professional organizations strengthens students' own positions and their commitment to act as advocates.

• Administration, Supervision, and Leadership requires active involvement in the field and the development of a targeted advocacy plan. Many students use this opportunity to build on their position statement paper from the Growth and Development course. Students in this class have made visits to their representatives on Capitol Hill and at the state capital, attended hearings, and written letters and sent e-mails on vital issues. They exchange Websites, share stories, and explain issues to one another.

—*Edyth Wheeler,*
Towson University

in the program. Some candidates (all doctoral candidates) demonstrate skills in conducting research and in presenting research findings to professional audiences.

7. Skills in Collaborating, Teaching, and Mentoring

Advanced program candidates demonstrate the flexible, varied skills needed to work collaboratively and effectively with other adults in professional roles.

The specifics depend on the professional role(s) and focus area(s) emphasized in the program. In some cases the skills emphasized are supervisory, as for administrators; in other cases they are directly related to adult learning and pedagogy. In all cases, given the importance of collaboration in contemporary professional work, collaborative skills are essential, including collaboration across disciplines and roles.

8. Advocacy Skills

Advanced program candidates demonstrate competence in articulating and advocating for sound professional practices and public policies for the positive development and learning of all young children.

Whatever their specialization, all candidates can identify and analyze public policy issues, build collaborations or effective coalitions, and communicate early childhood issues to a wide range of stakeholders and decision makers. All candidates of advanced programs are knowledgeable about evidence-based approaches to promoting early learning, development, and family strengths, to advocate for appropriate care and education for young children and their families.

9. Leadership Skills

Advanced program candidates reflect on and use their abilities and opportunities to think strategically, build consensus, create change, and influence better outcomes for children, families, and the profession.

Leadership does not automatically flow from an advanced degree, but advanced programs create opportunities for all candidates to assess and strengthen their unique leadership potential. Master teachers, program directors, state prekindergarten specialists, Head Start administrators, teacher educators, and other professionals carry the potential to exert positive leadership as an individual and in concert with others. Analysis of the meaning and development of leadership should be part of all candidates' programs, and ongoing assessment of leadership growth, though difficult, also needs to be integrated into the program.

III. Additional Specialized Competencies

Beyond the core standards and essential professional tools, programs may identify additional competencies essential to particular focus areas or specializations. Examples might be knowledge of the legislative process for candidates specializing in public policy and advocacy, or skills in personnel and fiscal management for candidates in an early childhood administration program. Programs with such additional competencies should identify them in clear performance language and include criteria by which the program assesses these competencies.

In their Program Report, programs should (if relevant) insert these additional competencies where noted, providing documentation of learning opportunities and candidate performance in the same way as requested for the core standards and essential professional tools.

References and Resources

The following resources supplement those in NAEYC's Initial Licensure Standards document, emphasizing early childhood leadership and specializations in areas such as accomplished early childhood teaching, administration, policy and advocacy, and early childhood teacher education as well as general recommendations for graduate professional education.

Blackwell, P.J., & M.E. Diez. 1998. *Toward a new vision of master's education for teachers.* Washington, DC: National Council for Accreditation of Teacher Education (NCATE).

Bloom, P.J. 2000. *Circle of influence: Implementing shared decision making and participative management.* Lake Forest, IL: New Horizons.

Bloom, P.J, & M. Sheerer. 1992. The effect of leadership training on child care program quality. *Early Childhood Research Quarterly* 7: 579-94.

Bredekamp, S. 1996. Early childhood education. In *Handbook of research on teacher education,* ed. J. Sikula, 323-47. New York: Simon & Schuster Macmillan.

Carter, M., D. Curtis, D.C. Baxter, B. Hieronymous, & B. Jones. 1995. *Training teachers: A harvest of theory and practice.* Redmond, WA: Redleaf Press.

Cronin, S., L. Derman-Sparks, S. Henry, C. Olatunji, & S. York. 1998. *Future vision, present work: Learning from the culturally relevant anti-bias leadership project.* St. Paul, MN: Redleaf Press.

Culkin, M.L., ed. 2000. *Managing quality in young children's programs: The leader's role.* New York: Teachers College Press.

Darling-Hammond, L., & S. Sykes, eds. 1999. *Teaching as the learning profession: Handbook of policy and practice.* San Francisco: Jossey-Bass.

Diez, M.E., & P.J. Blackwell. 2001. *Quality assessment for quality outcomes: Implications for the design and implementation of advanced master's programs.* Washington, DC: National Council for Accreditation of Teacher Education (NCATE).

Diez, M.E., & P.J. Blackwell. 2002. *Collaboration for teacher development: Implications for the design and implementation of advanced master's programs.* Washington, DC: National Council for Accreditation of Teacher Education (NCATE).

Feeney, S., & N.K. Freeman. 1999. *Ethics and the early childhood educator: Using the NAEYC code.* Washington, DC: NAEYC.

Feeney, S., N.K. Freeman, & E. Moravcik. 2000. *Teaching the NAEYC code of ethical conduct.* Washington, DC: NAEYC.

Glazer, J.S. 1986. *The master's degree: Tradition, diversity, innovation.* ASHE-ERIC Higher Education Report no. 6. Washington, DC: Association for the Study of Higher Education (ASHE). Gov. Doc. #ED 1.310/2:279260.

Goffin, S.G., & D.E. Day, eds. 1994. *New perspectives in early childhood teacher education: Bringing practitioners into the debate.* New York: Teachers College Press.

Jensen, M.A., & M.A. Hannibal. 1999. *Issues, advocacy, and leadership in early education.* 2d ed. Boston: Allyn & Bacon.

Jones, E. 1986. *Teaching adults: An active-learning approach.* Washington, DC: NAEYC.

Kagan, S.L. 1991. *United we stand: Collaboration for child care and early education services.* New York: Teachers College Press.

Kagan, S.L., & B. Bowman, eds. 1997. *Leadership in early care and education.* Washington, DC: NAEYC.

NAEYC. 1996. *Guidelines for preparation of early childhood professionals.* Washington, DC: Author. [G]

National Board for Professional Teaching Standards (NBPTS). 2001. *Early childhood generalist standards* (Second edition). http://new.nbpts.org/standards/complete/ec_gen_2ed.pdf

Neugebauer, R., ed. 1998. *Art of leadership: Managing early childhood organizations.* Redmond, WA: Child Care Information Exchange.

Robinson, A., & D. Stark. 2001. *Advocates in action: Making a difference for young children.* Washington, DC: NAEYC.

Tom, A. 1999. Reinventing master's degree study for experienced teachers. *Journal of Teacher Education* 50 (4): 245–54.

Appendix A

**Alignment of NAEYC core standards for advanced programs
and NBPTS Early Childhood/Generalist Standards**

	NBPTS Early Childhood/Generalist Standards								
NAEYC Advanced Core Standards	1. Understanding Young Children	2. Equity, Fairness, and Diversity	3. Assessment	4. Promoting Child Development and Learning	5. Knowledge of Integrated Curriculum	6. Multiple Teaching Strategies for Meaningful Learning	7. Family and Community Partnerships	8. Professional partnerships	9. Reflective Practice
1. Promoting Child Development and Learning	X			X	X				
2. Building Family and Community Relationships							X		
3. Observing, Documenting, and Assessing to Support Young Children and Families			X		X				
4. Teaching and Learning 4a. Connecting with children and families	X	X							
4b. Using developmentally effective approaches	X	X	X	X	X	X			
4c. Understanding content knowledge in early education					X				
4d. Building meaningful curriculum					X	X			
5. Growing as a Professional								X	X

Appendix B

Expectations for evidence, aligned with NAEYC's 2002 Advanced Standards

Background

NAEYC has detailed rubrics for each key element of its five Initial Licensure Standards, with each rubric describing three levels of performance. The rubrics are used by initial licensure programs and by reviewers as important tools in the submission and review of baccalaureate and five-year programs.

For its Advanced Standards, NAEYC has used the same five "core standards" as are in its Initial Standards. But in creating performance expectations for the advanced level, NAEYC has chosen to take a different approach. Rather than modifying the rubrics and levels of candidate performance developed for initial programs, NAEYC has at the advanced level chosen to emphasize the kinds of evidence that programs will need to provide to show that their candidates possess important competencies within the programs' areas of focus. Neither "rubrics" nor "criteria" seems exactly right for this approach; instead, NAEYC calls these "expectations for evidence."

As seen below, the expectations for evidence do not address each core standard and essential professional tool separately, because advanced master's and doctoral programs in early childhood education have many possible specializations that may result in different combinations and emphases. NAEYC's Advanced Standards document describes four such specializations but encourages a program to combine, add to, or modify these in ways that fit with their mission and community needs—as long as the program does have focus and depth, and as long as the program addresses the core standards and essential professional tools in a coherent way.

Together with the detailed expectations in the Program Report Outline, and the Advanced Standards document's many narrative examples of how candidates in various specializations might document their competence, the outline below gives institutions and reviewers guidance as to the kind of evidence needed to show that candidates and programs are meeting the NAEYC standards.

Opportunities, assessments, outcomes

Advanced programs submitting Program Reports for NAEYC review are asked to show evidence that in each of the following domains, the program has high-quality **Opportunities, Assessments,** and **Outcomes.** NAEYC expects programs to present evidence that gives satisfactory answers to these questions, adapted from the Advanced standards of the National Association of School Psychologists (NASP):

Opportunities—How does the program provide the knowledge and skills necessary for the development of competencies in a domain?

Assessments—How does the program assess and monitor the development of candidate competency in a domain?

Outcomes—How does the program determine that candidates have attained acceptable competence in a domain?

Core standards

Opportunities: Program evidence shows that candidates are provided with multiple, developmental opportunities to extend their knowledge, skills, and dispositions related to each of the five core standards domains (Promoting Child Development and Learning; Building Family and Community Relationships; Observing, Documenting, and Assessments to Support Children and Families; Teaching and Learning; Growing as a Professional). These opportunities—which could include course work, independent study, portfolio development, field or internship experiences, and capstone experiences such as comprehensive examinations and theses—build on candidates' prior competence at the initial licensure level and are tailored to the program's and candidates' primary areas of professional specialization (e.g., Early Childhood Accomplished Teacher; Early Childhood Administrator; Early Childhood Policy and Advocacy Specialist; Early Childhood Teacher Educator/Researcher). The Program Report Outline requires that programs describe "Opportunities to Learn" in each area.

Assessments: Program evidence shows that candidates' competence in the core standards areas is assessed through multiple measures and at multiple points during the program, including at entry into the program. These assessments could include internship supervisors' ratings, results on National Board assessments, comprehensive examination results, evaluations of professional portfolios, etc. Assessments are tailored to the program's and candidates' primary areas of professional specialization.

Outcomes: Program evidence—focused on key transitions and decision points in the program, and summarized, aggregated, and reported in the Program Report—shows that advanced candidates have developed knowledge, skills, and professional dispositions related to the core standards, at a level that will allow them to be effective in their professional work and to have a positive effect on young children and families.

Essential professional tools

Opportunities: Program evidence shows that candidates are provided with multiple, developmental opportunities to extend their knowledge, skills, and dispositions related to each of the nine essential professional tools for early childhood advanced candidates. These opportunities—which could include course work, independent study, portfolio development, field or internship experiences, and capstone experiences such as comprehensive examinations and theses—allow candidates to develop and use these competencies in relevant professional work and in ways closely connected to the NAEYC core standards. The Program Report Outline requires that programs describe "Opportunities to Learn" in each area.

Assessments: Program evidence shows that candidates' competence in using each of the Essential professional tools is assessed through multiple measures and at multiple points during the program. Assessments are tailored to the program's and candidates' primary areas of professional specialization and emphasize application of multiple skills to significant professional issues.

Outcomes: Program evidence—focused on key transitions and decision points in the program, as summarized, aggregated, and reported in the Program Report—shows that advanced candi-

dates have developed knowledge, skills, and professional dispositions related to the essential professional tools, at a level that will allow them to be effective in their professional work and to have a positive effect on young children and families.

Additional specialized competencies

Not all programs will add specialized competencies beyond those reflected in the NAEYC core standards and essential professional tools.

Opportunities: For programs whose specializations require additional competencies, program evidence shows that these competencies have been clearly identified and described in performance terms for candidates, and that their relation to the NAEYC core standards is evident. Candidates are provided with multiple, developmental opportunities to build their knowledge, skills, and dispositions related to each of the additional specialized competencies identified by their program. These opportunities—which could include course work, independent study, portfolio development, field or internship experiences, and capstone experiences such as comprehensive examinations and theses—also allow candidates to use all of the essential professional tools for early childhood advanced candidates. The Program Report Outline requires that programs describe "Opportunities to Learn" in each area.

Assessments: Program evidence shows that candidates' competence in the additional areas identified by the program is assessed through multiple measures and at multiple points during the program. Assessments help candidates make connections between this specialized work and the NAEYC core standards, and the assessments emphasize application of multiple skills to significant professional issues.

Outcomes: Program evidence—focused on key transitions and decision points in the program, as summarized, aggregated, and reported in the Program Report—shows that advanced candidates have developed knowledge, skills, and professional dispositions related to any additional specialized competencies identified by the program, at a level that will allow them to be effective in their professional work and to have a positive effect on young children and families.

Appendix C

Advanced Standards Work Group

NAEYC gratefully acknowledges the expertise and commitment of the members of the Advanced Standards Work Group:

Nancy Barbour, Kent State University

Jerlean Daniel, University of Pittsburgh

Marlene Henriques, National Board for Professional Teaching Standards (NBPTS)

Joan Isenberg, George Mason University, and National Board for Professional Teaching Standards (NBPTS)

Marjorie Lee, National-Louis University

John Johnston, University of Memphis

Brent McBride, University of Illinois

Frances Rust, New York University

Sylvia Sanchez, George Mason University

Roberta Schomburg, Carlow College

Edyth Wheeler, Towson State University

NAEYC Staff
Marilou Hyson, Associate Executive Director for Professional Development
Parker Anderson, Assistant Director for Professional Development

NAEYC expresses its appreciation to the many professional organizations that have provided feedback on the revisions to the standards for advanced programs. Feedback was sought from numerous groups, including:

AACTE (American Association of Colleges for Teacher Education)

ACCESS (American Associate Degree Early Childhood Educators)

ACEI (Association for Childhood Education International)

AFT (American Federation of Teachers)

CEC (Council for Exceptional Children)

Council for Professional Recognition

DEC (Division for Early Childhood, Council for Exceptional Children)

ECRQ (*Early Childhood Research Quarterly*) Consulting Editors Panel

NAECS/SDE (National Association of Early Childhood Specialists in State Departments of Education)

NAECTE (National Association for Early Childhood Teacher Educators)

NAEYC's Professional Development Panel

NBPTS (National Board for Professional Teaching Standards)

NEA (National Education Association)

In addition to members of the Advanced Standards Work Group, numerous individuals also offered constructive recommendations. Paula Jorde Bloom, of National-Louis University, and Alan Tom, of the University of North Carolina at Chapel Hill, made special contributions.

Institutional affiliations reflect those held by the members at the time the Work Group was convening.

Contents

Introduction   93

   Overview   93

   NAEYC's standards for early childhood professional preparation   94

   Associate degree preparation for early childhood professionals   96

   Processes and timelines for revision   102

   Components and organization   103

Standards Summary   106

Standards   107

   Standard 1. Promoting Child Development and Learning   107

   Standard 2. Building Family and Community Relationships   109

   Standard 3. Observing, Documenting, and Assessing to Support
     Young Children and Families   110

   Standard 4. Teaching and Learning   112

   Standard 5. Becoming a Professional   114

Supportive Skills   116

   Skills in Self-Assessment and Self-Advocacy   116

   Skills in Mastering and Applying Foundational Concepts from General Education   116

   Written and Verbal Communication Skills   116

   Skills in Making Connections between Prior Knowledge/Experience
     and New Learning   117

   Skills in Identifying and Using Professional Resources   118

References and Resources   118

   Publications   118

   Websites   122

Appendix
   A: Associate Standards Work Group   123

NAEYC Standards for Early Childhood Professional Preparation

Associate Degree Programs

Approved by NAEYC Governing Board, July 2003

Introduction

Overview

This document represents a major revision of NAEYC's standards for associate degree early childhood programs, replacing the "Guidelines for Early Childhood Professional Preparation Programs" issued in 1994. It begins with an introduction that outlines the history, purpose, and current knowledge base for NAEYC's vision for high-quality early childhood professional preparation. That vision is reflected in NAEYC's standards for associate, initial licensure (baccalaureate and five-year), and advanced (master's or doctoral) programs.

With that background, this document presents the defining characteristics of associate degree programs within a continuum of early childhood professional preparation, from community-based training through baccalaureate and graduate study. In the first section, it describes the broad context of U.S. community college programs and students; the characteristics and goals of students enrolled in early childhood associate degree programs; the ways in which high-quality programs are responding to those characteristics and goals; the challenges and opportunities created for associate degree programs by current trends in the early childhood field; and implications for this version of NAEYC's standards for high-quality associate degree programs. This document also describes the scope and purpose of these Associate Standards, distinguishing between professional preparation standards and the larger context of program accreditation.

The next section describes the processes and timeline that culminated in this Associate Standards document. In revising its 1994 Guidelines for associate degree programs, NAEYC relied on collaboration with leaders in associate degree programs, as well as extensive feedback from a wide range of stakeholders, to ensure that these new standards rest on a sound foundation.

Finally, this document presents the standards themselves, together with other related components of a strong standards and assessment system. As readers will see, the five core standards for associate degree programs are identical to those in NAEYC's Initial Licensure Standards and Advanced Standards documents. Each of the five shared standards describes the essential knowledge, skills, and dispositions that should be present in a well-prepared early childhood professional. However, this does not mean that programs at the associate, baccalaureate, and advanced levels are or should be equivalent. The breadth and depth of mastery expected from students, the kinds of learning opportunities provided by programs, and the nature of the evidence demonstrating competence in relation to each element of the standards should differ considerably across the different levels and types of higher education programs. Strong associate degree early childhood programs are not beefed-up versions of community training workshops, nor are they watered-down or speeded-up versions of four- or five-year teacher education programs. Thus, in this and in its other standards documents NAEYC intends to affirm the connectedness of early childhood professional preparation as well as the unique characteristics of the various settings in which early childhood educators are prepared.

NAEYC's standards for early childhood professional preparation

History

These Associate Standards are part of a larger history of standards-setting efforts by NAEYC, in early childhood professional preparation as well as in other areas.

NAEYC is one of 19 "specialty professional association" members of the National Council for Accreditation of Teacher Education (NCATE) that have issued standards. In 1980, NAEYC began developing "guidelines" for higher education programs preparing early childhood profession- als. Those Guidelines, for programs preparing "candidates" (future early childhood teachers) at the baccalaureate or initial master's degree level in NCATE-affiliated institutions, were first approved in 1982. Guidelines for advanced master's/doctoral degree programs and for associate degree programs were first developed and approved in 1988. The set of Guidelines was last revised and approved in 1994 (see NAEYC 1996a). Like their successors, those Guidelines echoed consistent themes across levels and settings of professional preparation.

Most recently, in 1999 NAEYC began signifi- cant revision of the 1994 Guidelines for the initial licensure level, and later for the advanced level. The revision was prompted both by NCATE's revising of its overall standards for "professional education units" and by new research findings and trends in early education. A major goal, both for NCATE and for NAEYC, was to create more fully performance-based standards that would place less focus on courses and credit hours and more focus on "outputs"—evidence that students had mastered the competencies reflected in the standards and so could positively influence children's learning. NAEYC's new Initial Licen- sure Standards were approved by NCATE in 2001. By Spring 2003, all four- or five-year early childhood teacher education programs seeking NCATE accreditation must provide NAEYC with documentation to show they are in compliance with those 2001 Initial Licensure Standards. Similarly, in 2002 NCATE approved NAEYC's new Advanced Standards. By Spring 2004, all

advanced master's and doctoral early childhood professional preparation programs seeking NCATE accreditation must comply with those 2002 Advanced Standards.

Revision of the 1994 Guidelines for associate degree programs began in 2002, and NAEYC's Governing Board approved the revised standards in July 2003.

Like all NAEYC position statements, the standards for early childhood professional preparation are "living documents," and as such will be regularly updated and revised.

Purpose

As this brief description shows, NAEYC's efforts to develop and promote standards for high-quality professional preparation have a long history. NAEYC's purpose has been not only to develop standards for institutions seeking external accreditation but also to develop an evidence-based consensus that reflects a shared vision across sectors of the early childhood field. Thus, NAEYC has encouraged all higher educa- tion institutions, as well as other groups, to use its standards as a guide in planning curriculum, training experiences, assessment strategies, and other components of high-quality professional development—whatever the setting and target audience.

Current issues and challenges

In every sector of the early childhood educa- tion community, including associate degree programs, professional preparation faces new challenges. The introduction to NAEYC's 2001 Initial Licensure Standards describes some of these challenges—and related opportunities; among them is the increased diversity of children and families in early childhood programs, from infant/toddler child care through the primary grades. That increased diversity is seen in the greater numbers of children from culturally and linguistically diverse communities, as well as in the growing numbers of children with disabilities and other special learning needs who are served in early childhood programs. High-quality early childhood programs will need to respond to that diversity inclusively and effectively.

The increased attention given to children's early years by federal and state policy makers also has implications for the development and revision of professional preparation standards. Soon, as a component of the federal No Child Left Behind legislation, all public school classrooms must be staffed by "highly qualified teachers" (as defined by states), with many paraprofessionals in public schools required to have a minimum of two years of college or the equivalent. State prekindergarten programs typically require an associate or bachelor's degree for lead teachers, and by the end of 2003 one half of all Head Start lead teachers must possess at least an associate degree in early childhood education or a related field. Access to professional education and to professional career pathways is becoming increasingly important for the many early childhood practitioners currently working with young children. Yet those calls for greater formal education have not been matched by public investments in salaries and working conditions for early childhood staff, especially in the community child care programs that serve the vast majority of children under age 5.

Beyond classroom-level qualifications, the early childhood field is increasingly committed to identifying and supporting a more diverse group of talented leaders. The leadership gap is clear: While as many as one third of the nation's early childhood teaching staff in child care centers and preschools are women of color, the field's leadership currently reflects neither the diversity of the workforce nor the diversity of the children served (Center for the Child Care Workforce 1993; Kagan & Bowman 1997). High-quality associate degree programs offer a promising route toward closing that gap. Associate degree early childhood programs play a critical role in providing access to higher education—and to the positions that require such education—for many groups, especially those currently underrepresented in professional leadership roles.

Knowledge base

NAEYC's new Associate, Initial Licensure, and Advanced Standards are grounded in a rapidly expanding knowledge base about what young children need in order to develop well and in a set of core values about young children and their education.

What research shows young children need. As reports from the National Research Council such

A uniform standard

Because New Jersey does not have a unified articulation system, each community college negotiates a separate transfer agreement with each four-year school; accepted courses vary significantly from institution to institution. Our project for a unified approach to course transfer used the Draft NAEYC Standards for Associate Programs as a uniform standard for evaluating community college courses.

Support from The Schumann Fund for New Jersey allowed the New Jersey Professional Development Center for Early Care and Education to provide grants to five community colleges for a program review. Participants have strengthened links between objectives and assessment, infused more appropriate early childhood course content, examined the role of practicum experiences in course outcomes, and improved sequencing of content throughout the degree programs. They have established stricter entrance and exit standards, including academic skills, to ensure that students will successfully meet the admission requirements of the four-year colleges. Discussions have begun with some four-year colleges to re-evaluate the distribution of early childhood content between the associate degree and bachelor's degree programs.

The project has also fostered dialogue among faculty, administration, and advisement personnel at both the community colleges and the four-year colleges about the needs of early childhood degree candidates and the goals of the teacher preparation programs.

—*Florence Nelson*,
Kean University

as *Eager to Learn* (2001b) and *From Neurons to Neighborhoods* (2000) emphasize, young children are far more capable intellectually and socially than many had previously believed. Young children benefit from well-planned, intentionally implemented, culturally relevant curriculum that both supports and challenges them. Research also has shown what kinds of experiences are essential to building later competence in such critical areas as language and literacy and mathematics and in social skills and emotional understanding and self-regulation. The knowledge base also emphasizes the need for close relationships between young children and adults, including caregivers and teachers, and between teachers and children's families. Such relationships, and the secure base that they create, are investments in children's later social, emotional, and academic competence. These are only a few examples of the developmental and educational research base from which NAEYC's core standards for professional preparation are derived; the resources at the end of this document and the discussion in NAEYC's Initial Licensure Standards document expand on these ideas.

The knowledge base and the role of associate degree programs. Because of the depth of knowledge and skill required to implement the kinds of experiences that this knowledge base suggests, the *Eager to Learn* report recommends that groups of children age 3 and older be led by teachers holding at least a baccalaureate degree with specialized preparation in child development and early childhood education. High-quality associate degree programs lay a foundation for that in-depth preparation, both through their strong general education in the humanities, mathematics, science, and other areas, and by introducing students to a variety of learning opportunities in child development and early childhood curriculum and pedagogy. In addition, strong associate degree programs provide effective preparation for students who intend to work in roles that do not require teacher licensure. Later sections of this document describe those varied roles for associate programs in more detail.

Field experiences. A key component of each of NAEYC's standards, at every level, is hands-on field or clinical experiences, whether this is doctoral students' immersion in applied research,

advanced master's students' systematic inquiry into their own classroom practices, or associate and initial licensure students' observations and direct experiences in early childhood settings or in home visits. National reports on the characteristics of high-quality professional preparation, and other national standards such as NCATE's, consistently emphasize the need for continuous interplay of theory, research, and practice, and the significance of field experiences as part of that process. The "professional development schools" movement underscores the importance of identifying high-quality sites for education professionals to develop or refine their skills with competent mentorship and supervision.

NAEYC's 1994 Guidelines included a separate "Field Experiences" standard; the new Associate, Initial Licensure, and Advanced Standards do not. But this in no way suggests that field experiences are less important now than in the past. Indeed, such experiences represent one of the primary ways in which students at every level can link knowledge, skills, and professional dispositions into a coherent whole and apply these to promoting children's learning. Thus, supervised field experiences in high-quality settings are a key part of any program's system for assessing its students' competencies in relation to the standards.

Core values in professional preparation. In addition to the common research base and common emphasis on the centrality of field experiences, these NAEYC standards for associate degree programs and its standards for initial licensure and advanced programs share a core set of values that cannot be easily quantified but are critically important. These affirm the value of, for example, play in children's lives; reciprocal relationships with families; child development knowledge as a foundation for professional practice; practices and curricula that are culturally respectful and responsive; ethical behavior and professional advocacy; and in-depth field experiences in high-quality professional preparation.

Associate degree preparation for early childhood professionals

While they may share these values, knowledge base, and core standards, all associate degree programs and institutions that offer associate degrees have characteristics, missions, opportunities, and challenges that uniquely distinguish them. As noted earlier, associate degree programs are not—and do not aspire to be—compressed versions of baccalaureate degree programs. It is neither possible nor desirable to replicate in two years what four- or even five-year programs attempt to do in preparing early childhood professionals. At the same time, it is beyond the scope of this document to describe the many possible ways in which associate programs might be organized and the many possible roles that such programs might play within a system of early childhood professional preparation.

However, the following sections describe the broad context of U.S. community college programs and students; the characteristics and goals of students enrolled in early childhood associate degree programs; the ways in which high-quality associate degree early childhood programs are responding to those characteristics and goals; the challenges and opportunities created for programs by recent trends in the early childhood field; and implications for the new NAEYC standards for high-quality associate degree programs.

The U.S. community college context

Community colleges and associate degree programs have undergone major changes even in their recent history, moving from primarily vocational goals to a far more diverse and dynamic set of aims. Community colleges' current scope, populations served, significance within the larger higher education system, and degree options all reflect those changes.

The scope. More than 10 million students are on our nation's community college campuses. Forty-four (44) percent of all U.S. undergraduates are community college students. Increasing numbers of elementary school teachers receive all of their mathematics, science and technology, and other content course work at community colleges (Moore 1997).

Student diversity. Nationally, 30 percent of all community college students are students of color. Of culturally and linguistically diverse undergraduate students in the United States, a majority are enrolled in community colleges. This includes 46 percent of all African American, 55 percent of all Hispanic, 46 percent of all Asian/Pacific

Islander, and 55 percent of all Native American undergraduate students. More than half of all Hispanic and African American students who enter college following graduation from high school enter two-year institutions (Phillippe & Patton 2000).

Increasing access to higher education. Associate degree programs often have the explicit mission of increasing access to higher education programs. More than 80 percent of community college students work either full- or part-time (Phillippe & Patton 2000), and many are the first in their families to attend college. Access to postsecondary education can be impeded by cost, location, scheduling, or students' previous educational experiences. The community college system has attempted to remove these barriers by being responsive to community needs. Consequently, most community colleges offer courses in English as a second language and remedial courses in reading, writing, and mathematics for students who need that additional support.

Degree options for community college students. As part of their effort to be responsive to students' varied needs, community colleges offer a variety of educational or degree options. The American Association of Community Colleges (AACC) recommends the following terminology: The Associate of Arts (A.A.) degree generally emphasizes the arts, humanities, and social sciences; typically, three quarters of the work required is general education course work. The Associate of Sciences (A.S.) degree generally requires one half general education course work, with substantial mathematics and science. The Associate in Applied Science (A.A.S.) degree prepares the student for direct employment, with one third of the course work in general education. While many students who seek A.A.S. degrees do not intend to transfer, these degrees are not intended to create barriers to transfer. "The [A.A.S.] degree programs must be designed to recognize this dual possibility and to encourage students to recognize the long-term career possibilities that continued academic study will create" (AACC 1998).

Early childhood associate degree programs, like other community college programs, may offer students one or more of these degrees. That variability was taken into account when developing these standards for associate degree programs.

Tennessee's articulated system

Tennessee Early Childhood Training Alliance (TECTA) is a statewide early childhood training and professional recognition system administered by higher education to include orientation training through advanced degree programs. The TECTA system is based on the belief that all early childhood education personnel need professional knowledge and skills to provide appropriate care for young children. The goal is improving the quality of early childhood education by providing articulated preparation programs.

Five early childhood education courses prepare family child care providers to go through the CDA (Child Development Associate) assessment process and also transfer into the Associate of Applied Science (A.A.S.) degree in early childhood education. The A.A.S. degree articulates to any of the Tennessee Board of Regents' four-year institutions.

—*Judy Green*,
TECTA

The real world

Our Hispanic-serving institution is located in a rural area where distance creates real challenges for students and faculty. Many students are underprepared for college work and have not experienced success in school. Families tend to show little support for higher education, and students' confidence is low. More than 90 percent of the early childhood education students are working in Head Start or child care. Some are grandmothers or primary caregivers for others, taking significant responsibility for children as well as for other family members. Complex, multiple responsibilities are the rule, not the exception.

For example, one student works as a full-time teacher in a Head Start program while taking six to nine credits each semester toward her associate degree to meet the Head Start higher education mandate. At the same time she is coping with family challenges, including caring for her aging parents and her seriously ill husband who is awaiting a heart transplant. It is not unusual for her to be called out of class for messages.

—*Martha Muñoz and Joanne Floth*,
Central Arizona College

Characteristics of programs and their students

Numbers and characteristics. The general characteristics and mission of community colleges are reflected in specialized associate degree programs. According to estimates from Early and Winton's (2001) national sample, more than 700 institutions of higher education offer associate degree programs in early childhood education. Many of the students enrolled in those programs represent cultural and linguistic minorities; as in the general community college population, early childhood students in two-year programs are proportionately more diverse than in four-year programs.

Increasing numbers of students entering early childhood associate degree programs have been working—most in child care or Head Start programs (Early & Winton 2001). Many of those students continue to work while attending college part-time. These students are taking the lead in their own education, developing long-term career goals as they improve the quality of their current work with young children and families.

Career goals and pathways. The career goals of students in associate degree early childhood programs vary. For some, the degree may enhance their current position, build on a prior Child Development Associate (CDA) credential, and perhaps lead to greater responsibilities in the setting where they work. Although these work settings vary widely, Early and Winton's (2001) data suggest that proportionately more associate degree students work, or plan to work, with infants and toddlers than do students in four-year programs, and that many entering students have been working in family child care or child care administrative positions.

Other associate degree students are entering the early childhood field from an entirely different career. Some students are planning to transfer into a four-year college, heading either toward teacher certification or toward other work in the early childhood field. A strong general education foundation together with an introduction to early childhood professional issues and skills is often the combination these students seek. Still other students enter a community college program with a relatively limited set of objectives (e.g., to take one course that meets a child care licensing requirement or to receive college credit for work toward the CDA) but find unexpected pleasure and challenge in higher education. With support, such students often continue through the associate degree toward a baccalaureate degree and beyond.

Most early childhood associate degree programs focus on preparing students for direct work with young children in classroom settings. However, associate degree students may have other professional goals (many requiring further education immediately or later in students' careers) including but not limited to:

Early childhood educator roles such as early childhood classroom teacher, family child care provider, Head Start teacher, or paraprofessional in the public schools;

Home-family support roles such as home visitor, family advocate, child protective services worker, or parent educator; or

Professional support roles such as early childhood administrator in a child care or Head Start program, staff trainer, peer/program mentor, or advocate at the community, state, or national level.

Responding to student and community needs

Associate degree programs have great opportunities to meet the diverse needs of their students in ways that are responsive, flexible, and innovative.

Providing a foundation for multiple roles and pathways. Associate degree early childhood programs focus on providing solid foundational knowledge, field experiences, and common skills and strategies that prepare students for multiple roles within the early childhood field. In combination with this program-specific foundation, general education courses strengthen students' conceptual knowledge in multiple areas that are important for all educated individuals, including those responsible for young children's learning. Some programs are focused more on transfer and others more on immediate entry into the career. Whatever the balance, in all cases high-quality associate degree programs promote both general and professional education in an integrated fashion.

Supportive relationships

Just as with young children, we build our work with college students from a secure base of relationships and trust. At our institution we start even before students enroll. Many students are intimidated by the prospect of attending college, so the program arranges college orientations and placement assessments right at their child care center or Head Start program. They attend the orientations as a group and can support one another as they transition to campus together.

Once students are enrolled we continue to provide intensive advising and support. This approach is both developmental and "intrusive," as it addresses work and family life as well as academics. Throughout the year we keep in touch with students, checking on their progress, helping them stay on task and persist with their education. We actively refer students to tutoring services and other special help as needed.

One group of family child care providers living near the Mexican border has a remarkable rate of success, with 67 graduating from the program last year. This group became a close-knit learning community. Their learning started with local orientations and a one-credit course offered in their own community and taught by a bilingual adjunct faculty member from the college. Bilingual students supported their monolingual Spanish-speaking classmates. The faculty member served as mentor for the group, finding out what their individual needs were, registering them for classes, and bringing them to campus as their confidence grew. Weekly potluck dinners have strengthened relationships and celebrated successes over the past two years.

—*Martha Muñoz and Joanne Floth,*
Central Arizona College

Universal articulation

Universal articulation is a feature of higher education in New Mexico. Several unique features make it possible. At each level (associate, bachelor's, master's):

• All institutions of higher education share a common core of content in their coursework, thereby guaranteeing each student's level of competence when exiting the program, regardless of the particular institution

• There is a common set of courses used at all institutions of higher education with approved early childhood education programs.

These features enable students to transfer between associate or bachelor's programs easily. Rather than having to repeat courses or material already mastered, they can transfer credits and enter new programs where they left off.

Expanding online learning

Distance education provides college course access to working professionals, people in rural areas or with long commutes to a college campus, and mothers with young children. Several community colleges in New York State were already offering early childhood courses online when a grant opportunity came through the state's Office of Children and Families–SUNY (State University of New York) Research Foundation for innovative projects. A call went out to community colleges in New York State that might be interested in collaborating to expand the number and breadth of early childhood courses offered online. Nine colleges were ready to pursue such a project.

Broome Community College took the lead. We assessed what was already offered among the nine colleges and where courses seemed to be missing. Each college then selected courses it would expand or develop over the next year. Twenty-seven new courses were developed. By careful planning and course transfer, a student can now patch together totally online the early childhood portion of an associate degree.

—Barbara Nilsen,
Broome Community College

Meeting immediate needs while keeping doors open. Early childhood students who are already working in the field need high-quality professional course work offered concurrently with strong general education. Students who need time to succeed in developmental reading, writing, and mathematics courses also need time to develop confidence, skills, and career goals before deciding whether to seek transfer into a four-year institution. Early tracking of students into nontransfer or "terminal" programs can perpetuate the idea that little education is needed to teach our youngest children. In addition, premature tracking may create unnecessary barriers to students' future options—a serious concern given the opportunities for these students to become part of a more diverse leadership pool for the early childhood field. Many associate degree programs are attempting to keep these doors open through "career programs" (programs that are primarily aimed at enhancing one's current career) that still maintain transfer options.

Meeting the challenge of transfer and articulation. Historically, associate degree graduates, even those who have not been counseled into "nontransfer" options, have faced serious obstacles in attempting to transfer credits to a four-year program. In recent years, however, a growing number of associate degree programs and baccalaureate programs have attempted to develop links that support students' movement from one educational program to another. This process is generally referred to as *articulation*. The connections are intended to serve as one component of a relatively seamless system of professional development. Despite some institutional barriers on both sides, there has been progress in a number of states to create smoother articulation—and some state legislatures are requiring institutions to craft "articulation agreements" between all two- and four-year programs. If successful, these connections promote more continuity across the professional development system and allow greater numbers of associate degree students to have the option of moving forward in higher education without losing credits or repeating content already mastered.

Serving today's students with creative solutions. The diversity of degrees, career goals, and transfer options within associate degree programs creates challenges for faculty and administrators, but it also creates opportunities for programs to be responsive, creative, and flexible. Greater numbers of associate degree programs are offering distance learning, noncredit to credit course work, courses offered at worksites, and specialized courses that focus on particular settings and roles such as family child care.

Implications for NAEYC's Associate Standards

Support for flexibility, innovation, and articulation is increasingly necessary as early childhood associate degree programs work to meet the needs of students and the profession today. At the same time, the current national attention to early childhood education is likely to produce significant changes over the next decade—including new roles for associate degree programs as states and others reset teacher qualifications and redesign systems of early education. Collaboratively developed and aligned, early childhood education standards can provide a solid and common foundation to support both articulation and innovation, meeting the needs and incorporating the wisdom of local communities, families, and practitioners. Standards for this diverse array of associate degree programs must promote innovation and flexibility while ensuring equivalent standards of quality for all students.

As it does for initial licensure programs, NAEYC cautions associate programs against the superficial "mile wide and inch deep" model of professional preparation. The challenges are especially daunting in associate degree programs, which vary so greatly (both between and within programs) in degree options, the relative focus on general education, transfer and articulation or current career enhancement, and the constraints on the number and type of courses they may offer.

Looking at the standards in this document, associate degree program faculty will be challenged to weigh breadth versus depth (standard by standard and element by element) within the context of their own program, student needs (including the need to acquire concepts and skills in general education), and the realities of a two-year time frame. Again, the answer is not replicating or compressing the approach used in four-

and five-year licensure programs. An associate degree program that specializes in early childhood education has a responsibility to address all of the standards, just not in the same way or at the same depth as baccalaureate programs would. In some cases, the decision may be simply to expose students to a particular issue in a general or introductory way; in other cases, the primary focus for associate students may be on developing some specific skills, with in-depth theory and research linkages left for possible study in a four-year institution. Certain aspects of a standard may appear especially important for students in an associate program, with other aspects requiring less focused attention. Like houses that start out with the same foundation and framework but look entirely different as rooms are added, combined, altered, and personalized, each associate program may implement these standards in distinctive ways—as long as what is implemented is of uniformly high quality.

In developing the Associate Standards in this document, NAEYC and its colleagues in community college and other professional settings have attempted to respect and reflect the unique characteristics of associate degree programs, while also connecting the standards to the entire continuum of early childhood professional preparation.

Standards and program accreditation

The standards that follow describe what well-prepared graduates of associate degree early childhood programs should know and be able to do within the framework of NAEYC's five core standards: child development and learning; family and community relationships; observation, documentation, and assessment; teaching and learning; and professionalism.

That limited scope means that several important issues are not addressed. For example, these Associate Standards do not detail a number of features from NAEYC's 1994 Guidelines that had been adapted from the former NCATE standards for accreditation of professional education units. Those features included expectations for the design of professional education (including the conceptual framework, general studies, field experiences, and so on); the characteristics, qualifications, and assessment of students;

Enhancing CCC programs

The City Colleges of Chicago (CCC) is a network of seven community colleges that provides affordable, quality education to students from Chicago and beyond. In January 2003 the McCormick Tribune Foundation of Chicago awarded CCC a two-year grant of $1 million to launch a districtwide initiative to enhance its child develop- ment degree programs. The goals of this initiative are to:

• align programs with NAEYC's standards;

• coordinate program standards and course offerings across the seven colleges;

• provide professional development opportunities for all faculty and lab school directors;

• align lab school practices with the research-based theory and practice being taught;

• increase the number of high-quality practicum sites;

• enhance academic advisement and other supports;

• establish additional articulation agreements with universities in and around Chicago;

• enhance CCC's presence on local, state, and national efforts related to early childhood education.

This work is a collaboration of CCC's child development faculty, administrators, and lab school staff. In addition, an advisory board consisting of local, state, and national leaders in early childhood education and teacher training guides the initiative and creates cutting-edge strategies for achieving project goals.

—*Jana Fleming,*
City Colleges of Chicago

faculty characteristics, qualifications, and professional development; and the administration of the early childhood program (including governance and re-source issues).

In the accreditation system for baccalaureate, master's, and doctoral programs at NCATE-affiliated institutions, NAEYC does not review those broader aspects (except for the early childhood conceptual framework). Rather, those aspects are addressed by NCATE in its review of the institution's overall "professional education unit," using unit-level standards that NCATE revised in 2000.

These aspects of associate programs are addressed in NAEYC's Early Childhood Associate Degree Accreditation review. A Self-Study report followed by a site visit assesses the program's mission and role in the community, program of studies, student characteristics and supports, faculty qualifications and composition, infrastructure, learning opportunities, key assessments related to the five NAEYC core standards, and evidence of student performance. An accreditation commission makes accreditation decisions. More information on NAEYC Early Childhood Associate Degree Accreditation is available at www.naeyc.org.

Processes and timelines for revision

This new NAEYC standards document, like the 1994 Guidelines for associate degree programs it replaces, has been the product of a close collaboration with ACCESS, the national organization of American Associate Degree Early Childhood Educators. ACCESS leaders have been key participants in the work group that drafted these standards. That collaboration, as well as continuing feedback and critiques from associate degree faculty, has been essential to ensure credibility, vision, and linkage with community colleges' distinctive missions and contexts.

Revision of the 1994 Guidelines began with the assumption that the five core standards NAEYC had developed for its new Initial Licensure and Advanced Standards were both appropriate and significant for associate degree programs too. By building each set of standards from a common core, NAEYC wished to affirm the continuity and connectedness of early childhood professional preparation. Discussions of that proposed approach at conference sessions and other forums confirmed that it would receive widespread support from teacher educators and others, so long as distinctions were made in how programs addressed and assessed the common standards.

Before beginning this revision, NAEYC and ACCESS sought comments from stakeholders regarding the 1994 Guidelines, focusing on elements that should be retained and those that might be altered or enhanced. Faculty felt strongly that programs needed a balance between standards that were overly prescriptive or restrictive, and those that would be so vague as to offer no guidance. As with the Initial Licensure and Advanced Standards revisions, there was general support for retaining the five key categories of child development, family relationships, assessment, curriculum and teaching practices, and professionalism. The critical importance of high-quality field experiences was also affirmed. The work group and others in the field also believed that the document needed to highlight the distinctive and often complex nature of preparation at the associate level (for example, the mix of programs primarily preparing students for transfer and programs primarily preparing students for immediate employment or enhancing their current credentials).

Earlier versions were shared at sessions at NAEYC's 2002 National Institute for Early Childhood Professional Development and at NAEYC's 2002 Annual Conference. Written and verbal comments at those sessions influenced further revisions leading to this current document, which was posted with an electronic feedback form on NAEYC's and ACCESS's Websites. In addition, comments were sought from a wide range of individuals and groups with particular expertise and with various kinds of interest in associate degree standards, including those involved in four- and five-year teacher education programs.

In July 2003, NAEYC's Governing Board reviewed and approved this Associate Standards document, as it reviews and approves all Association position statements. In August 2003, ACCESS endorsed the standards.

Components and organization

The standards that follow include a number of interconnected components. Those components, and their organization, are outlined below:

Core standards

As described earlier, NAEYC's core Associate Standards are identical to those in its Initial Licensure and Advanced Standards documents. There are five core standards, each of which describes in a few sentences what well-prepared students should know and be able to do. For example, Standard 1 is:

Promoting Child Development and Learning—Students prepared in associate degree programs use their understanding of young children's characteristics and needs, and of multiple interacting influences on children's development and learning, to create environments that are healthy, respectful, supportive, and challenging for all children.

It is important to note, then, that the standard is not just that students know something "about" child development and learning—the expectations are more specific and complex than that.

Supporting explanations

Like the Initial Licensure and Advanced Standards documents, this Associate Standards document includes rationales, or "supporting explanations," for each core standard. For associate degree programs, each supporting explanation offers a general description of why that standard is important, but also emphasizes the specific aspects that may be appropriate to emphasize in associate programs—linked to but not identical with how the standard might be addressed in baccalaureate or advanced programs. The discussion in the supporting explanations is supplemented by the references and resources at the end of this document.

Key elements

To help readers understand what the expectations are for each standard, this document identifies three to five "key elements" within each standard. In effect, the key elements unpack the meaning of that standard to clarify its most important features. Again, these key elements are identical in NAEYC's Initial Licensure, Advanced, and Associate Standards documents, yet would be implemented and assessed quite differently at each level. To continue with the example above, for Standard 1, Promoting Child Development and Learning, its key elements are:

1a: Knowing and understanding young children's characteristics and needs

1b: Knowing and understanding the multiple influences on development and learning

1c: Using developmental knowledge to create healthy, respectful, supportive, and challenging learning environments

Examples of opportunities to learn and practice

NAEYC wants this Associate Standards document to be as useful as possible to faculty and others concerned with developing the competencies of associate degree students. For this reason, under each key element are listed examples of how associate degree programs might help students learn and practice the knowledge, skills, and professional dispositions within that aspect of that standard. Such opportunities may be found both in general education and in the early childhood program—and ideally, would be integrated throughout. Again, the extent of these opportunities will appropriately vary depending on the extent of early childhood and related course work and field experiences within the associate degree program.

For example, under Key Element 1a: Knowing and understanding young children's characteristics and needs, this document suggests:

Opportunities to learn this content would typically include course work in child development, emphasizing current research and its applications. This builds a foundation for practice and for further study. When connected with in-class support, high-quality field experiences can also serve as rich opportunities for students to observe and describe children's characteristics and needs, as members of cultures and communities, as part of an age group and as individuals. Case study assignments are powerful teaching tools.

Examples of evidence and assessments of students' growth

Immediately following the examples of opportunities to learn and practice are examples of ways that faculty might assess or document student growth and development—both quantitatively and qualitatively. Continuing with Key Element 1a: Knowing and understanding young

Summer seminar

Many of our students take a great many of their courses off campus, at their workplace or online. To create a greater sense of community the college offers a one-week "Summer Seminar" on campus. A grant pays for tuition and books. Students come from all over the state—one group helicoptered from the bottom of the Grand Canyon and others travel from urban programs in Phoenix. Students live and work together, staying in residence life, eating all meals on campus, sharing their cultures, adjusting to 113-degree heat, and taking an intensive three-credit course with technology embedded throughout.

Enthusiasm for the college experience is enormous, with waiting lists every year. They discover the larger world of early childhood education. They experience a richly diverse community of Native American, African American, Anglo, and Latino classmates, finding that despite their differences they have much in common. Family child care providers, center staff, Head Start teachers—all share a set of values and dedication to young children.

—*Martha Muñoz and Joanne Floth,*
Central Arizona College

children's characteristics and needs, the suggestion is:

> Students might demonstrate competence in this key element by, for example, successfully completing a child development course, receiving positive ratings of knowledge and understanding in a case study project or child observation assignment, developing and using an informal checklist, or developing lesson plans that take into account children's cultural and developmental characteristics and needs.

As always, the examples (of opportunities and of evidence) are intended to be suggestions, not prescriptions. Associate degree program faculty are invited to use, adapt, and expand the examples to fit their own context and the scope and nature of their program.

Supportive skills

In order to support the effective use of the knowledge, skills, and dispositions described in Standards 1–5, well-prepared graduates of associate degree programs also need a set of skills that cut across those five domains. The section of this document that follows the standards describes five such skills: (1) skills in self-assessment and self-advocacy; (2) skills in mastering and applying foundational skills from general education; (3) written and verbal communication skills; (4) skills in making connections between prior knowledge/experience and new learning; and (5) skills in identifying and using professional resources.

Again, examples are given of how associate degree faculty might offer students opportunities to learn and practice these skills and examples of what evidence might demonstrate students' competence in each skill area—both to enhance their current work and, in many cases, to lay the foundation for successful completion of a baccalaureate degree and beyond.

References and resources

The final section of this document provides key references and resources. These are intended to highlight critical issues in professional preparation, to identify the research base for each standard, and to suggest resources for faculty to explore further as they review and enhance their own programs.

Some notes on the terminology used in this document

"**Students prepared in associate degree programs**" refers to those who are preparing for professional positions serving young children and their families.

"**Use**" refers to application in practice, always soundly based on professional knowledge. "**Know**" refers to possession of key information. "**Understand**" includes analysis and reflection.

"**All children**" means *all*: children with developmental delays or disabilities, children who are gifted and talented, children whose families are culturally and linguistically diverse, children from diverse socioeconomic groups, and other children with individual learning styles, strengths, and needs. Note that NAEYC uses the term *children,* rather than *students,* to reflect the focus on all aspects of development and learning and to remind ourselves that children have identities outside of their classroom roles.

The term "**field experiences**" includes observations, field work, practica, and student teaching or other "clinical" experiences such as home visiting.

The term "**culture**" includes ethnicity, racial identity, economic class, family structure, language, and religious and political beliefs, which profoundly influence each child's development and relationship to the world.

Standards Summary

These core standards are identical to NAEYC's Initial Licensure core standards; however, associate programs distinguish themselves from initial licensure programs in the scope and depth of preparation. In addition, the term *students prepared in associate degree programs* is used rather than the term *candidates* that NCATE uses in accrediting initial licensure and advanced programs.

Standard 1. Promoting Child Development and Learning

Students prepared in associate degree programs use their understanding of young children's characteristics and needs, and of multiple interacting influences on children's development and learning, to create environments that are healthy, respectful, supportive, and challenging for all children.

Standard 2. Building Family and Community Relationships

Students prepared in associate degree programs know about, understand, and value the importance and complex characteristics of children's families and communities. They use this understanding to create respectful, reciprocal relationships that support and empower families, and to involve all families in their children's development and learning.

Standard 3. Observing, Documenting, and Assessing to Support Young Children and Families

Students prepared in associate degree programs know about and understand the goals, benefits, and uses of assessment. They know about and use systematic observations, documentation, and other effective assessment strategies in a responsible way, in partnership with families and other professionals, to positively influence children's development.

Standard 4. Teaching and Learning

Students prepared in associate degree programs integrate their understanding of and relationship with children and families; their understanding of developmentally effective approaches to teaching and learning; and their knowledge of academic disciplines to design, implement, and evaluate experiences that promote positive development and learning for all young children.

Sub-Standard 4a. Connecting with children and families

Students know, understand, and use positive relationships and supportive interactions as the foundation for their work with young children.

Sub-Standard 4b. Using developmentally effective approaches

Students know, understand, and use a wide array of effective approaches, strategies, and tools to positively influence children's development and learning.

Sub-Standard 4c. Understanding content knowledge in early education

Students understand the importance of each content area in young children's learning. They know the essential concepts, inquiry tools, and structure of content areas, including academic subjects, and can identify resources to deepen their understanding.

Sub-Standard 4d. Building meaningful curriculum

Students use their own knowledge and other resources to design, implement, and evaluate meaningful, challenging curriculum that promotes comprehensive developmental and learning outcomes for all young children.

Standard 5. Becoming a Professional

Students prepared in associate degree programs identify and conduct themselves as members of the early childhood profession. They know and use ethical guidelines and other professional standards related to early childhood practice. They are continuous, collaborative learners who demonstrate knowledgeable, reflective and critical perspectives on their work, making informed decisions that integrate knowledge from a variety of sources. They are informed advocates for sound educational practices and policies.

Standards

The following standards are identical to NAEYC's Initial Licensure core standards. In its position statements and publications about the continuum of early childhood professional preparation, and in the core competencies outlined in many state early childhood career development systems, NAEYC affirms the value of having a common set of outcomes shared by all in the profession, whatever their preparation or professional role.

As described earlier in this document, however, associate programs distinguish themselves from initial licensure programs in the scope and depth of preparation. In addition, in the standards below, the term *students* or *graduates* of associate programs is used rather than the term *candidates* that NCATE uses in accrediting initial licensure and advanced programs.

Standard 1. Promoting Child Development and Learning

Students prepared in associate degree programs use their understanding of young children's characteristics and needs, and of multiple interacting influences on children's development and learning, to create environments that are healthy, respectful, supportive, and challenging for all children.

Supporting explanation

All early childhood professionals base their practice on a sound foundation of child development knowledge. Many students enter associate degree programs with years of experience in child care, Head Start, or other settings in which they observe children's development on a daily basis. Associate degree programs build on this experience by connecting experience with relevant theoretical and research knowledge. Programs provide those working in teaching or paraprofessional roles with current, research-based, culturally informed knowledge that students draw upon in their daily interactions with young children. Programs ensure that students know what the children in their programs are like, what the reasons may be for similarities and differences among children of the same and different ages, and what the major

Aligning with NAEYC standards

The Early Childhood Education Department recently revised its curriculum using the NAEYC professional preparation standards. At the same time the department developed a system for course and program assessment that is both formative and summative. The system requires faculty to identify processes, resources, and teaching and learning tools that work and/or need revision or development.

The department faces the challenge of instituting and evaluating the curriculum and assessment process while preparing adjuncts across all teaching and learning formats (noncredit to credit, distance- and classroom-based learning) to revise their courses and pedagogy so all students receive comparable opportunities. The opportunity before us is to use the challenges presented by the development of this system to intentionally adopt a quality improvement model that will lead us through the transition.

—*Rebecca Gorton*,
Northampton Community College

Infusing exceptionality

Northampton Community College has spent the last few years working on a series of projects to infuse exceptionality into each course in our early childhood education program. Currently we are working on ways to introduce our students to assistive technology, working simple adaptation and accommodation assignments into each of our courses. We formed a regional consortium of two- and four-year colleges to work on course revisions.

—*Alison Lutton*,
Northampton Community College

cognitive, language, physical/motor, social, and emotional needs are among the children with whom students will be working.

Independently or as part of a team, associate degree graduates show that they can communicate with young children in healthy, developmentally appropriate ways and that they can help create environments that promote children's development by building on cultural, individual, and developmental characteristics. This foundation can enrich graduates' ability to create engaging, play-oriented learning environments that reflect current knowledge, incorporating developmentally and culturally appropriate practices for all children, including those with disabilities. (Standard 4, Teaching and Learning, describes these skills and knowledge in more detail.) To broaden students' abilities to use child development knowledge in varied professional roles, associate degree programs also help students become more articulate about the nature and importance of the child development foundations of early childhood education, and become better able to communicate these foundations to families and other adults. In addition, this foundation prepares those transferring to baccalaureate programs for later, more in-depth study of child development and learning.

Key elements of Standard 1

1a. Knowing and understanding young children's characteristics and needs

Opportunities to learn. Opportunities to learn this content would typically include course work in child development, emphasizing current research and its applications. This builds a foundation for practice and for further study. When connected with in-class support, high-quality field experiences can also serve as rich opportunities for students to observe and describe children's characteristics and needs, as members of cultures and communities, as part of an age group, and as individuals. Case study assignments are powerful teaching tools.

Evidence of growth. Students might demonstrate competence in this key element by, for example, successfully completing a child development course, receiving positive ratings of knowledge and understanding in a case study project or child observation assignment,

developing and using an informal checklist, or developing lesson plans that take into account children's cultural and developmental characteristics and needs.

1b. Knowing and understanding the multiple influences on development and learning

Opportunities to learn. Associate degree programs create a foundation for this complex area by helping students observe and discuss the many examples they see in their work and field experience settings, perhaps with a child case study focus. Students' reflections on their own development provide additional insight.

Evidence of growth. Students' growing understanding may be seen in their responses to vignettes or actual classroom events, when students begin to offer more complex, culturally informed explanations for children's characteristics and behavior. Portfolio entries that focus on individual children's strengths and needs may also reveal students' levels of understanding.

1c. Using developmental knowledge to create healthy, respectful, supportive, and challenging learning environments

Opportunities to learn. Opportunities to learn and practice these skills arise in almost every course and field experience in an associate degree program, whether these courses and experiences are extensive or limited by the nature of the program. Faculty can routinely include "what does this mean for my work with young children?" assignments in child development courses, helping students link theoretical and research knowledge to practice. A program might alert students to the key features of positive learning environments by asking them to explain how their activity/lesson plans attend to the *healthy, respectful, supportive,* and *challenging* dimensions.

Evidence of growth. These activity/lesson plans—and their implementation—can be assessed to see how well students incorporate knowledge of children's development within cultures and communities, and how effectively they demonstrate a focus on health, respect, support, and challenge. Faculty might also use these dimensions as part of field experience evaluations.

Standard 2. Building Family and Community Relationships

Students prepared in associate degree programs know about, understand, and value the importance and complex characteristics of children's families and communities. They use this understanding to create respectful, reciprocal relationships that support and empower families and to involve all families in their children's development and learning.

Supporting explanation

Family and community contexts must be well understood and valued by all early childhood professionals, whatever their degree or role. Before, during, and after graduation, associate degree students may have frequent opportunities to interact with families and members of their communities. Associate degree programs help students better understand the families with whom they work, adding research-based knowledge of family dynamics, family development, and culturally responsive practices. This knowledge creates a foundation for further study and also improves graduates' ability to work successfully with families in a variety of roles. Programs also develop students' skills, even at a beginning level, in creating supportive individual relationships with families, communicating with and supporting all families, including those from diverse cultures and those whose children have disabilities or other special needs. Finally, associate degree programs ensure that graduates know how to find help and support from colleagues and from community agencies in addressing difficult family situations.

Associate degree programs help students move beyond stereotyped perceptions of families to a respectful appreciation of challenges facing families of young children. With this foundation, associate program graduates are prepared either for further study of these issues in baccalaureate programs or for roles as effective practitioners who can assist families of young children in promoting their development and learning.

Well-prepared associate degree students will demonstrate that they know, understand, and can use information about family characteristics and needs to better support and communicate with the families of children they serve. At a foundational level, associate degree programs help students learn to work independently or as part of an education team to build respectful relationships, communicate helpfully with families about their children's development and learning, and use varied strategies to support family involvement.

Key elements of Standard 2

2a. Knowing about and understanding family and community characteristics

Opportunities to learn. Associate degree programs can use students' work and field experience settings to explore and discuss these characteristics and their implications for building relationships and communicating with families. Guided readings, panels of diverse family and community members, and visits to a variety of communities can broaden students' horizons.

Evidence of growth. Students' growth in knowledge and understanding may be seen, for example, in their portfolio or journal descriptions of the families and communities in which children live. Assessment of this work needs to include attention to growth in understanding of and respect for diversity, as well as assessment of students' foundational understanding of how children's development and learning may be influenced by family and community contexts. It is important for students to demonstrate understanding that young children's racial identities are a significant aspect of their development and that the concept of "race" has a socially constructed, rather than a biological, basis.

2b. Supporting and empowering families and communities through respectful, reciprocal relationships

Opportunities to learn. Faculty can introduce students to the importance of staff-family relationships through readings and course assignments. Field experiences and students' work sites offer many opportunities to observe and construct relationships, independently or as part of a team. Role plays and other simulations can broaden students' knowledge of and responsiveness to family diversity. Students can learn more about how to support families by creating resource guides to local community agencies.

Evidence of growth. Logs, portfolio entries, and supervisors' evaluations allow faculty to see students' progress in this area, tracking students' growing ability to see families' and communities' strengths and contributions to the teaching-learning process.

2c. Involving families and communities in their children's development and learning

Opportunities to learn. Even if time in the associate degree program is limited, well-designed assignments may prompt students to design and implement family involvement activities, following research-based best practices. In other cases, role plays or other simulations may be effective, or students may read about or observe exemplary family involvement programs. Field experiences can build in family involvement assignments that foster flexible responses to families' and children's diversity—in culture, language, and economic circumstances.

Evidence of growth. Depending on a program's characteristics and context, students might demonstrate their competence by documenting and displaying actual examples of family involvement activities in a class project; creating a portfolio or resource guide that others could use; or analyzing and responding to a written scenario in which families of diverse cultures or families whose children have disabilities seem reluctant to become involved with the program.

Standard 3. Observing, Documenting, and Assessing to Support Young Children and Families

Students prepared in associate degree programs know about and understand the goals, benefits, and uses of assessment. They know about and use systematic observations, documentation, and other effective assessment strategies in a responsible way, in partnership with families and other professionals, to positively influence children's development and learning.

Supporting explanation

In order to construct early childhood environments that are responsive to the learning needs of young children, early childhood professionals—whatever their roles—must engage in an ongoing cycle of inquiry within their classrooms and work settings. Information gained from this process is used for curriculum development, tracking children's progress, communicating with families and other professionals, and documenting the impact of programs on children's lives.

As future participants in this process, associate degree students must have a foundational understanding of the goals, benefits, and uses of assessment. Even at a beginning level, they should know that responsible assessment is done in an ethically grounded manner and is based on sound professional standards. In addition, programs ensure that students pay close attention to issues of confidentiality in gathering and reporting information about children and families.

As part of this foundational understanding, associate degree students are introduced to the value of careful observation, documentation, and other appropriate assessment strategies. This would include a solid awareness of the connection between the assessment process and planning for meaningful curriculum. Curriculum that engages young children in the process of learning is based on the documented interests and abilities of the children. Likewise, early childhood professionals must develop the knowledge, skills, and dispositions needed to work in partnership with families and other professionals in order to gather data that documents the developmental progression, individual needs, and progress toward learning within the classroom (DEC 2001). Associate degree programs can help students begin to develop these competencies.

Associate degree students who have direct contact with children need skills for engaging in deliberate, planful observation. They need to understand the various strategies for observing and assessing, how to choose appropriate strategies, and how to record and analyze what they observe, looking for the interest, curiosity, and uniqueness of each child. They should be aware of commonly adopted standardized assessments that are used for accountability and identification of special needs, and they should know what responsibilities they may have in contributing information to these assessments. Students should also understand the need to communicate valid, reliable information to families and other professionals who support children's learning and development.

Early childhood professionals may also work with children, families, and other agencies in nonclassroom settings. The need to gather information and report it to families, agencies, and other professionals requires skills such as clear and concise oral and written communication; understanding of family structures and family development; participating as part of an educational team; contributing to program evaluation; and understanding local, state, and national standards as these standards apply to their own work settings and roles.

Within a two-year program that also provides strong general education, associate degree students cannot fully develop all these competencies in family and community relationships. However, they should gain a basic understanding, positive dispositions, and foundational skills.

Key elements of Standard 3

3a. Understanding the goals, benefits, and uses of assessment

Opportunities to learn. The foundations of this understanding may be developed in a number of courses including child development, curriculum, and teaching strategies. Students can observe capable teachers using assessment to guide their planning and to communicate with families and specialists. Associate degree students can engage in guided practice with a particular focus on classroom observation.

Evidence of growth. Students' progress may be seen, for example, in role plays in which they explain assessment's goals and benefits to colleagues or families. Students might create group projects in which they pool and document their knowledge of assessment's varied uses.

3b. Knowing about and using observation, documentation, and other appropriate assessment tools and approaches

Opportunities to learn. In associate degree programs, the emphasis should be on the practical uses of assessment to inform daily planning for children. Many opportunities to learn and practice may be embedded in field experiences or may extend students' current assessment practices at their work site. Assign-

ments in multiple courses (e.g., child development, curriculum, nutrition) can emphasize careful observation using a variety of tools. Structured observation projects or case studies hone students' skills and increase their awareness of and responses to all forms of diversity, including family structure, ethnicity, racial identity, and religious beliefs. Class "assessment displays" can expand students' acquaintance with a broader array of assessment approaches, especially if students teach one another.

Evidence of growth. Faculty and field experience supervisors have multiple ways to evaluate student progress in this area. Observations can be rated for their objectivity and in-depth description; lesson plans and other assignments can be examined to see how well assessments are incorporated; written responses to hypothetical situations may show students' knowledge of appropriate assessment strategies.

3c. Understanding and practicing responsible assessment

Opportunities to learn. Associate degree faculty introduce ethical issues in assessment through readings (including NAEYC's Code of Ethical Conduct and other position statements); interviews and discussions with master teachers may also shed light on current challenges and assessment trends.

Evidence of growth. Although associate degree students do not have the training to administer many standardized or complex assessment measures, faculty can gauge students' progress through noting the degree of objectivity, fairness, and absence of bias in child observations, and in students' adherence to confidentiality as they share assessment results.

3d. Knowing about assessment partnerships with families and other professionals

Opportunities to learn. Associate program faculty can introduce students to this concept through, for example, panel discussions or videos in which families or specialists share their efforts to work closely with teachers in collecting and using assessment information. Students may seek families' insights into their child's development and behavior.

Evidence of growth. Progress in understanding this key aspect of assessment may be seen, for example, in students' journals based on field experiences or work settings, as well as in their responses to hypothetical scenarios.

Standard 4. Teaching and Learning

Students prepared in associate degree programs integrate their understanding of and relationships with children and families; their understanding of developmentally effective approaches to teaching and learning; and their knowledge of academic disciplines to design, implement, and evaluate experiences that promote positive development and learning for all young children.

Supporting explanation

Associate degree graduates work as professionals in diverse settings that require foundational knowledge of the ways young children learn, as well as competencies to support that learning. Research has shown a direct relationship between the level of teacher knowledge and quality of work with children, especially in the impact on children's language development, social skills, and learning. Recent studies of early literacy and brain development clearly indicate the key role of the early childhood professional in providing appropriate learning experiences for young children. The complex nature of this standard requires the ability to use reflective practices that incorporate knowledge of individual and family development with meaningful curriculum. The students will demonstrate competence in a variety of strategies that respect diverse learners and reflect best practices.

Students at the associate degree level have opportunities to implement and support the implementation of meaningful teaching and learning for young children in settings that include, but are not limited to, child care centers, preschool settings, home-based or family child care and as paraprofessionals in kindergarten-primary classrooms. These students frequently create the first relationships and the first learning environments for young children and their families outside the home. It is important for them to demonstrate competencies in applying principles of child development and current research on early learning to effective curriculum

planning and implementation. Their knowledge of best practices in the classroom is translated into supporting, planning, and evaluating learning that promotes development of the whole child.

Although further education will add greater depth, associate degree students demonstrate their knowledge of teaching and learning through individualized approaches to children and families, supporting a curriculum that takes into account culturally valued content and that adapts content for children who are diverse in ability, temperament, and learning style. Students need to demonstrate beginning competencies in using a variety of strategies to positively impact young children's development and learning.

Sub-Standard 4a: Connecting with children and families

Students know, understand, and use positive relationships and supportive interactions as the foundation for their work with young children.

Associate degree graduates are most often found in settings with children from birth through age 5. Knowledge of theories and practices that recognize the critical importance of supportive relationships is essential for these early years. Programs help students use their understanding of children's individual and cultural characteristics (including abilities, learning styles, temperaments, and developmental profiles) to facilitate positive adult-child relationships.

Sub-Standard 4b: Using developmentally effective approaches

Students know, understand, and use a wide array of effective approaches, strategies, and tools to positively influence children's development and learning.

Current research emphasizes the need to use a continuum of strategies to meet children's varied learning needs. Associate degree programs introduce and provide opportunities for students to explore a number of curriculum models that address the development of the whole child, including understanding the role of guidance and problem solving to support children's growth. Associate degree students also gain a foundational understanding of the differences between best practices for different age groups and developmental levels.

Sub-Standard 4c: Understanding content knowledge in early education

Students understand the importance of each content area in young children's learning. They know the essential concepts, inquiry tools, and structure of content areas, including academic subjects, and can identify resources to deepen their understanding.

Teachers of young children approach any content knowledge area with an understanding of the young child's emerging skills. However, the associate degree graduate addresses this content knowledge in the context of the whole child, and also with a well-grounded understanding of the foundations of language, literacy, mathematics, and other key content areas. Teachers of young children understand that learning occurs through a relationship-based, meaningful curriculum that emphasizes play, integration, and active learning and that incorporates experiences in creative arts, music/movement, motor development, and health/safety/nutrition. Although further education will add greater depth, programs prepare students to recognize core foundational concepts that build toward later learning, attending to the very different learning and developmental characteristics of infants, toddlers and twos, preschoolers, and school-agers.

Sub-Standard 4d: Building meaningful curriculum

Students use their own knowledge and other resources to design, implement, and evaluate meaningful, challenging curriculum that promotes comprehensive developmental and learning outcomes for all young children.

Associate degree graduates are aware of the breadth of these outcomes, including positive outcomes in language development, literacy, mathematics, science, social/emotional competence, approaches to learning, physical health, and the creative arts. At an introductory level, students demonstrate that they can implement curriculum that uses the conceptual knowledge they are acquiring through general education,

that appropriately reflects the importance of play as the tool of learning in the early years, and that is likely to promote positive developmental outcomes. They demonstrate the ability to be flexible, individually and as part of a team, in adapting curriculum to meet the interests and needs of culturally diverse children and of children with exceptionalities. They demonstrate skills in modifying curriculum in light of evaluation and feedback from supervisors.

Key elements of Standard 4

4a. Knowing, understanding, and using positive relationships and supportive interactions

Opportunities to learn. Opportunities to learn and practice begin with an introduction, generally in a child development course, to the critical importance of relationships and to the relevant research base. Students' reflections on their own personal and work experience help make this point. Journals, field experience notes, and well-designed assignments can prompt students to reflect on and plan how to develop and maintain positive relationships with young children, including those with diverse backgrounds and abilities.

Evidence of growth. Direct observations and evaluation of students' interactions with young children will help document their ability to create and sustain relationships. Because all students can improve in this critical area, evidence of growth in skills at relationship building is essential.

4b. Knowing, understanding, and using effective approaches, strategies, and tools for early education

Opportunities to learn. Associate degree programs offer students multiple opportunities to begin to learn and practice a variety of teaching techniques—through observations, simulated teaching, and applications in field experiences and work settings. Faculty introduce students to the professional knowledge base that supports the use of a "continuum of teaching strategies" adapted to development, individual, and cultural characteristics.

Evidence of growth. Students' growth can be documented through student learning logs, supervisors' observations, analysis of lesson or activity plans, and many other ongoing assessments.

4c. Knowing and understanding the importance, central concepts, inquiry tools, and structures of content areas or academic disciplines

Opportunities to learn. Associate program faculty connect early childhood courses to what students are learning in general education, helping students identify which aspects of, for example, mathematics or science may be most engaging and important for young children. Programs create many opportunities to strengthen content knowledge on language and literacy-readings with discussion, reports on position statements on literacy and mathematics as well as national or state content standards, Internet exploration, guided classroom observations, etc.

Evidence of growth. The foundations of content knowledge may be assessed not only by performance in general education courses but also by students' explanation and application of that knowledge (at least at a beginning level) in designing activities.

4d. Using own knowledge and other resources to design, implement, and evaluate meaningful, challenging curriculum to promote positive outcomes

Opportunities to learn. Faculty offer opportunities for students to see multiple models of excellent curriculum through direct observation or videos. Program expectations for students' activity plans or project plans call for discussion of meaningfulness and challenge.

Evidence of growth. Performance in field experiences offers the most valid assessment, taking into account growth over time and the opportunities that may be available for students within the associate degree program. In this as in other areas, those opportunities, and therefore the depth of skill expected, will vary depending on the focus and scope of the program.

Standard 5. Becoming a Professional

Students prepared in associate degree programs identify and conduct themselves as members of the early childhood profession. They know and use ethical guidelines and other professional standards related to early childhood practice. They are continuous, collaborative learners who demonstrate knowledgeable, reflective, and critical perspectives on their work, making informed decisions that integrate knowledge from a variety of sources. They are informed advocates for sound educational practices and policies.

Supporting explanation

The variety of professional roles played by associate degree graduates requires an array of skills for interacting competently, capably, and collaboratively with culturally, linguistically, and ability diverse children, adults, and partners in diverse home and community settings. Most early childhood professionals will have daily opportunities to apply current knowledge and demonstrate ethical decision making. Skills in the areas of communication, collaboration with family and professional partners, and providing/accepting consultation are essential to the coordination of each child's learning experiences and opportunities, and associate degree students can begin to develop these skills. Whatever their position, associate degree graduates must function in a manner that demonstrates positive regard for the roles and responsibilities of team members, who may include support staff, peers, and supervisory personnel. Students at the associate, baccalaureate, and advanced program levels are at different points in their growth as professionals; nevertheless, the commitment of all students to becoming lifelong learners will enhance the quality of teaching available to each young child and support the vitality of the early childhood field. And, at each level and point in professional growth, a commitment to and knowledge of advocacy is essential—though the form that advocacy takes, and the background gained in the professional preparation program, will vary considerably.

Typically, associate degree graduates maintain daily contact with children, families, and collaborating partners in home and community settings. They will be expected to enter the lives of families at the individual level and to gather and share information in a manner that is helpful, knowledgeable, and discreet. They will need to know how to balance the program/curriculum with knowledge of policies and guidelines for ethical decision making and appropriate linkages/referrals.

Skills for time and priority management will be essential to ensure opportunities for ongoing self-reflection and improvement. Because associate degree graduates often play essential roles in community settings that serve children of diverse cultures and abilities (e.g., early intervention, Head Start/Early Head Start), they will need to know about and be prepared to collaborate with diverse partners (e.g., speech-language pathologists, bilingual education specialists). Additionally, graduates who eventually function in professional support roles (e.g., administrators, mentors, trainers, advocates) must acquire a range of skills for supporting the development of staff, colleagues, and families. Some but not all of these skills may be incorporated into associate degree programs; others will await further study.

Key elements of Standard 5

5a. Identifying and involving oneself with the early childhood field

Opportunities to learn. Associate degree programs tailor opportunities to learn and practice to students' individual work histories and goals, providing resources that expand students' current knowledge of the field. Student organizations and involvement in NAEYC Affiliates are other examples of such opportunities.

Evidence of growth. Evaluation of progress may be based, for example, on evidence of professional activities, as well as on personal mission statements, reflective essays, or group presentations.

5b. Knowing about and upholding ethical standards and other professional guidelines

Opportunities to learn. Associate degree faculty can introduce students to the key principles of NAEYC's Code of Ethical Conduct. Students can share with one another the standards or other guidelines relevant to their work role (e.g., Head Start Performance Standards).

Evidence of growth. Faculty can assess ethical understanding through student responses to real or hypothetical ethical dilemmas. Presentations and reports on other professional guidelines are other sources of information on student progress.

5c. Engaging in continuous, collaborative learning to inform practice

Opportunities to learn. Group projects and other collaborative assignments will hone students' skills. Faculty can also identify and recommend resources for further study for students whose basic skills are in place. Students who are working or involved in field experiences can describe challenging classroom situations and seek out resources that can help them address the situation successfully.

Evidence of growth. Faculty know students are progressing if they are rated by peers or coworkers as good team members, if they document their efforts to seek new information even when not required, and when their classroom performance is enhanced by their own learning efforts.

5d. Integrating knowledgeable, reflective, and critical perspectives on early education

Opportunities to learn. Associate degree programs build a foundation for reflective practice while also grounding students in essential skills. Continuous modeling and prompting of students to ask "why?" will create multiple opportunities to learn and practice. Attendance at professional meetings, as well as viewing and discussing dialogues about professional issues, will expose associate degree students to complex perspectives that may differ from their own.

Evidence of growth. Student logs, journals, and portfolios, developed over time, are promising tools with which to assess students' increasing levels of knowledge, critical thinking, and reflection.

5e. Engaging in informed advocacy for children and the profession

Opportunities to learn. Because so many associate degree students are working in the field, some opportunities to learn and practice can be created on site—i.e., students can talk with families and colleagues about children's or the profession's needs, using approaches learned in courses or from reading. Role plays and other simulations can present students with hypothetical situations in which advocacy skills are needed. Class speakers, interactions with community partners and programs that can help support culturally, linguistically, and ability diverse children and families, trips to professional meetings, Web investigations, and more, can broaden students' knowledge of effective advocacy.

Evidence of growth. Students' growth in advocacy skills can be assessed in a variety of ways, including evaluations of their ability to apply principles of effective advocacy in assignments or projects. Students' ability to identify situations that call for advocacy, in their own workplace or community, is another sign of competence in this area.

Supportive Skills

In order to support the effective use of the knowledge, skills, and dispositions described in Standards 1–5, well-prepared graduates of associate degree programs also need a set of skills that cut across these five domains. These skills are outlined below, along with examples of opportunities to learn and practice these skills. In some cases, these opportunities may be incorporated into general education courses, and in other cases they might be provided as part of the early childhood program or through collaborative efforts across units of the institution. Finally, examples show how students might demonstrate competence in each of these areas.

Skills in Self-Assessment and Self-Advocacy

Associate degree students are often at a key decision point in their professional lives, entering or re-entering higher education after extended work experiences or making decisions about further education beyond the associate degree. Therefore, skills in assessing one's own goals, strengths, and needs are critical, as is learning how to advocate for one's own professional needs.

Opportunities to learn. Opportunities to practice and learn these skills may occur, for example, in career counseling and advisement upon entry into the program and at key decision points thereafter. Student organizations and professional development events may also make a contribution. Courses may include role plays to strengthen self-advocacy

skills. Student portfolios may include personal mission statements and self-assessments of growth over time.

Evidence of growth. Students' growth in these skills may be seen in assessments of changes over time and in the actual professional decisions made by students as they move through the program and beyond.

Skills in Mastering and Applying Foundational Concepts from General Education

General education has value for its own sake—as part of the background of an educated person— and for the value added to practitioners' ability to implement a conceptually rich curriculum. Both in immediate employment as an early childhood professional and in preparing for further baccalaureate study, associate degree graduates are enriched by understanding foundational concepts from areas including science, mathematics, literature, and the behavioral and social sciences.

Opportunities to learn. Opportunities to learn and practice are provided in high-quality general education courses selected to support students' goals and in intentional linkages between the general education and professional curriculum—for example, in team-taught courses and in assignments that call on students to apply general education concepts as they plan activities for young children.

Evidence of growth. Students' acquisition of these skills may be seen, for example, in their successful mastery of general education objectives, in their written and oral rationales for activities, and in ratings of the conceptual accuracy and richness of their curriculum plans.

Written and Verbal Communication Skills

Well-prepared associate degree graduates have strong skills in written and verbal communication. These skills allow them to provide positive language and literacy experiences for children, and they also support professional communications with families and colleagues. Students going on to baccalaureate study need skills sufficient to ensure success in upper-division academic work. In addition, technological literacy is an essential component of this set of skills.

Opportunities to learn. Opportunities to learn and practice are based on the program's assessment of individual students' strengths and needs. Some students will need more intensive support because of linguistic diversity or inadequate secondary preparation. Course work, labs, and assignments in both general and professional education courses should offer developmentally sequenced opportunities to gain communicative competence and build technological literacy.

Evidence of growth. Students' mastery of these skills may be seen, for example, in successful completion of relevant courses, performance on communication and technological aspects of assignments, and competent use of communication skills in field experiences.

Skills in Making Connections between Prior Knowledge/Experience and New Learning

All professionals need these skills, but they are especially important in supporting the learning of associate degree students who have worked for years in early care and education. Well-prepared associate degree graduates are able to respect and draw upon their past or current work experience and also reflect critically upon it, enriching and altering prior knowledge with new insights. These skills will, over time, enable graduates to respond to the evolving mandates and priorities of the early childhood field.

Opportunities to learn. Opportunities to learn and practice these skills are numerous; almost every assignment can prompt students to use and reflect on their experiences. Class discussions of work situations, logs, and portfolios can be used to encourage students to make connections. Student presentations related to their current work allow students to share and validate that experience.

Evidence of growth. Progress in making productive connections may be seen in students' growing ability to articulate relevant

Embedding humanities

Several community colleges across the country were involved in a project sponsored by the Community College Humanities Association and funded by the National Endowment for the Humanities. The purpose was to provide models of how teacher education programs at the associate degree level could make a stronger link to humanities to better prepare future teachers. Many projects involved learning communities linking an introductory education course with a course in composition, children's literature, or history.

Each college in the project identified a team to develop a program to meet the needs of that college's unique context and institutional culture. Each team was mentored by another college team that had already implemented some form of education/humanities link. The grant provided for a beginning planning conference, mentor visits to the campuses, and a concluding conference where the teams presented their projects.

—*Barbara Nilsen*,
Broome Community College

Hands-on skills

The early childhood education associate degree program has given me a different perspective on the importance of blending my learning in the college classroom with hands-on skills with children. I have learned about issues in the profession that have renewed my enthusiasm for learning. Early childhood education is ever changing and needs professionals with multiple skills who are eager to learn and discover.

—*Lorraine Kaiser*,
student, Iowa Lakes Community College

Impact

In the associate degree early childhood program I have learned skills that I use daily as a teacher in Head Start. I am more self-confident and have a sense of accomplishment in working with children.

—*Val Lowe*,
student, Iowa Lakes Community College

theory and research that either affirms or calls into question their experience—often seen in journals and portfolios, but also in interviews and presentations.

Skills in Identifying and Using Professional Resources

Even the best associate program cannot provide in-depth knowledge and skills in all areas. Therefore, well-prepared graduates should know how to identify and use credible professional resources from multiple sources, allowing them to better serve children and families with a wide range of cultures, languages, needs, and abilities.

Opportunities to learn. Opportunities to learn and practice these skills may occur within many courses and field experiences—for example, through Internet assignments, library research, discussions with other members of teaching teams who have other specializations, and so on.

Evidence of growth. Students' growth in this area may be evidenced, for example, by portfolio artifacts, resources used in lesson plans or other field assignments, or in class presentations.

References and Resources

Publications

[Numbers in brackets denote items pertinent to one or more of the five standards; "G" denotes items of *General* usefulness.]

Althouse, R., M.H. Johnson, & S.T. Mitchell. 2003. *The colors of learning: Integrating the visual arts into the early childhood curriculum.* New York: Teachers College Press; and Washington, DC: NAEYC. [4]

American Association of Colleges for Teacher Education (AACTE). 2002. *The community college role in teacher education: A case for collaboration.* AACTE issue paper prepared by A.M. Schuhmann. Washington, DC: Author. [G]

American Association of Community Colleges (AACC). 1998. *AACC position on the associate degree.* Washington, DC: Author. [G]

American Association of Community Colleges (AACC). n.d. *Reexamining the community college mission.* Washington, DC: Author. [G]

August, D., & K. Hakuta, eds. 1998. *Educating language-minority children.* Washington, DC: National Academy Press. [1,4]

Barnett, S.W., & S.S. Boocock. 1998. *Early care and education for children in poverty: Promises, programs, and long-term results.* Albany, NY: State University of New York Press. [G]

Barnett, W.S., J.W. Young, & L.J. Schweinhart. 1998. How preschool education influences long-term cognitive development and school success. In *Early care and education for children in poverty,* eds. W.S. Barnett & S.S. Boocock, 167–84. Albany, NY: State University of New York Press. [G]

Barrera, I. 1996. Thoughts on the assessment of young children whose sociocultural background is unfamiliar to the assessor. In *New visions for the developmental assessment of infants and young children,* eds. S.J. Meisels & E. Fenichel, 69–84. Washington, DC: ZERO TO THREE/ National Center for Infants, Toddlers, and Families. [3]

Beckman, P.J. 1996. *Strategies for working with families of young children with disabilities.* Baltimore, MD: Brookes. [2]

Bellm, D., M. Whitebook, & P. Hnatiuk. 1997. *The Early Childhood Mentoring Curriculum: A handbook for mentors.* Washington, DC: Center for the Child Care Workforce. [G]

Bergen, D., R. Reid, & L. Torelli. 2001. *Educating and caring for very young children: The infant/toddler curriculum.* New York: Teachers College Press. [4]

Berk, L.E., & A. Winsler. 1995. *Scaffolding children's learning: Vygotsky and early childhood education.* Washington, DC: NAEYC. [1]

Bodrova, E., & D.J. Leong. 1996. *Tools of the mind: The Vygotskian approach to early childhood education.* Upper Saddle River, NJ: Prentice Hall. [4]

Bowman, B.T., ed. 2002. *Love to read: Essays in developing and enhancing early literacy skills of African American children.* Washington, DC: National Black Child Development Institute. [4]

Bredekamp, S., & C. Copple, eds. 1997. *Developmentally appropriate practice in early childhood programs.* Rev. ed. Washington, DC: NAEYC. [G]

Bredekamp, S., & T. Rosegrant, series & vol. eds. 1992. *Reaching potentials. Vol. 1: Appropriate curriculum and assessment for young children.* Washington, DC: NAEYC. [3,4]

Bredekamp, S., & T. Rosegrant, series & vol. eds. 1995. *Reaching potentials. Vol. 2: Transforming early childhood curriculum and assessment.* Washington, DC: NAEYC. [3,4]

Burns, M.S., P. Griffin, & C.E. Snow, eds. 1999. *Starting out right: A guide to promoting children's reading success.* Washington, DC: National Academy Press. [4]

Campbell, F.A., R. Harms, J.J. Sparling, & C.T. Ramey. 1998. Early childhood programs and success in school: The Abecedarian study. In *Early care and education for children in poverty,* eds. W.S. Barnett & S.S. Boocock, 145–66. Albany, NY: State University of New York Press. [G]

Campbell, P.S., & C. Scott-Kassner, eds. 1995. *Music in childhood, from preschool through the early grades.* Belmont, CA: Wadsworth. [4]

Center for the Child Care Workforce. 1993. *The national child care staffing study–revisited: Four years in the life of center-based child care.* Washington, DC: Author. [G]

Chafel, J., ed. 1997. *Families and early childhood education.* Advances in Early Education and Day Care, vol. 9. Stamford, CT: JAI Press. [2]

Chang, H.N., A. Muckelroy, & D. Pulido-Tobiassen. 1996. *Looking in, looking out: Redefining child care and early education in a diverse society.* San Francisco, CA: California Tomorrow. [G]

Chang, H.N., J.O. Edwards, C. Alvarado, D. Pulido-Tobiassen, & C.L. Morgan. 1999. *Transforming curriculum, empowering faculty: Deepening teachers' understanding of race, class, culture, and language.* San Francisco, CA: California Tomorrow. [G]

Child Mental Health Foundations and Agencies Network. 2000. *A good beginning: Sending America's children to school with the social and emotional competence they need to succeed.* Bethesda, MD: National Institute of Mental Health, Office of Communications and Public Liaison. [4]

Clements, D.H., J. Sarama, & A.M. DiBiase, eds. In press. *Engaging young children in mathematics: Findings of the National 2000 Conference on Standards for Preschool and Kindergarten Mathematics Education.* Hillsdale, NJ: Erlbaum. [4]

Cohen, D.H., V. Stern, & N. Balaban. 1997. *Observing and recording the behavior of young children.* 4th ed. New York: Teachers College Press. [1]

Copley, J.V. 2000. *The young child and mathematics.* Washington, DC: NAEYC. [4]

Copley, J.V., ed. 1999. *Mathematics in the early years.* Reston, VA: National Council of Teachers of Mathematics; and Washington, DC: NAEYC. [4]

Curtis, D., & M. Carter. 1996. *Reflecting children's lives: A handbook for planning child-centered curriculum.* St. Paul, MN: Redleaf Press. [4]

Curtis, D., & M. Carter. 2000. *The art of awareness: How observation can transform your teaching.* St. Paul, MN: Redleaf Press. [3,4]

Dickinson, D.K., & P.O. Tabors, eds. 2001. *Beginning literacy with language.* Baltimore, MD: Brookes. [4]

Division for Early Childhood (DEC). 2001. *DEC recommended practices: Indicators for quality in programs for infants and young children with special needs and their families.* Reston, VA: Division for Early Childhood, Council for Exceptional Children. [G,2]

Dodge, D. 2000. *Connecting content, teaching, and learning.* Washington, DC: Teaching Strategies. [3,4]

Dodge, D. 2002. *The creative curriculum for early childhood.* Washington, DC: Teaching Strategies. [3,4]

Doyle, M.B. 2002. *Paraprofessional's guide to the inclusive classroom.* Baltimore, MD: Brookes. [G]

Driscoll, A., & N.G. Nagel. 2002. *Early childhood education, birth–8: The world of children, families, and educators.* 2d ed. Boston: Allyn & Bacon. [G]

Dunst, C.J., C.M. Trivette, & A.G. Deal. 1994. *Supporting and strengthening families: Methods, strategies, and practices.* Vol. 1. Cambridge, MA: Brookline Books. [2]

Early, D.M., & P.J. Winton. 2001. Preparing the workforce: Early childhood teacher preparation at 2- and 4-year institutions of higher education. *Early Childhood Research Quarterly* 16 (3): 285–306. [G]

Edwards, P.A., H.M. Pleasants, & S.H. Franklin. 1999. *A path to follow: Learning to listen to parents.* Portsmouth, NH: Heinemann. [2]

Epstein, A.S., L.J. Schweinhart, & L. McAdoo. 1996. *Models of early childhood education.* Ypsilanti, MI: High/Scope Press. [4]

Epstein, J.L., M.G. Sanders, & L.A. Clark. 1999. *Preparing educators for school-family-community partnerships: Results of a national survey of colleges and universities.* Baltimore, MD: Center for Research on the Education of Students Placed at Risk. [2]

Falk, B. 2000. *The heart of the matter: Using standards and assessment to learn.* Portsmouth, NH: Heinemann. [3]

Feeney, S., & N.K. Freeman. 1999. *Ethics and the early childhood educator: Using the NAEYC code.* Washington, DC: NAEYC. [5]

Feeney, S., N.K. Freeman, & E. Moravcik. 2000. *Teaching the NAEYC code of ethical conduct.* Washington, DC: NAEYC. [5]

Fillmore, L.W., & C.E. Snow. 2000. *What teachers need to know about language.* Washington, DC: Office of Educational Research and Improvement. [4]

Fishbaugh, M.S.E. 2000. *The collaboration guide for early career educators.* Baltimore, MD: Brookes. [G]

Forman, G., & B. Fyfe. 1998. Negotiated learning through design, documentation, and discourse. In *The hundred languages of children: The Reggio Emilia approach—Advanced reflections,* 2d ed., eds. C. Edwards, L. Gandini, & G. Forman, 239–60. Greenwich, CT: Ablex. [4]

Fund for Instructional Improvement, California Community College's Chancellor's Office. 1996. *Race, class, culture, language: A deeper context for early childhood education.* Santa Barbara, CA: Author. [G]

Gandini, L., & C.P. Edwards. 2001. *Bambini: The Italian approach to infant/toddler care.* New York: Teachers College Press. [4]

Gardner, H. 1993. *Frames of mind: The theory of multiple intelligences.* New York: Basic Books. [1]

Gartrell, D. 2002. *A guidance approach for the encouraging classroom.* Albany, NY: Delmar. [1]

Genishi, C., ed. 1992. *Ways of assessing young children and curriculum: Stories of early childhood practice.* New York: Teachers College Press. [3,4]

Gregory, E., ed. 1997. *One child, many worlds: Early learning in multicultural communities.* New York: Teachers College Press. [2]

Guralnick, M.J., ed. 2001. *Early childhood inclusion: Focus on change.* Baltimore, MD: Brookes. [G]

Harbin, G.L., R.A. McWilliam, & J.J. Gallagher. 2000. Services for young children with disabilities and their families. In *Handbook of early childhood intervention,* 2d ed., eds. J.P. Shonkoff & S.J. Meisels, 387–415. New York: Cambridge University Press. [G]

Harms, T., R. Clifford, & D. Cryer. 1998. *Early Childhood Environment Rating Scale (ECERS-R).* Rev. ed. New York: Teachers College Press. [4]

Hart, B., & T.R. Risley. 1995. *Meaningful differences in everyday experience of young American children.* Baltimore, MD: Brookes. [4]

Heath, S.B. 1983. *Ways with words: Language, life, and work in communities and classrooms.* New York: Cambridge University Press. [4]

Helm, J.H., & S. Beneke, eds. 2003. *The power of projects. Meeting contemporary challenges in early childhood classrooms: Strategies and solutions.* New York: Teachers College Press; and Washington, DC: NAEYC. [3,4]

Helm, J.H., & L. Katz. 2001. *Young investigators: The project approach in the early years.* New York: Teachers College Press. [3]

Helm, J.H., S. Beneke, & K. Steinheimer. 1998. *Windows on learning: Documenting young children's work.* New York: Teachers College Press. [3]

Hemmeter, M.L., G.E. Joseph, B.J. Smith, & S. Sandall. 2001. *DEC recommended practices program assessment: Improving practices for young children with special needs and their families.* Denver, CO: Sopris West Educational Services. [G,2]

Hohmann, M., & D.P. Weikart. 1995. *Educating young children: Active learning practices for preschool and child care programs.* Ypsilanti, MI: High/Scope Press. [4]

Hull, K., J. Goldhaber, & A. Capone. 2002. *Opening doors: Introduction to inclusive early childhood education.* Boston: Houghton Mifflin. [G]

Johnson, J., & J.B. McCracken, eds. 1994. *The early childhood career lattice: Perspectives on professional development.* Washington, DC: NAEYC. [5]

Johnson, L.J., M.J. LaMontagne, P.M. Elgas, & A.M. Bauer. 1998. *Early childhood education: Blending theory, blending practice.* Baltimore, MD: Brookes. [G]

Jones, E. 1986. *Teaching adults: An active learning approach.* Washington, DC: NAEYC. [G]

Jones, E., ed. 1993. *Growing teachers: Partnerships in staff development.* Washington, DC: NAEYC. [G]

Kagan, S.L., & B.T. Bowman, eds. 1997. *Leadership in early care and education.* Washington, DC: NAEYC. [G]

Kaiser, B., & J.S. Rasminsky. 1999. *Meeting the challenge: Effective strategies for challenging behaviors in early childhood environments.* Ottawa, Canada: Canadian Child Care Federation. [4]

Katz, L.G., & S.C. Chard. 2000. *Engaging children's minds: The project approach.* 2d ed. Greenwich, CT: Ablex. [4]

Kirkpatrick, L. 2001. *Multicultural strategies for community colleges: Expanding faculty diversity.* ERIC Digest No. ED455902. Los Angeles: ERIC Clearinghouse for Community Colleges. [G]

Ladson-Billings, G. 2001. *Crossing over to Canaan: The journey of new teachers in diverse classrooms.* San Francisco: Jossey-Bass. [5]

Lally, J.R. 1995. *Caring for infants and toddlers in groups: Developmentally appropriate practice.* Arlington, VA: ZERO TO THREE/National Center for Clinical Infant Programs. [4]

Lamb, M., ed. 1999. *Parenting and child development in "nontraditional" families.* Mahwah, NJ: Erlbaum. [2]

Lee, E., D. Menkart, & M. Okazawa-Rey, eds. 1998. *Beyond heroes and holidays: A practical guide to K–12 antiracist, multicultural education and staff development.* Washington, DC: Network of Educators on the Americas. [4]

Levin, D.E. 2003. *Teaching young children in violent times: Building a peaceable classroom.* 2d ed. Cambridge, MA: Educators for Social Responsibility; and Washington, DC: NAEYC. [G]

Losardo, A., & A. Notari-Syverson. 2001. *Alternative approaches to assessing young children.* Baltimore, MD: Brookes. [3]

Lynch, E.W., & M.J. Hanson. 1998. *Developing cross-cultural competence: A guide for working with children and their families.* 2d ed. Baltimore, MD: Brookes. [1,2]

McAfee, O., & D. Leong. 2002. *Assessing and guiding young children's development and learning.* 3d ed. Boston: Allyn & Bacon. [1,3]

McCarthy, J., J. Cruz, & N. Ratcliff. 1999. *Early childhood teacher education licensure patterns and curriculum guidelines: A state by state analysis.* Washington, DC: Council for Professional Recognition. [G]

McWilliam, P.J., P.J. Winton, & E.R. Crais. 1996. *Practical strategies for family-centered intervention.* San Diego, CA: Singular Publishing Group. [2]

Moore, E. 1997. Race, class, and education. In *Leadership in early care and education,* eds. S.L. Kagan & B.T. Bowman, 69–74. Washington, DC: NAEYC. [G]

Mussen, P., ed. 1997. *Handbook of child psychology.* 5th ed. New York: Wiley. [1]

NAEYC. 1996a. *Guidelines for preparation of early childhood professionals.* Washington, DC: Author. [G]

NAEYC. 1996b. *Technology and young children: Ages 3 through 8.* Position Statement. Washington, DC: Author. [G]

NAEYC. 1997. *Licensing and public regulation of early childhood programs.* Position Statement. Washington, DC: Author. [5]

NAEYC. 1998. *Accreditation criteria and procedures of the National Academy of Early Childhood Programs.* Position Statement. Washington, DC: Author. [G]

National Council of Teachers of Mathematics (NCTM). 2000. *Principles and standards for school mathematics.* Reston, VA: Author. [4]

National Institute of Child Health and Human Development. 2000. *Report of the National Reading Panel. Teaching children to read: An evidence-based assessment of the scientific research literature on reading and its implications for reading instruction.* NIH Publication No. 00-4769. Washington, DC: U.S. Government Printing Office. [4]

National Institute on Early Childhood Development and Education, U.S. Department of Education. 2000. *New teachers for a new century: The future of early childhood professional preparation.* Jessup, MD: U.S. Department of Education, ED Publishing. [G]

National Research Council. 1998. *Preventing reading difficulties in young children,* eds. C.E. Snow, M.S. Burns, & P. Griffin. Committee on the Prevention of Reading Difficulties in Young Children, Commission on Behavioral and Social Sciences and Education. Washington, DC: National Academy Press. [4]

National Research Council. 1999. *How people learn: Brain, mind, experience, and school,* eds. J.D. Bransford, A.L. Brown, & R.R. Cocking. Committee on Developments in the Science of Learning, Commission on Behavioral and Social Sciences and Education. Washington, DC: National Academy Press. [G]

National Research Council. 2001a. *Adding it up: Helping children learn mathematics,* eds. J. Kilpatrick, J. Swafford, & B. Findell. Mathematics Learning Study Committee, Center for Education, Division of Behavioral and Social Sciences and Education. Washington, DC: National Academy Press. [4]

National Research Council. 2001b. *Eager to learn: Educating our preschoolesrs,* eds. B.T. Bowman, M.S. Donovan, & M.S. Burns. Committee on Early Childhood Pedagogy, Commission on Behavioral and Social Sciences and Education. Washington, DC: National Academy Press. [G]

National Research Council and Institute of Medicine. 2000. *From neurons to neighborhoods: The science of early childhood development,* eds. J.P. Shonkoff & D.A. Phillips. Board on Children, Youth, and Families, Commission on Behavioral and Social Sciences and Education. Washington, DC: National Academy Press. [G,1]

National Institute on Early Childhood Development and Education, U.S. Department of Education. 2000. *New teachers for a new century: The future of early childhood professional preparation.* Jessup, MD: U.S. Department of Education, ED Publishing. [G]

National Reading Panel. 2000. *Report of the National Reading Panel: Teaching children to read: An evidence-based assessment of the scientific research literature on reading and its implications for reading instruction.* Washington, DC: National Institute of Child Health and Human Development, National Institutes of Health. [4]

Neelly, L.P. 2001. Developmentally appropriate music practice: Children learn what they live. *Young Children* 56 (3): 32–43. [4]

Neuman, S.B., & D.K. Dickinson. 2001. *Handbook of early literacy research.* New York: Guilford. [4]

Neuman, S.B., C. Copple, & S. Bredekamp. 1999. *Learning to read and write: Developmentally appropriate practices for young children.* Washington, DC: NAEYC. [4]

New Standards/Speaking and Listening Committee. 2001. *Speaking and listening for preschool through third grade.* Washington, DC: National Center on Education and the Economy. [4]

Nora, A. n.d. *Reexamining the community college mission.* Washington, DC: American Association of Community Colleges. Available only online at www.aacc.nche.edu/ Content/NavigationMenu/ResourceCenter/ Projects_Partnerships/Current/NewExpeditions/ IssuePapers/Reexamining_the_Community_ College_Mission.htm. [G]

Peisner-Feinberg, E.S., M.R. Burchinal, R.M. Clifford, M.L. Culkin, C. Howes, S.L. Kagan, N. Yazejian, P. Byler, J. Rustici, & J. Zelazo. 1999. *The children of the Cost, Quality, and Outcomes Study go to school.* Chapel Hill: University of North Carolina at Chapel Hill, Frank Porter Graham Child Development Center. [G]

Phillippe, K.A., & M. Patton. 2000. *National profile of community colleges: Trends and statistics.* 3d ed. Washington, DC: Community College Press, American Association of Community Colleges. [G]

Pickett, A.L., & K. Gerlach, eds. 1997. *Supervising paraeducators in school settings: A team approach.* Austin, TX: PRO-ED, Inc. [G]

Pickett, A.L., B. Semrau, K. Faison, & J. Formanek. 2002. *A core curriculum and training program to prepare paraeducators to work in center and home-based programs for young children with disabilities from birth to age five.* 3d ed. Logan, UT: National Resource Center for Paraprofessionals. [G]

Project Zero, Cambridgeport School, Cambridgeport Children's Center, Ezra H. Baker School, & John Simpkins School. 2003. *Making teaching visible: Documenting individual and group learning as professional development.* Cambridge, MA: Project Zero. [3]

Recruiting New Teachers (RNT). 2002. *Tapping potential: Community college students and America's teacher recruitment challenge.* Belmont, MA: Author. [G]

Reynolds, A.J., J.A. Temple, D.L. Robertson, & E.A. Mann. 2001. Long-term effects of an early childhood intervention on educational achievement and juvenile arrest: A 15-year follow-up of low-income children in public schools. *Journal of the American Medical Association* 285 (18): 2339–46. [G]

Rosin, P., A.D. Whitehead, L.I. Tuchman, G.S. Jesien, A.L. Begun, & L. Irwin. 1996. *Partnerships in family-centered care: A guide to collaborative early intervention.* Baltimore, MD: Brookes. [2]

Sandall, S., M. McLean, & B. Smith. 2000. *DEC recommended practices in early intervention/early childhood special education.* Longmont, CO: Sopris West Educational Services. [G]

Seefeldt, C. 1995. Transforming curriculum in social studies. In *Reaching potentials. Vol. 2: Transforming early childhood curriculum and assessment,* eds. S. Bredekamp & T. Rosegrant, 145–66. Washington, DC: NAEYC. [4]

Seefeldt, C. 2001. *Social studies for the preschool/primary child.* 6th ed. Upper Saddle River, NJ: Prentice Hall/ Merrill. [4]

Shartrand, A.M., H.B. Weiss, H.M. Kreider, & M.E. Lopez. 1997. *New skills for new schools.* Washington, DC: U.S. Department of Education. [2]

Shore, R. 1997. *Rethinking the brain: New insights into early development.* New York: Families and Work Institute. [G]

Sims, W.L. ed.; J. Cassidy, A. Freshwater, & C.D. Mack, assoc. eds. 1995. *Strategies for teaching: Prekindergarten music.* Reston, VA: National Association for Music Education (MENC). [4]

Snell, M.E., & R. Janney. 2000. *Teachers' guides to inclusive practices: Collaborative teaming.* Baltimore, MD: Brookes. [G]

Southern Poverty Law Center. 1997. *Starting small: Teaching tolerance in preschool and early grades.* Montgomery, AL: Author. [G]

Stayton, V.D., P.S. Miller, & L.A. Dinnebeil. 2003. *DEC personnel preparation in early childhood special education: Implementing the DEC recommended practices.* Denver, CO: Sopris West Educational Services. [G]

Tabors, P.O. 1997. *One child, two languages: A guide for preschool educators of children learning English as a second language.* Baltimore, MD: Brookes. [4]

Tabors, P.O. 1998. What early childhood educators need to know: Developing effective programs for linguistically and culturally diverse children and families. *Young Children* 53 (6): 20–26. [1,4]

Tabors, P.O., & C.E. Snow. 2001. Young bilingual children and early literacy development. In *Handbook of early literacy research,* eds. S.B. Neuman & D.K. Dickinson, 159–78. New York: Guilford. [4]

Tertell, E.A., S.M. Klein, & J.L. Jewett, eds. 1998. *When teachers reflect: Journeys toward effective, inclusive practice.* Washington, DC: NAEYC. [5]

Townsend, B.K., & J.M. Ignash, eds. 2003. *The role of the community college in teacher education.* New Directions for Community Colleges, no. 121. San Francisco, CA: Jossey-Bass. [G]

Turnbull, A.P., & H.R. Turnbull. 1997. *Families, professionals, and exceptionality: A special partnership.* 3d ed. Columbus, OH: Merrill. [2]

Van Scoter, J., E. Ellis, & J. Railsback. 2001. *Technology in early childhood education: Finding a balance.* Portland, OR: Northwest Regional Education Laboratory. [4]

Von Blackensee, L. 1999. *Technology tools for young learners.* Larchmont, NY: Eye on Education. [4]

Vygotsky, L.S. 1978. *Mind in society: The development of higher psychological processes.* Cambridge, MA: Harvard University Press. [1]

Wolery, M., & J.S. Wilbers, eds. 1994. *Including children with special needs in early childhood programs.* Washington, DC: NAEYC. [G]

Wolpert, E. (for the Committee for Boston Public Housing). 1999. *Start seeing diversity: The basic guide to an antibias classroom.* Saint Paul, MN: Redleaf Press. [G]

Yelland, N.J., ed. 2000. *Promoting meaningful learning: Innovations in educating early childhood professionals.* Washington, DC: NAEYC. [5]

Websites

American Alliance for Health, Physical Education, Recreation, and Dance, www.aahperd.org

American Associate Degree Early Childhood Educators, www.accessece.org

American Association of Colleges for Teacher Education, www.aacte.org

American Association of Community Colleges, www.aacc.nche.edu

Center for Community College Policy, www.communitycollegepolicy.org

Center for Evidence-Based Practices, www.evidencebasedpractices.org/projects.php

Center for the Improvement of Early Reading Achievement, www.ciera.org

Center on the Social and Emotional Foundations for Early Learning, http://csefel.uiuc.edu

CEO Forum on Education and Technology, Self-Assessment for Teacher Preparation, www.ceoforum.org

Children and Computers, www.childrenandcomputers.com

Community College Research Center, Teachers College/ Columbia University, www.tc.columbia.edu/ccrc/

Council for Exceptional Children, www.cec.sped.org

Division for Early Childhood, www.dec-sped.org

ERIC Clearinghouse on Assessment and Evaluation, http://ericae.net

ERIC Clearinghouse for Community Colleges, www.gseis.ucla.edu/ERIC/eric.html

International Reading Association, www.reading.org

League for Innovation in the Community College, www.league.org

MENC: National Association for Music Education, www.menc.org

MuSICA: Music and Science Information Computer Archive, www.musica.uci.edu

National Association for Bilingual Education, www.nabe.org

National Association for Early Childhood Teacher Educators, www.naecte.org

National Association of Community College Teacher Education Programs, www.nacctep.org/index.html

National Center for Research on Evaluation, Standards, and Student Testing, http://cresst96.cse.ucla.edu

National Center on Education and the Economy, www.ncee.org

National Clearinghouse for English Language Acquisition and Language Instruction Educational Programs, www.ncela.gwu.edu

National Council of Teachers of Mathematics, www.nctm.org

National Early Childhood Technical Assistance Center, www.nectac.org

National Education Goals Panel, www.negp.gov

National Educational Technology Standards Projects, http://cnets.iste.org

National Geographic Society, National Standards for Geography, www.nationalgeographic.com/xpeditions/standards/

National Institute for Early Education Research, http://nieer.org/

Program for Infant/Toddler Caregivers, www.pitc.org

Technology & Young Children (NAEYC Technology & Young Children Interest Forum), http://techandyoungchildren.org/index.shtml

ZERO TO THREE, www.zerotothree.org

Appendix A

Associate Standards Work Group

NAEYC gratefully acknowledges the expertise and commitment of the members of the Associate Standards Work Group:

Nancy Barbour, Kent State University

Camille Catlett, Frank Porter Graham Child Development Institute, University of North Carolina at Chapel Hill

Alison Lutton, Northampton Community College; and president, American Associate Degree Early Childhood Educators (ACCESS)

ReJean Schulte, Cuyahoga Community College–Western Campus

NAEYC Staff

Marilou Hyson, Associate Executive Director for Professional Development

Mary Duru, Professional Development Specialist

Institutional affiliations reflect those held by the members at the time the Work Group was convening.

Council for Exceptional Children, Division for Early Childhood
CEC/DEC

About the CEC/DEC Standards for Early Childhood Special Education Teachers

The Council for Exceptional Children (CEC) and its Division for Early Childhood (DEC) have long worked to develop and implement standards for beginning early childhood special education teachers. For more than 15 years these standards have provided direction to colleges and universities that prepare teachers, as well as to states as they develop new licensure frameworks for early childhood special educators.

In 1999, CEC began the process of reexamining *all* of its standards to ensure that special education standards effectively addressed changes in the field and were appropriate for developing performance-based accountability systems at both the institution and state levels. DEC took the lead in reexamining its standards for early childhood special educators.

Back in 1995, DEC, with NAEYC and the Association of Teacher Educators (ATE), had approved a set of standards. DEC decided to completely revise that set to reflect current best practice in the field. A revised set of standards was field-validated by members of CEC, DEC, and NAEYC. Representatives of NAEYC and DEC participated in the final decision-making discussions. The final set of standards reproduced in this volume was approved by the CEC Professional Standards and Practice Committee in 2001.

Using these standards for NCATE approval

Special education programs

If an institution offers undergraduate and/or graduate programs in early childhood special education, it must respond to the CEC program standards. Institutions should carefully note that CEC considers any program that prepares candidates for their first special education license to be "initial," whether such programs are at the graduate or undergraduate level.

Blended programs

Some schools have merged their programs for the preparation of early childhood education teachers and of early childhood special education teachers into a single ("blended") preservice preparation program.

Such institutions may submit a combined Program Report to NCATE, following the NAEYC standards. However, that combined Program Report must also include responses to the CEC Content Standards, following the instructions in CEC's "Guidelines for the Preparation of the Special Education Program Report" available at www.cec.sped.org.

The combined Program Report will be reviewed by members representing the CEC *and* NAEYC. If approved, the program will be nationally recognized by both CEC and NAEYC.

For more

For further information, please contact the Council for Exceptional Children at cecprof@cec.sped.org.

Contents

Introduction   129

Standards   129

Standard 1: Foundations   129

Standard 2: Development and Characteristics of Learners   130

Standard 3: Individual Learning Differences   131

Standard 4: Instructional Strategies   132

Standard 5: Learning Environments and Social Interactions   132

Standard 6: Language   133

Standard 7: Instructional Planning   134

Standard 8: Assessment   135

Standard 9: Professional and Ethical Practice   136

Standard 10: Collaboration   137

CEC Special Education Content Standards

For All Beginning Special Education Teachers of Early Childhood Students

Introduction

The CEC Special Education Content Standards consist of 10 narrative standards. These same 10 standards are used by CEC to review all special education programs. Under the performance-based review procedures, it is expected that faculty will use the knowledge and skill base both in the Common Core and in the Early Childhood area of specialization to inform their curriculum development to ensure that the Content Standards are met.

Please note that a program is not expected to include a response to each of the knowledge and skills. Programs must respond to the 10 Content Standards, not to each of the knowledge and skills. The program's evaluation system should ensure that the program's assessment system comprehensively addresses each of the 10 standards.

Beginning special educators demonstrate their mastery of each standard through their mastery of the knowledge ("K") and skills ("S") of the CEC Common Core ("CC") and the Early Childhood ("EC") area of specialization.

Terminology used in the standards

"**Individual with exceptional learning needs (ELN)**" is used throughout to include individuals with disabilities and individuals with exceptional gifts and talents. "**Exceptional condition**" is used throughout to include both single and coexisting conditions. These may be two or more disabling conditions or exceptional gifts or talents coexisting with one or more disabling conditions.

"**Special curricula**" is used throughout to denote curricular areas not routinely emphasized or addressed in general curricula; for example, social, communication, motor, independence, self-advocacy.

Standards

Standard 1: Foundations

Special educators understand the field as an evolving and changing discipline based on philosophies, evidence-based **principles and theories**, relevant **laws and policies**, diverse and **historical** points of view, and **human issues** that have historically influenced and continue to influence the field of special education and the education and treatment of individuals with exceptional needs both in school and society. Special educators understand how these **influence professional practice**, including assessment, instructional planning, implementation, and program evaluation. Special educators understand how **issues of human diversity** can impact families, cultures, and schools, and how these complex human issues can interact with issues in the delivery of special education services. They understand the **relationships of organizations of special education** to the organizations and functions of schools, school systems, and other agencies. Special educators use this knowledge as a ground upon which to construct their own personal understandings and philosophies of special education.

Knowledge

CC1-K1   Models, theories, and philosophies that form the basis for special education practice.

CC1-K2   Laws, policies, and ethical principles regarding behavior management planning and implementation.

CC1-K3   Relationship of special education to the organization and function of educational agencies.

CC1-K4   Rights and responsibilities of students, parents, teachers, and other professionals and schools related to exceptional learning needs.

CC1-K5   Issues in definition and identification of individuals with exceptional learning needs, including those from culturally and linguistically diverse backgrounds.

CC1-K6   Issues, assurances, and due process rights related to assessment, eligibility, and placement within a continuum of services.

CC1-K7   Family systems and the role of families in the educational process.

CC1-K8   Historical points of view and contribution of culturally diverse groups.

CC1-K9   Impact of the dominant culture on shaping schools and the individuals who study and work in them.

CC1-K10   Potential impact of differences in values, languages, and customs that can exist between the home and school.

EC1-K1   Historical and philosophical foundations of services for young children both with and without exceptional learning needs.

EC1-K2   Trends and issues in early childhood education and early childhood special education.

EC1-K3   Law and policies that affect young children, families, and programs for young children.

Skills

CC1-S1   Articulate personal philosophy of special education.

Standard 2: Development and Characteristics of Learners

Special educators know and **demonstrate respect** for their students first as unique human beings. Special educators understand the **similarities and differences in human development** and the characteristics between and among individuals with and without exceptional learning needs (ELN). Moreover, special educators understand how **exceptional conditions** can **interact** with the domains of human development and they **use this knowledge to respond to the varying abilities and behaviors of individuals** with ELN. Special educators understand how the experiences of individuals with ELN can impact families, as well as the individual's ability to learn, interact socially, and live as fulfilled contributing members of the community.

Knowledge

CC2-K1   Typical and atypical human growth and development.

CC2-K2   Educational implications of characteristics of various exceptionalities.

CC2-K3   Characteristics and effects of the cultural and environmental milieu of the individual with exceptional learning needs and the family.

CC2-K4   Family systems and the role of families in supporting development.

CC2-K5   Similarities and differences of individuals with and without exceptional learning needs.

CC2-K6   Similarities and differences among individuals with exceptional learning needs.

CC2-K7   Effects of various medications on individuals with exceptional learning needs.

EC2-K1   Theories of typical and atypical early childhood development.

EC2-K2   Effect of biological and environmental factors on pre-, peri-, and post-natal development.

EC2-K3   Influence of stress and trauma, protective factors and resilience, and supportive relationships on the social and emotional development of young children.

EC2-K4 Significance of sociocultural and political contexts for the development and learning of young children who are culturally and linguistically diverse.

EC2-K5 Impact of medical conditions on family concerns, resources, and priorities.

EC2-K6 Childhood illnesses and communicable diseases.

Skills

[none]

Standard 3: Individual Learning Differences

Special educators understand the **effects that an exceptional condition** can have **on an individual's learning** in school and throughout life. Special educators understand that the beliefs, traditions, and values across and within cultures can affect relationships among and between students, their families, and the school community. Moreover, special educators are **active and resourceful in seeking to understand how primary language, culture, and familial backgrounds interact with the individual's exceptional condition** to impact the individual's academic and social abilities, attitudes, values, interests, and career options. The understanding of these learning differences and their possible interactions **provides the foundation** upon which **special educators individualize instruction** to provide meaningful and challenging learning for individuals with ELN.

Knowledge

CC3-K1 Effects an exceptional condition(s) can have on an individual's life.

CC3-K2 Impact of learners' academic and social abilities, attitudes, interests, and values on instruction and career development.

CC3-K3 Variations in beliefs, traditions, and values across and within cultures and their effects on relationships among individuals with exceptional learning needs, family, and schooling.

CC3-K4 Cultural perspectives influencing the relationships among families, schools, and communities as related to instruction.

Interdisciplinary committees

One of the challenges that blended early childhood and early childhood special education programs often face is how to involve faculty and staff across multiple departments and programs, as well as students and community representatives, in the ongoing development, implementation, and evaluation of the program.

We have addressed this challenge by establishing an interdisciplinary committee that includes representation from all departments and programs in which students take professional education courses; undergraduate and graduate students; and representatives from community agencies (for example, public schools, Head Start, early intervention) that support our programs as field sites and in other ways. Committee members have developed strong working relationships and even have written and implemented grants together, presented at national and state conferences, and coauthored manuscripts.

—*Vicki D. Stayton,*
Western Kentucky University

"Virtual family"

We use a simulation in our family courses to help students become more sensitive and aware of what a family who has a child with a disability may encounter. A family member typically coteaches these courses and assumes primary responsibility for the "virtual family" project, which is conducted online.

Each student receives a description of a newborn infant who presents some real-life challenges (for example, failed the newborn hearing screening, diagnosed with Down syndrome, prematurity). Acting as virtual parents, students name their baby, provide a personal family context (for example, decide to be married, divorced, a single parent), and discuss their initial reaction to their infant's situation. Several times throughout the semester the scenarios are changed (the child with impaired hearing receives a cochlear implant, grandparents have problems coping, additional disabilities are identified, early intervention services are initiated, the first IEP meeting is scheduled, the child goes to kindergarten). Again the students discuss their family situation, how they cope, supports they receive, programs they and their child participate in, and so on. A series of guiding questions focus their online discussions. At the end of the semester the students reflect on what they learned, how they felt, and how they would use this experience in their future work with young children and their families.

—*Judith A. Niemeyer,*
University of North Carolina at Greensboro

CC3-K5 Differing ways of learning of individuals with exceptional learning needs, including those from culturally diverse backgrounds, and strategies for addressing these differences.

Skills

EC3-S1 Use intervention strategies with young children and their families that affirm and respect family, cultural, and linguistic diversity.

Standard 4: Instructional Strategies

Special educators posses a repertoire of evidence-based **instructional strategies to individualize instruction** for individuals with ELN. Special educators select, adapt, and use these instructional strategies to promote **positive learning results in general and special curricula** and to appropriately **modify learning environments** for individuals with ELN. They enhance the **learning of critical thinking, problem solving, and performance skills** of individuals with ELN, and increase their self-awareness, self-management, self-control, self-reliance, and self-esteem. Moreover, special educators emphasize the **development, maintenance, and generalization** of knowledge and skills across environments, settings, and the lifespan.

Knowledge

[none]

Skills

CC4-S1 Use strategies to facilitate integration into various settings.

CC4-S2 Teach individuals to use self-assessment, problem solving, and other cognitive strategies to meet their needs.

CC4-S3 Select, adapt, and use instructional strategies and materials according to characteristics of the individual with exceptional learning needs.

CC4-S4 Use strategies to facilitate maintenance and generalization of skills across learning environments.

CC4-S5 Use procedures to increase the individual's self-awareness, self-management, self-control, self-reliance, and self-esteem.

CC4-S6 Use strategies that promote successful transitions for individuals with exceptional learning needs.

EC4-S1 Use instructional practices based on knowledge of the child, family, community, and the curriculum.

EC4-S2 Use knowledge of future educational settings to develop learning experiences and select instructional strategies for young children.

EC4-S3 Prepare young children for successful transitions.

Standard 5: Learning Environments and Social Interactions

Special educators actively **create learning environments** for individuals with ELN that foster cultural understanding, safety and emotional well-being, positive social interactions, and **active engagement** of individuals with ELN. In addition, special educators **foster environments in which diversity is valued** and individuals are taught to live harmoniously and productively in a culturally diverse world. Special educators shape **environments to encourage the independence**, self-motivation, self-direction, personal empowerment, and self-advocacy of individuals with ELN. Special educators **help their general education colleagues integrate individuals** with ELN in regular environments and engage them in meaningful learning activities and interactions. Special educators use **direct motivational and instructional interventions** with individuals with ELN to teach them to respond effectively to current expectations. When necessary, special educators can safely **intervene with individuals with ELN in crisis**. Special educators coordinate all these efforts and provide **guidance and direction to paraeducators and others**, such as classroom volunteers and tutors.

Knowledge

CC5-K1 Demands of learning environments.

CC5-K2 Basic classroom management theories and strategies for individuals with exceptional learning needs.

CC5-K3 Effective management of teaching and learning.

CC5-K4   Teacher attitudes and behaviors that influence behavior of individuals with exceptional learning needs.

CC5-K5   Social skills needed for educational and other environments.

CC5-K6   Strategies for crisis prevention and intervention.

CC5-K7   Strategies for preparing individuals to live harmoniously and productively in a culturally diverse world.

CC5-K8   Ways to create learning environments that allow individuals to retain and appreciate their own and each others' respective language and cultural heritage.

CC5-K9   Ways specific cultures are negatively stereotyped.

CC5-K10   Strategies used by diverse populations to cope with a legacy of former and continuing racism.

EC5-K1   Medical care considerations for premature, low-birth-weight, and other young children with medical and health conditions.

Skills

CC5-S1   Create a safe, equitable, positive, and supportive learning environment in which diversities are valued.

CC5-S2   Identify realistic expectations for personal and social behavior in various settings.

CC5-S3   Identify supports needed for integration into various program placements.

CC5-S4   Design learning environments that encourage active participation in individual and group activities.

CC5-S5   Modify the learning environment to manage behaviors.

CC5-S6   Use performance data and information from all stakeholders to make or suggest modifications in learning environments.

CC5-S7   Establish and maintain rapport with individuals with and without exceptional learning needs.

CC5-S8   Teach self-advocacy.

CC5-S9   Create an environment that encourages self-advocacy and increased independence.

CC5-S10   Use effective and varied behavior management strategies.

CC5-S11   Use the least intensive behavior management strategy consistent with the needs of the individual with exceptional learning needs.

CC5-S12   Design and manage daily routines.

CC5-S13   Organize, develop, and sustain learning environments that support positive intracultural and intercultural experiences.

CC5-S14   Mediate controversial intercultural issues among students within the learning environment in ways that enhance any culture, group, or person.

CC5-S15   Structure, direct, and support the activities of paraeducators, volunteers, and tutors.

CC5-S16   Use universal precautions.

EC5-S1   Implement nutrition plans and feeding strategies.

EC5-S2   Use health appraisal procedures and make referrals as needed.

EC5-S3   Design, implement, and evaluate environments to assure developmental and functional appropriateness.

EC5-S4   Provide a stimuli-rich indoor and outdoor environment that employs materials, media, and technology, including adaptive and assistive technology.

EC5-S5   Maximize young children's progress in group and home settings through organization of the physical, temporal, and social environments.

Standard 6: Language

Special educators understand **typical and atypical language development** and the ways in which exceptional conditions can interact with an individual's experience with and use of language. Special educators use individualized strategies to **enhance language development** and **teach communication skills** to individuals with ELN. Special educators are familiar with **augmentative, alternative, and assistive technologies** to support and enhance communication of individuals with exceptional needs. Special educators match their communication methods to an individual's language proficiency and cultural and linguistic differences. Special educators provide **effective language models** and they use communication strategies and resources to **facilitate understanding of subject matter for individuals with ELN whose primary language is not English.**

Knowledge

CC6-K1   Effects of cultural and linguistic differences on growth and development.

CC6-K2   Characteristics of one's own culture and use of language and the ways in which these can differ from other cultures and uses of languages.

CC6-K3   Ways of behaving and communicating among cultures that can lead to misinterpretation and misunderstanding.

CC6-K4   Augmentative and assistive communication strategies.

Skills

CC6-S1   Use strategies to support and enhance communication skills of individuals with exceptional learning needs.

CC6-S2   Use communication strategies and resources to facilitate understanding of subject matter for students whose primary language is not the dominant language.

EC6-S1   Support and facilitate family and child interactions as primary contexts for learning and development.

Standard 7: Instructional Planning

Individualized decision-making and instruction is at the center of special education practice. Special educators develop **long-range individualized instructional plans** anchored in both general and special curricula. In addition, special educators systematically translate these individualized plans into carefully selected **shorter-range goals and objectives** taking into consideration an individual's abilities and needs, the learning environment, and a myriad of cultural and linguistic factors. Individualized instructional plans emphasize **explicit modeling** and **efficient guided practice** to assure acquisition and fluency through maintenance and generalization. Understanding of these factors as well as the implica-

tions of an individual's exceptional condition, guides the special educator's selection, adaptation, and creation of materials, and the use of powerful instructional variables. Instructional plans are **modified based on ongoing analysis of the individual's learning progress.** Moreover, special educators facilitate this instructional planning in a **collaborative context** including the individuals with exceptionalities, families, professional colleagues, and personnel from other agencies as appropriate. Special educators also develop a variety of **individualized transition plans**, such as transitions from preschool to elementary school and from secondary settings to a variety of postsecondary work and learning contexts. Special educators are comfortable using **appropriate technologies** to support instructional planning and individualized instruction.

Knowledge

CC7-K1   Theories and research that form the basis of curriculum development and instructional practice.

CC7-K2   Scope and sequences of general and special curricula.

CC7-K3   National, state or provincial, and local curricula standards.

CC7-K4   Technology for planning and managing the teaching and learning environment.

CC7-K5   Roles and responsibilities of the paraeducator related to instruction, intervention, and direct service.

Skills

CC7-S1   Identify and prioritize areas of the general curriculum and accommodations for individuals with exceptional learning needs.

CC7-S2   Develop and implement comprehensive, longitudinal individualized programs in collaboration with team members.

CC7-S3   Involve the individual and family in setting instructional goals and monitoring progress.

CC7-S4   Use functional assessments to develop intervention plans.

CC7-S5   Use task analysis.

CC7-S6   Sequence, implement, and evaluate individualized learning objectives.

CC7-S7   Integrate affective, social, and life skills with academic curricula.

CC7-S8   Develop and select instructional content, resources, and strategies that respond to cultural, linguistic, and gender differences.

CC7-S9   Incorporate and implement instructional and assistive technology into the educational program.

CC7-S10   Prepare lesson plans.

CC7-S11   Prepare and organize materials to implement daily lesson plans.

CC7-S12   Use instructional time effectively.

CC7-S13   Make responsive adjustments to instruction based on continual observations.

CC7-S14   Prepare individuals to exhibit self-enhancing behavior in response to societal attitudes and actions.

EC7-S1   Implement, monitor, and evaluate Individualized Family Service Plans (IFSPs) and Individualized Education Plans (IEPs).

EC7-S2   Plan and implement developmentally and individually appropriate curriculum.

EC7-S3   Design intervention strategies incorporating information from multiple disciplines.

EC7-S4   Implement developmentally and functionally appropriate individual and group activities including play, environmental routines, parent-mediated activities, group projects, cooperative learning, inquiry experiences, and systematic instruction.

Standard 8: Assessment

Assessment is integral to the decision making and teaching of special educators, and special educators use **multiple types of assessment information** for a variety of educational decisions. Special educators use the results of assessments to help identify exceptional learning needs and to develop and implement individualized instructional programs, as well as to adjust instruction in response to ongoing learning progress. Special educators understand the **legal policies and ethical principles of measurement and assessment** related to referral, eligibility, program planning, instruction, and placement for individuals with ELN, including those from culturally and linguistically diverse back-

grounds. Special educators understand **measurement theory and practices** for addressing issues of validity, reliability, norms, bias, and interpretation of assessment results. In addition, special educators understand the appropriate **use and limitations** of various types of assessments. Special educators collaborate with families and other colleagues to assure **nonbiased, meaningful assessments and decision making**. Special educators conduct **formal and informal assessments** of behavior, learning, achievement, and environments to design learning experiences that support the growth and development of individuals with ELN. Special educators use assessment information to **identify supports and adaptations** required for individuals with ELN to access the general curriculum and to participate in school, system, and statewide assessment programs. Special educators **regularly monitor the progress** of individuals with ELN in general and special curricula. Special educators **use appropriate technologies** to support their assessments.

Knowledge

CC8-K1   Basic terminology used in assessment.

CC8-K2   Legal provisions and ethical principles regarding assessment of individuals.

CC8-K3   Screening, pre-referral, referral, and classification procedures.

CC8-K4   Use and limitations of assessment instruments.

CC8-K5   National, state or provincial, and local accommodations and modifications.

Skills

CC8-S1   Gather relevant background information.

CC8-S2   Administer nonbiased formal and informal assessments.

CC8-S3   Use technology to conduct assessments.

CC8-S4   Develop or modify individualized assessment strategies.

CC8-S5   Interpret information from formal and informal assessments.

CC8-S6   Use assessment information in making eligibility, program, and placement decisions for individuals with exceptional learning needs, including those from culturally and/or linguistically diverse backgrounds.

CC8-S7   Report assessment results to all stake-holders using effective communication skills.

CC8-S8   Evaluate instruction and monitor progress of individuals with exceptional learning needs.

CC8-S9   Create and maintain records.

EC8-S1   Assess the development and learning of young children.

EC8-S2 Select, adapt, and use specialized formal and informal assessments for infants, young children, and their families.

EC8-S3   Participate as a team member to integrate assessment results in the development and implementation of Individualized Family Service Plans (IFSPs) and Individualized Education Plans (IEPs).

EC8-S4   Assist families in identifying their concerns, resources, and priorities.

EC8-S5   Participate and collaborate as a team member with other professionals in conducting family-centered assessments.

EC8-S6   Evaluate services with families.

Standard 9: Professional and Ethical Practice

Special educators are guided by the profession's ethical and professional practice standards. Special educators practice in multiple roles and complex situations across wide age and developmental ranges. Their practice requires ongoing attention to **legal matters** along with serious professional and **ethical considerations**. Special educators engage in **professional activities** and participate in learning communities that benefit individuals with ELN, their families, colleagues, and their own professional growth. Special educators view themselves as **lifelong learners** and regularly reflect on and adjust their practice. Special educators are aware of how their own and others attitudes, behaviors, and ways of communicating can influence their practice. Special educators understand that culture and language can interact with exceptionalities, and are **sensitive to the many aspects of diversity** of individuals with ELN and their families. Special educators actively plan and engage in activities that foster their professional growth and keep

them **current with evidence-based best practices.** Special educators know their own limits of practice and practice within them.

Knowledge

CC9-K1   Personal cultural biases and differences that affect one's teaching.

CC9-K2   Importance of the teacher serving as a model for individuals with exceptional learning needs.

CC9-K3   Continuum of lifelong professional development.

CC9-K4   Methods to remain current regarding research-validated practice.

EC9-K1   Organizations and publications relevant to the field of early childhood special education.

Skills

CC9-S1   Practice within the CEC Code of Ethics and other standards of the profession.

CC9-S2   Uphold high standards of competence and integrity and exercise sound judgment in the practice of the professional.

CC9-S3   Act ethically in advocating for appropriate services.

CC9-S4   Conduct professional activities in compliance with applicable laws and policies.

CC9-S5   Demonstrate commitment to developing the highest education and quality-of-life potential of individuals with exceptional learning needs.

CC9-S6   Demonstrate sensitivity for the culture, language, religion, gender, disability, socio-economic status, and sexual orientation of individuals.

CC9-S7   Practice within one's skill limit, and obtain assistance as needed.

CC9-S8   Use verbal, nonverbal, and written language effectively.

CC9-S9   Conduct self-evaluation of instruction.

CC9-S10   Access information on exceptionalities.

CC9-S11   Reflect on one's practice to improve instruction and guide professional growth.

CC9-S12   Engage in professional activities that benefit individuals with exceptional learning needs, their families, and one's colleagues.

EC9-S1   Recognize signs of child abuse and neglect in young children, and follow reporting procedures.

EC9-S2   Use family theories and principles to guide professional practice.

EC9-S3   Respect family choices and goals.

EC9-S4   Apply models of team process in early childhood.

EC9-S5   Advocate for enhanced professional status and working conditions for early childhood service providers.

EC9-S6   Participate in activities of professional organizations relevant to the field of early childhood special education.

EC9-S7   Apply research and effective practices critically in early childhood settings.

EC9-S8   Develop, implement, and evaluate a professional development plan relevant to one's work with young children.

Standard 10: Collaboration

Special educators routinely and effectively **collaborate with families, other educators, related service providers, and personnel from community agencies in culturally responsive ways.** This collaboration assures that the needs of individuals with ELN are addressed throughout schooling. Moreover, special educators embrace their special role as advocates for individuals with ELN. Special educators promote and advocate the learning and well being of individuals with ELN across a wide range of settings and a range of different learning experiences. Special educators are viewed as specialists by a myriad of people who actively seek their collaboration to effectively include and teach individuals with ELN. Special educators are a **resource to their colleagues** in understanding the laws and policies relevant to individuals with ELN. Special educators use collaboration to **facilitate the successful transitions** of individuals with ELN across settings and services.

Knowledge

CC10-K1   Models and strategies of consultation and collaboration.

CC10-K2   Roles of individuals with exceptional learning needs, families, and school and

Community liaison

Our community liaison is a parent of a child with a disability. She participates part-time in course activities and program development; she also serves as a liaison between family members and university faculty.

The community liaison works with faculty in the graduate and undergraduate programs to coordinate class assignments and in-class activities that specifically relate to families and participates in program development. For example, she arranges panels of family members, and then leads the panel discussions with our students.

Faculty consider the community liaison integral to the program. While this person is not on the university payroll, faculty have advocated for her support from a variety of sources (state contracts, Parent Advocacy Center, federal funds, indirect funds from the university).

—*Judith A. Niemeyer,*
University of North Carolina at Greensboro

Collaborating

Collaborating with birth–3 providers and early childhood teachers in our community is an important part of the university's early childhood special education personnel preparation program. We could not do our jobs as faculty without the assistance of these professionals who mentor our students and help them apply book knowledge to the real world. Early childhood teachers in the community provide safe environments where our students can practice what they learn in their classes, try out new skills, and not be afraid of failing.

We strive to develop self-reflective teachers. So we urge cooperating professionals and university supervisors to encourage our students to continually reflect on what worked well, why it worked well, what they might do differently, and what they need to consider in the future.

— *Michaelene Ostrosky,*
University of Illinois at Urbana-Champaign

community personnel in planning of an individualized program.

CC10-K3   Concerns of families of individuals with exceptional learning needs and strategies to help address these concerns.

CC10-K4   Culturally responsive factors that promote effective communication and collaboration with individuals with exceptional learning needs, families, school personnel, and community members.

EC10-K1   Dynamics of team building, problem solving, and conflict resolution.

Skills

CC10-S1   Maintain confidential communication about individuals with exceptional learning needs.

CC10-S2   Collaborate with families and others in assessment of individuals with exceptional learning needs.

CC10-S3   Foster respectful and beneficial relationships between families and professionals.

CC10-S4   Assist individuals with exceptional learning needs and their families in becoming active participants in the educational team.

CC10-S5   Plan and conduct collaborative conferences with individuals with exceptional learning needs and their families.

CC10-S6   Collaborate with school personnel and community members in integrating individuals with exceptional learning needs into various settings.

CC10-S7   Use group problem-solving skills to develop, implement, and evaluate collaborative activities.

CC10-S8   Model techniques and coach others in the use of instructional methods and accommodations.

CC10-S9   Communicate with school personnel about the characteristics and needs of individuals with exceptional learning needs.

CC10-S10   Communicate effectively with families of individuals with exceptional learning needs from diverse backgrounds.

CC10-S11   Observe, evaluate, and provide feedback to paraeducators.

EC10-S1   Assist the family in planning for transitions.

EC10-S2   Communicate effectively with families about curriculum and their child's progress.

EC10-S3   Apply models of team process in early childhood settings.

EC10-S4   Apply various models of consultation in early childhood settings.

EC10-S5   Establish and maintain positive collaborative relationships with families.

EC10-S6   Provide consultation and instruction specific to services for children and families.

About the DEC Recommended Practices in Personnel Preparation

As the nature of services to young children with special needs changes, so must the ways professionals are prepared to work with these children and their families. In recent years the early childhood education field has seen a major shift toward developmentally appropriate practices for all children, including children who have disabilities or special needs. Developmentally appropriate practices are practices that meet the developmental, cultural, and individual needs of children. Because children's needs may differ, the practices may vary from child to child. Professionals working with young children and their families understand the importance of tailoring learning opportunities to the needs of the learners, whether they are typically developing children, gifted children, or children who have developmental delays or disabilities.

In addition to recognizing and respecting children's individual learning needs, the field recognizes the value of inclusion and natural learning environments for young children. Inclusion supports the right of all children, regardless of abilities, to participate actively in natural settings within their communities; natural settings are those in which any child with no disability would spend time. The term "inclusive settings" is usually used to refer to preschool and school-age programs, such as child care centers, Head Start classrooms, and kindergartens; "natural environments" extends also to settings where infants and toddlers usually learn and develop, such as parent-child playgroups, library story time, Gymboree classes, playgrounds, community events, and family homes.

The Division of Early Childhood (DEC) recognizes the importance of fully including children who have special needs in community-based programs and natural environments. To read more about DEC's position on inclusion, visit the DEC Website at www.dec-sped.org and follow the links to its position paper on inclusion.

The move toward inclusion shifts the focus away from direct service delivery by specialists in early intervention and early childhood special education to an indirect form of service delivery that reflects a more consultative approach. This means that instead of focusing their efforts on the child directly, professionals must often focus their attention on the child's primary caregiver or other adults who work with the child on a daily basis. While it is critical that special education professionals have a strong foundation in child- and family-focused intervention and assessment strategies, they must also have the knowledge and skills needed to transmit this information to the child's primary caregiver through a consultative approach (Buysse & Wesley 1993; Dinnebeil & McInerney 2000; McWilliam, Wolery, & Odom 2000).

Rethinking professional development

In 2000 DEC published the results of a group of comprehensive studies designed to identify a set of "recommended practices" to guide professionals' work with children with special needs and their families (Sandall, McLean, & Smith 2000).

Through their work on the DEC Recommended Practices project, leaders in the field of early childhood special education, including Vicki Stayton and Pat Miller, recognized the importance of high-quality personnel preparation (a term encompassing the preparation of teachers as well as other professionals who work with children and families). They identified a number of practices empirically linked to effective service delivery. Those practices are in the areas of

- family participation in personnel preparation,

- interdisciplinary and interagency collaboration,

- the design and sequence of learning activities,

- integrating cultural and linguistic diversity throughout personnel preparation programs,

- developing and maintaining high-quality field experiences that give students opportunities to practice and refine emerging skills,

- including faculty members from a variety of disciplines in an integrated or interdisciplinary approach, and

- designing and sequencing professional development (i.e., inservice) activities that help professionals learn and grow professionally.

An outgrowth of that work is the publication *Personnel Preparation in Early Childhood Special Education: Implementing the DEC Recommended Practices* (Stayton, Miller, & Dinnebeil 2003). In this book the editors identify early childhood special education teacher education programs across the country that implement the recommended practices. They offer these programs as case examples illustrating the successes and challenges faced by program developers. These case examples provide practical information for teacher educators interested in designing or revising programs.

Recommended practices for personnel preparation

Described more fully in DEC's two publications, the seven recommended practices briefly are as follows:

Family participation in personnel preparation. Given the high value placed on family-centered practices in early intervention, professionals need opportunities for meaningful interactions with families in the context of a professional preparation program. Students learn about working with families in many ways—through class lectures, class simulations, and supervised home visits with families, as well as interviews and informal conversations. High-quality personnel preparation programs find multiple ways to include family members in learning activities.

Teaming

The seminar Working with Peers incorporates DEC's Recommended Practices in interdisciplinary planning and collaboration. The course is jointly taught by two instructors, one who teaches the preschool practicum and seminar class in the Family and Human Development Department and one who teaches early childhood special education specialization courses in the Special Education Department.

The instructors organize the students into teams according to their practicum classroom settings. Each team includes students from early childhood elementary education, special education, and communicative disorders, depending on class enrollment. The first three weeks are spent discussing teaming in general, roles and resources of team members, and the processes teams use to complete assignments.

After the first three weeks of instruction, the students spend the hour of class time in their team meetings, working together to complete assignments that focus on specific children whom the team members select. Since each member has different information, the students spend time during team meetings . . .

Interdisciplinary and interagency collaboration. High-quality services for children and their families are interdisciplinary in nature, because children's developmental problems are seldom limited to one developmental domain. Those who work with children with special needs and their families must be prepared to collaborate with professionals from a variety of backgrounds, including general early childhood teachers, social workers, occupational and physical therapists, and speech/language pathologists. Preparation for interdisciplinary work must include opportunities to learn alongside professionals from a variety of backgrounds.

Design and sequence of learning activities. Consistent with what we know about children's learning (Bredekamp & Rosegrant 1992, 12–18), strong personnel preparation programs must design and sequence learning activities just as carefully to meet the needs of their adult students. Learning begins with awareness and culminates in application, and students must be provided with differentiated opportunities to meet the learning goals.

Integrating cultural and linguistic diversity throughout personnel preparation programs. As the demographics of American society change, early childhood professionals must be able to work with other professionals with cultural or linguistic backgrounds different from their own. High-quality personnel preparation programs integrate ethnic, cultural, and linguistic diversity in meaningful ways throughout a student's learning experiences; attention is not limited to a "diversity course." Students learn to work with peers, professionals, children, and family members who represent a range of linguistic, ethnic, and cultural backgrounds. Students are also provided with opportunities to explore and reflect on their own cultures and how their beliefs influence their interactions with others.

Developing and maintaining high-quality field experiences. Integration of knowledge occurs most efficiently when learners can apply new knowledge in a variety of settings. Professionals preparing to work with young children who have special needs must have opportunities to practice and refine their skills in real-world settings. These include, but are not limited to, inclusive classrooms, community-based programs such as story time at the library, child care or Head Start classrooms, and family homes. Learners in professional preparation programs must have access to skilled professionals who can model effective practices as well as provide meaningful feedback to improve learners' skills and performance.

Including faculty members from a variety of disciplines in an integrated or interdisciplinary approach. As stated earlier, providing interdisciplinary services to children represents high-quality service delivery practice; therefore, professionals must be prepared to work with other professionals from many disciplines. Effective professional preparation programs mirror this recommended interdisciplinary approach to service delivery by including faculty members from a variety of disciplines to share their perspectives and present information from diverse sources.

sharing the information to develop a quality case study.

Each week students are encouraged to start the meeting by completing an agenda form to guide the meeting for the day. One student, who had no previous experiences working on teams, reported that this form was one of the most helpful tools for her when working with others. She continued to use this agenda form three semesters later as president of the student organization in her department, and the semester following that as she worked with other teachers in her student teaching placements. She included these forms in her student teaching portfolio as ways to work with other teachers in the field. She received a Teacher of the Month award in her district in her first year of teaching; in her e-mail sharing this information, she said it was easy for her now to work with the other teachers because she had so much practice in her training.

—*Barbara Fiechtl*,
Utah State University

Designing and sequencing professional development (i.e., inservice) activities that help professionals learn and grow professionally. Learning is a continual process that does not end when a student graduates from a program and begins his or her professional career. Careful attention must be given to providing professional development experiences that allow teachers and other professionals to increase and deepen their level of knowledge and expertise related to working with children and families. Systems of comprehensive professional development should be provided by credentialing bodies such as state offices of education and should reflect the needs of professionals who work with children and families.

Conclusion

The fields of early childhood, early intervention, and early childhood special education are strongly connected in practice and must also be strongly connected in preparation programs. The principles described here are useful for any program that prepares individuals to work with children and families.

Readers interested in learning more about personnel preparation in the field of early childhood special education can contact the DEC Executive Office at (406) 243-5898 or visit the DEC Website at www.dec-sped.org.

References

Bredekamp, S., & T. Rosegrant, eds. 1992. *Reaching potentials. Vol. 1: Appropriate curriculum and assessment for young children.* Washington, DC: NAEYC.

Buysse, V., & P.W. Wesley. 1993. The identity crisis in early childhood special education: A call for professional role clarification. *Topics in Early Childhood Special Education* 13: 418–29.

Dinnebeil, L.A., & W. McInerney. 2000. Supporting inclusion in early childhood settings: The Tuesday morning teacher. *Young Exceptional Children* 4: 19–27.

McWilliam, R.A., M. Wolery, & S.L. Odom. 2001. Instructional perspectives in inclusive preschool classrooms. In *Early childhood inclusion: Focus on change,* ed. M.J. Guralnick, 503–30. Baltimore, MD: Brookes.

Miller, P., & V.D. Stayton. 1999. Higher education culture—A fit or misfit with reform in teacher education? *Journal of Teacher Education* 50: 290–302.

Sandall, S., M.E. McLean, & B.J. Smith. 2000. *DEC recommended practices in early intervention/early childhood special education.* Longmont, CO: Sopris West Educational Services.

Stayton, V.D., P.S. Miller, & L.A. Dinnebeil. 2003. *Personnel preparation in early childhood special education: Implementing the DEC Recommended Practices.* Longmont, CO: Sopris West Educational Services.

National Board
for Professional
Teaching Standards
NBPTS

About the NBPTS Early Childhood/Generalist Standards

The National Board for Professional Teaching Standards® (NBPTS) has established a volunteer certification process to recognize what accomplished teachers should know and be able to do. For all teachers who undertake it, the study of the standards and the completion of the certification process is an intense professional development activity. Although the standards primarily serve as the basis for this voluntary process for experienced teachers, the standards can also be used as a guide to what *all* accomplished teachers should know and be able to do. Colleges and universities across the country have incorporated the NBPTS standards into their preservice programs. Although the NBPTS standards for early childhood teachers were developed for individual teachers rather than for students, curriculum, or programs, the developers were careful to reflect both NAEYC's and NCATE's standards in their development.

The text that follows reproduces selected sections of NBPTS's publication *Early Childhood/Generalist Standards, 2d ed.* As outlined in the "Preface," the Five Core Propositions provide the philosophical basis for all of the NBPTS standards. The developers of both the first and the second editions of the Early Childhood/Generalist Standards began their discussions with these Propositions as they faced the task of writing documents that reflected how accomplished early childhood teaching would look in connection to each Proposition. The initial lists of important knowledge and actions produced by these committees showed a certain uniformity across disciplines and developmental units; however, the developers then wrote specific standards that reflect the uniqueness of the accomplished early childhood teacher.

The "Introduction" more specifically describes these unique qualities, presenting a more defined picture of that dedicated educator. The "Introduction" also presents a historical view of the development of these documents and an explanation of the organization of the standards. It is important to note that NBPTS recognizes the seamless quality of teaching and knows that, although the standards are listed and explained as separate entities, they occur concurrently in the classrooms of accomplished teachers.

The "Overview" of standards presents succinct standard statements, each describing one aspect of accomplished teaching. In the actual Early Childhood/Generalist Standards document, the nine standard statements are followed by elaborations, which provide a detailed picture of what accomplished early childhood teachers need to know, value, and do in order to fulfill the standards.

To access the complete, 70-page *Early Childhood/Generalist Standards, 2d ed.* publication, or for more information about the National Board for Professional Teaching Standards, please visit the NBPTS Website at www.nbpts.org.

Contents

Preface   147

    The philosophical context   147

    The certification framework   149

    Standards and assessment development   150

    Strengthening teaching and improving learning   151

Introduction   153

    Developing high and rigorous standards for accomplished practice   155

    The standards format   155

Standards (Overview)   156

Appendix

    A: Early Childhood/Generalist Standards Committee, 2d ed.   157

    B: Early Childhood/Generalist Standards Committee, 1st ed.   158

NBPTS Early Childhood/ Generalist Standards, 2d Ed.[1]

For Teachers of Students Ages 3–8

Preface

The world-class schools the United States requires cannot exist without a world-class teaching force; the two go hand in hand. Many accomplished teachers already work in the nation's schools, but their knowledge and skills are often unacknowledged and underutilized. Delineating outstanding practice and recognizing those who achieve it are important first steps in shaping the kind of teaching profession the nation needs. This is the core challenge embraced by the National Board for Professional Teaching Standards® (NBPTS). Founded in 1987 with a broad base of support from governors, teacher union and school board leaders, school administrators, college and university officials, business executives, foundations, and concerned citizens, NBPTS is a nonprofit, nonpartisan organization governed by a 63-member board of directors, the majority of whom are teachers. Committed to basic reform in education, NBPTS recognizes that teaching is at the heart of education and, further, that the single most important action the nation can take to improve schools is to strengthen teaching. To this end, NBPTS has embraced a three-part mission:

• to establish high and rigorous standards for what accomplished teachers should know and be able to do;

• to develop and operate a national voluntary system to assess and certify teachers who meet these standards; and

• to advance related education reforms for the purpose of improving student learning.

Dedication to this mission is elevating the teaching profession, educating the public about the demands and complexity of accomplished teaching practice, and making teaching a more attractive profession for talented college graduates with many other promising career options.

National Board Certification® is more than a system for recognizing and rewarding accomplished teachers. It offers both an opportunity to guide the continuing growth and development of the teaching profession and a chance to design ways to organize and manage schools so as to capitalize on the expertise of National Board Certified Teachers®. Together with other reforms, National Board Certification is a catalyst for significant change in the teaching profession and in education.

The philosophical context

The standards presented here lay the foundation for the Early Childhood/Generalist certificate. They represent a professional consensus on the aspects of practice that distinguish accomplished teachers. Cast in terms of actions that teachers take to advance student achievement, these standards also incorporate the essential knowledge, skills, dispositions, and commitments that

[1] Reprinted with permission from the National Board for Professional Teaching Standards, *Early Childhood/Generalist Standards, 2d Ed.*, www.nbpts.org. All rights reserved.

allow teachers to practice at a high level. Like all NBPTS standards, this standards document is grounded philosophically in the NBPTS policy statement *What Teachers Should Know and Be Able to Do*. That statement identifies five core propositions.

1. Teachers are committed to students and their learning.

Accomplished teachers are dedicated to making knowledge accessible to all students. They act on the belief that all students can learn. They treat students equitably, recognizing the individual differences that distinguish their students from one another and taking account of these differences in their practice. They adjust their practice, as appropriate, on the basis of observation and knowledge of their students' interests, abilities, skills, knowledge, family circumstances, and peer relationships.

Accomplished teachers understand how students develop and learn. They incorporate the prevailing theories of cognition and intelligence in their practice. They are aware of the influence of context and culture on behavior. They develop students' cognitive capacity and respect for learning. Equally important, they foster students' self-esteem; motivation; character; sense of civic responsibility; and respect for individual, cultural, religious, and racial differences.

2. Teachers know the subjects they teach and how to teach those subjects to students.

Accomplished teachers have a rich understanding of the subject(s) they teach and appreciate how knowledge in their subjects is created, organized, linked to other disciplines, and applied to real-world settings. While faithfully representing the collective wisdom of our culture and upholding the value of disciplinary knowledge, they also develop the critical and analytical capacities of their students.

Accomplished teachers command specialized knowledge of how to convey subject matter to students. They are aware of the preconceptions and background knowledge that students typically bring to each subject and of strategies and instructional resources that can be of assistance. Their instructional repertoire allows them to create multiple paths to learning the subjects they teach, and they are adept at teaching students how to pose and solve challenging problems.

3. Teachers are responsible for managing and monitoring student learning.

Accomplished teachers create, enrich, maintain, and alter instructional settings to capture and sustain the interest of their students. They make the most effective use of time in their instruction. They are adept at engaging students and adults to assist their teaching and at making use of their colleagues' knowledge and expertise to complement their own.

Accomplished teachers command a range of instructional techniques and know when to employ them. They are devoted to high-quality practice and know how to offer each student the opportunity to succeed.

Accomplished teachers know how to engage groups of students to ensure a disciplined learning environment and how to organize instruction so as to meet the schools' goals for students. They are adept at setting norms of social interaction among students and between students and teachers. They understand how to motivate students to learn and how to maintain their interest even in the face of temporary setbacks.

Accomplished teachers can assess the progress of individual students as well as the progress of the class as a whole. They employ multiple methods for assessing student growth and understanding and can clearly explain student performance to students, parents, and administrators.

4. Teachers think systematically about their practice and learn from experience.

Accomplished teachers are models of educated persons, exemplifying the virtues they seek to inspire in students—curiosity, tolerance, honesty, fairness, respect for diversity, and appreciation of cultural differences. They demonstrate capacities that are prerequisites for intellectual growth—the ability to reason, take multiple perspectives, be creative and take risks, and experiment and solve problems.

Accomplished teachers draw on their knowledge of human development, subject matter, and instruction, and their understanding of their students, to make principled judgments about sound practice. Their decisions are grounded not only in the literature of their fields but also in their experience. They engage in lifelong learning, which they seek to encourage in their students.

Striving to strengthen their teaching, accomplished teachers examine their practice critically; expand their repertoire; deepen their knowledge; sharpen their judgment; and adapt their teaching to new findings, ideas, and theories.

5. Teachers are members of learning communities.

Accomplished teachers contribute to the effectiveness of the school by working collaboratively with other professionals on instructional policy, curriculum development, and staff development. They can evaluate school progress and the allocation of school resources in light of their understanding of state and local educational objectives. They are knowledgeable about specialized school and community resources that can be engaged for their students' benefit and are skilled at employing such resources as needed.

Accomplished teachers find ways to work collaboratively and creatively with parents, engaging them productively in the work of the school.

The certification framework

Using the five core propositions as a springboard, NBPTS sets standards and offers National Board Certification in nearly 30 fields. These fields are defined by the developmental level of the students and the subject or subjects being taught. The first descriptor represents the four overlapping student developmental levels:

• Early Childhood, ages 3–8;

• Middle Childhood, ages 7–12;

• Early Adolescence, ages 11–15;

• Adolescence and Young Adulthood, ages 14–18+.

The second descriptor indicates the substantive focus of a teacher's practice. Teachers may select either a subject-specific or a generalist certificate at a particular developmental level. Subject-specific certificates are designed for teachers who

A voice for children

Since achieving National Board Certification, I am a more confident educator. Board certification provides a professional validation that early childhood educators often do not receive. I now take the initiative in discussions of educational practice, and I do not hesitate to share my views about developmentally appropriate practice. I am a kindergarten teacher trainer for my district, and through that work I have a direct impact on advancing appropriate early childhood education. Being a National Board Certified Teacher has given me the confidence to be an advocate for early childhood education.

—*Debbie Niezgoda*, NBCT®, kindergarten teacher

Reflection is key

I had a great need to know myself, and seeking National Board Certification was the way to do it. Through this process I discovered the joy of reflection. Although by nature I am reflective, I was not aware that there was a process I could go through that would direct my thoughts and energies into becoming a better teacher.

—*Ginger Gregory*, NBCT®, first grade teacher

emphasize a single subject area in their teaching (e.g., Early Adolescence/English Language Arts, Adolescence and Young Adulthood/Mathematics); generalist certificates are designed for teachers who develop student skills and knowledge across the curriculum (e.g., Early Childhood/Generalist, Middle Childhood/Generalist). For some subject-specific certificates, developmental levels are joined together to recognize the commonalities in teaching students at those developmental levels (e.g., Early and Middle Childhood/Art).

Standards and assessment development

Following a nationwide search for outstanding educators, a standards committee is appointed for each field. The committees are generally made up of 15 members who are broadly representative of accomplished professionals in their fields. A majority of committee members are teachers regularly engaged in teaching students in the field in question; other members are typically professors, experts in child development, teacher educators, and other professionals in the relevant discipline. The standards committees develop the specific standards for each field, which are then disseminated widely for public critique and comment and subsequently revised as necessary before their adoption by the NBPTS Board of Directors. Periodically, standards are updated so that they remain dynamic documents, responsive to changes in the field.

Determining whether or not candidates meet the standards requires performance-based assessment methods that are fair, valid, and reliable and that ask teachers to demonstrate principled, professional judgments in a variety of situations. A testing contractor specializing in assessment development works with standards committee members, teacher assessment development teams, and members of the NBPTS staff to develop assessment exercises and pilot test them with teachers active in each certificate field. The assessment process involves two primary activities: (1) the compilation of a portfolio of teaching practice over a period of time and (2) the demonstration of content knowledge through assessment center exercises. Teachers prepare their portfolios by videotaping their teaching, gathering student learning products and other teaching artifacts, and providing detailed analyses of their practice. At the assessment center, teachers write answers to questions that relate primarily to content knowledge specific to their fields.

The portfolio is designed to capture teaching in real-time, real-life settings, thus allowing trained assessors from the field in question to examine how teachers translate knowledge and theory into practice. It also yields the most valued evidence NBPTS collects—videos of practice and samples of student work. The videos and student work are accompanied by commentaries on the goals and purposes of instruction, the effectiveness of the practice, teachers' reflections on what occurred, and their rationales for the professional judgments they made. In addition, the portfolio allows candidates to document their accomplishments in contributing to the advancement of the profession and the improvement of schooling— whether at the local, state, or national level—and to document their ability to work constructively with their students' families.

Teachers report that the portfolio is a professional development vehicle of considerable power, in part because it challenges the historic isolation of teachers from their peers. It accomplishes this by actively encouraging candidates to seek the advice and counsel of their professional colleagues—whether across the hall or across the country—as they build their portfolios. It also requires teachers to examine the underlying assumptions of their practice and the results of their efforts in critical but healthy ways. This emphasis on reflection is highly valued by teachers who go through the process of National Board Certification.

The assessment center exercises are designed to complement the portfolio. They validate that the knowledge and skills exhibited in the portfolio are, in fact, accurate reflections of what candidates know and can do, and they give candidates an opportunity to demonstrate knowledge and skills not sampled in the portfolio because of the candidate's specific teaching assignment. For example, high school science teachers assigned to teach only physics in a given year might have difficulty demonstrating in their portfolio a broad knowledge of biology. Given that the NBPTS standards for science teachers place a high value on such capabilities, another strategy for data collection is necessary. The assessment center exercises fill this gap and otherwise augment the portfolio. Each candidate's work is examined by trained assessors who teach in the certificate field.

The National Board for Professional Teaching Standards believes that a valid assessment of accomplished practice must allow for the variety of forms sound practice takes. It must also sample the range of content knowledge that teachers possess and must provide appropriate contexts for assessments of teaching knowledge and skill. Teaching is not just about knowing things; it is about the use of knowledge—knowledge of learners and of learning, of schools and of subjects—in the service of helping students grow and develop. Consequently, NBPTS believes that the most valid teacher assessment processes engage candidates in the activities of teaching—activities that require the display and use of teaching knowledge and skill and that allow teachers the opportunity to explain and justify their actions.

In its assessment development work, NBPTS uses technology for assessment when appropriate; ensures broad representation of the diversity that exists within the profession; engages pertinent disciplinary and specialty associations at key points in the process; collaborates closely with appropriate state agencies, academic institutions, and independent research and education organizations; establishes procedures to detect and eliminate instances of external and internal bias with respect to age, gender, and racial and ethnic background of teacher-candidates; and selects the method exhibiting the least adverse impact when given a choice among equally valid assessments.

Once an assessment has been thoroughly tested and found to meet NBPTS requirements for validity, reliability, and fairness, eligible teachers may apply for National Board Certification. To be eligible, a teacher must hold a baccalaureate degree from an accredited institution; have a minimum of three years' teaching experience at the early childhood, elementary school, middle school, or high school level; and have held a valid state teaching license for those three years or, where a license is not required, have taught in schools recognized and approved to operate by the state.

Strengthening teaching and improving learning

The National Board's system of standards and certification is commanding the respect of the profession and the public, thereby making a difference in how communities and policy makers view teachers, how teachers view themselves, and how teachers improve their practice throughout their careers. National Board Certification has yielded such results in part because it has forged a national consensus on the characteristics of accomplished teaching practice in each field. The traditional conversation about teacher competence has focused on beginning teachers. The National Board for Professional Teaching Standards has helped broaden this conversation to span the entire career of teachers.

Developing standards of accomplished practice helps to elevate the teaching profession as the standards make public the knowledge, skills, and dispositions of accomplished teachers. However, making such standards the basis for National Board Certification promises much more. Since National Board Certification identifies accomplished teachers in a fair and trustworthy manner, it can offer career paths for teachers that will make use of their knowledge, wisdom, and expertise; give accomplished practitioners the opportunity to achieve greater status, authority, and compensation; and accelerate efforts to build more successful school organizations and structures.

By holding accomplished teachers to high and rigorous standards, National Board Certification encourages change along several key fronts:

• changing what it means to have a career in teaching by recognizing and rewarding accomplished teachers and by making it possible for teachers to advance in responsibility, status, and compensation without having to leave the classroom;

• changing the culture of teaching by accelerating growth in the knowledge base of teaching, by placing real value on professional judgment and accomplished practice in all its various manifestations, and by encouraging teachers to search for new knowledge and better practice through a steady regimen of collaboration and reflection with peers and others;

Collaboration and respect

During the National Board Certification process, I collaborated with a group consisting of a colleague from my school and four other teachers from my district. Being in this support group was one of the most positive experiences of my life. When April came and it was time to send in our completed application materials, we met at FedEx, cameras in hand, and took pictures as we each mailed "THE BOX." Afterwards we all went to celebrate.

Sending that box gave me feelings of satisfaction, relief, and fear. I knew that whether I became a National Board Certified Teacher or not, I had done my best. But what if I, the only African American in the group, didn't pass and they all did? Or what if my colleague passed and I didn't? Everyone knew we were involved in the NBPTS process: other colleagues, principal, parents, and students. What would they think of me? I am proud to say in November 2000 we received our results, and we all achieved National Board Certification and celebrated together again.

Receiving certification has opened new doors. Currently I serve as clinical faculty for North Carolina Agricultural and Technical State University in Greensboro. In this position one of my major roles is working with preservice elementary teachers.

—*Patricia Faison*, NBCT®,
third grade teacher

• changing the way schools are organized and managed by creating a vehicle that facilitates the establishment of unique teacher positions, providing accomplished teachers with greater authority and autonomy in making instructional decisions and greater responsibility for sharing their expertise to strengthen the practice of others;

• changing the nature of teacher preparation and ongoing professional development by laying a standards-based foundation for a fully articulated career development path that begins with prospective teachers and leads to accomplished teachers;

• changing the way school districts think about hiring and compensating teachers by encouraging administrators and school boards to reward excellence in teaching by seeking to hire accomplished teachers.

Although National Board Certification has been designed with the entire country in mind, each state and locality decides for itself how best to encourage teachers to achieve National Board Certification and how best to take advantage of the expertise of the National Board Certified Teachers in their midst. Across the country, legislation has been enacted that supports National Board Certification, including allocations of funds to pay for the certification fee for teachers, release time for candidates to work on their portfolios and prepare for the assessment center exercises, and salary supplements for teachers who achieve National Board Certification. Incentives for National Board Certification exist at the state or local level in all 50 states and in the District of Columbia.

As this support at the state and local levels suggests, National Board Certification is recognized throughout the nation as a rich professional development experience. Because National Board Certification provides states and localities with a way to structure teachers' roles and responsibilities more effectively and to allow schools to benefit from the wisdom of their strongest teachers, National Board Certification is a strong component of education reform in the United States.

Introduction

Early childhood teachers have the unique opportunity to introduce young children to the challenges and rewards of learning in classroom settings. Each year, teachers in early intervention programs, child care centers, and a variety of pre-kindergarten programs welcome 3- and 4-year-old children to the formal community of learners. Other early childhood professionals open the doors of kindergarten and primary grade classrooms. They facilitate the child's transition from the private world of home and family to the more public world of formal education.

These professionals relish their roles as the orchestrators of a cohesive community of young learners. They take pride in their ability to create a productive, safe, and enriching environment in which children with often vastly differing backgrounds, abilities, and needs work together successfully. They work to help children gain the knowledge, skills, habits, and dispositions toward learning that are essential for later success in school and in life.

Accomplished early childhood teachers enjoy and appreciate young children. They love children's unbridled enthusiasm and curiosity and the excitement they bring to their explorations and to the new things they learn each day. They are engaged by the variety and diversity of their charges across many dimensions—including their talents, interests, and cultures. They welcome the challenge and responsibility of guiding young children through their ever-expanding and dynamic worlds. They apply what they know about how children grow and develop to create learning experiences that allow their children to use the resources around them and their own abilities as pathways to learning.

Accomplished early childhood teachers nurture children's experiments with language, sounds, and images as they build their expressive repertoires. They also encourage children to expand their worlds to include new friends and experiences and a whole range of never-before-experienced emotions and feelings. These range from pride in their ability to demonstrate a unique skill to wonder and surprise at new observations such as exploring a found bird's nest or a complex pattern in a picture.

Accomplished early childhood teachers are aware that children do not come to them as empty vessels—they have begun to make sense of the world long before they arrive at school. Their primary goal is to help children understand themselves and the world around them as they develop the skills and knowledge essential for thinking, problem solving, and expanding their sense of confidence in their abilities.

As generalists, early childhood teachers develop skills and knowledge across all areas of the curriculum. In doing so, they draw on a wide range of subject matter knowledge and pedagogy. This foundation allows them to meet the needs of young children who grow and develop at different rates and to respond effectively to groups of boys and girls who—while the same age—are at vastly different points in their development. Whether teaching 3-year-olds in a child development center or 8-year-olds in the third grade, these teachers advance student understanding and respond to the capacity and interests of their children.

Today's early childhood teachers work with a rich mélange of eager learners from a wide range of backgrounds and a variety of experiences and personal challenges. They teach young children who are maturing, developing skills, and acquiring knowledge at different rates. Typically, this process occurs unevenly, rather than in a smoothly incremental fashion. Accomplished early childhood teachers are distinguished by their skill at recognizing and responding to the individual differences that children bring to the classroom. For example:

• Accomplished early childhood teachers create integrated curriculum to build on children's present knowledge and understandings and move them to more sophisticated and in-depth skills, knowledge, concepts, and performances. They calibrate their responses to children, designing learning experiences that fit the children's learning and developmental needs.

• Accomplished early childhood teachers employ a range of instructional strategies and resources to match the variety of children they teach and to provide each student with several ways of exploring important ideas, skills, and concepts. They understand how to work as facilitators, coaches, models, evaluators, managers, and advocates. They know how to use various forms of play; different strategies for grouping children; and different types of technology, media, and other instructional resources.

• Accomplished early childhood teachers observe and assess young children in the context of ongoing classroom life. They are skilled in collecting and interpreting a variety of evidence to evaluate where each child is in a sequence or continuum of learning and development. They know how to move from assessment to decisions about curriculum, social support, and teaching strategies to increase the prospects for successful learning and development.

• Accomplished early childhood teachers understand and respect the diverse cultures, values, languages, and family backgrounds of their class members, and they use community people and settings as resources for learning.

• Accomplished early childhood teachers involve parents and families as active partners in children's total development.

Like the conductor of a great orchestra, accomplished early childhood teachers make and execute dozens of complex decisions as they create the symphony that is their work with children. Each moment presents the opportunity for them to respond creatively to the unique challenges of classroom life. They analyze through formal and informal observations of individual children and of the overall environment and use their analyses to guide their judgments and responses. They reflect on their own performances—considering student progress, seeking the views of colleagues and parents, and thinking about current knowledge bases and options and the consequences of their choices.

While seeing to the needs of individuals, accomplished early childhood teachers also are responsible to the group. They can attend to the needs of each child while managing a sizable and active group enterprise. They make children feel special in the midst of a crowd, allowing them to experience the pleasure of being one of the group and making the group an enjoyable, harmonious place to be.

Support

I received a great deal of support in a year-long class I took at George Mason University. The entire class was teachers pursuing their National Board Certification. We were mentored throughout the process by a National Board Certified Teacher, Early Childhood/Generalist who was experienced in the standards and requirements.

More important, the class provided a cohort of teachers with whom I could discuss the standards and receive guidance and feedback on the portfolio entries. My classmates provided not only practical support but also emotional support during this very intense and sometimes stressful process. I learned from these very accomplished teachers, and my own teaching improved as a result of their advice and assistance.

—*Debbie Niezgoda*, NBCT®, kindergarten teacher

Candidate support providers

In many parts of the country "candidate support providers" work with teachers seeking National Board Certification, including Early Childhood/Generalist candidates. It is important that candidate support providers provide support that is nonjudgmental, honest, specific and direct, constructive, professional, and knowledgeable. One of the best ways to work with early childhood candidates struggling with the process of preparing for certification is to use questioning strategies that facilitate their deeper thinking.

—*Marlene Henriques*, NBCT®, George Mason University

Increasingly, society is appreciating and research is documenting the complexity and significance of learning during the early childhood period. More resources than ever before are provided to preschool, child care, kindergarten, and primary grade programs; and more healthy scrutiny is given to the quality of these environments and of those who work there. There is a growing recognition that high-quality early childhood teaching is vital to the educational development of all children, an awareness that erodes any misconception that young children are easier to teach than older children and therefore do not need the strongest teachers.

Developing high and rigorous standards for accomplished practice

In 1990, a committee of early childhood teachers and other educators with expertise in this field began the process of developing advanced professional standards for teachers of students ages 3 to 8. The Early Childhood/Generalist Standards Committee was charged with translating the five core propositions of the National Board for Professional Teaching Standards into a standards document that defines outstanding teaching in this field.

In 2000, a committee comprising original committee members and a new group of educators (including National Board Certified Teachers) was convened to examine and update as necessary the published Early Childhood/Generalist Standards. This second edition of the standards is the result of the committee's deliberations at meetings and their input into working drafts of the standards.

This NBPTS standards document describes in observable form what accomplished teachers should know and be able to do. The standards are meant to reflect the professional consensus at this point about the essential aspects of accomplished practice. The deliberations of the Early Childhood/Generalist standards Committee were informed by various national and state initiatives on student and teacher standards that have been operating concurrently with the development of NBPTS standards. As the understanding of teaching and learning continues to evolve over the next several years, Early Childhood/Generalist Standards will be updated again.

An essential tension of describing accomplished practice concerns the difference between the analysis and the practice of teaching. The former tends to fragment the profession into any number of discrete duties, such as designing learning activities, providing quality explanation, modeling, managing the classroom, and monitoring student progress. Teaching as it actually occurs, on the other hand, is a seamless activity.

Everything an accomplished teacher knows through study, research, and experience is brought to bear daily in the classroom through innumerable decisions that shape learning. Teaching frequently requires balancing the demands of several important educational goals. It depends on accurate observations of particular students and settings. And it is subject to revision on the basis of continuing developments in the classroom. The professional judgments that accomplished teachers make also reflect a certain improvisational artistry.

The paradox, then, is that any attempt to write standards that dissect what accomplished teachers know and are able to do will, to a certain extent, misrepresent the holistic nature of how teaching actually takes place. Nevertheless, the fact remains: Certain identifiable commonalties characterize the accomplished practice of teachers. The nine standards that follow are designed to capture the craft, artistry, proficiency, and understandings—both deep and broad—that contribute to the complex work that is accomplished teaching.

The standards format

Accomplished teaching appears in many different forms, and it should be acknowledged at the outset that these specific standards are not the only way it could have been described. No linearity, atomization, or hierarchy is implied in this vision of accomplished teaching, nor is each standard of equal weight. Rather, the standards are presented as aspects of teaching that are analytically separable for the purposes of this standards document, but that are not discrete when they appear in practice.

Early Childhood/Generalist Standards, 2d ed.

For Teachers of Students Ages 3–8

Overview

The National Board for Professional Teaching Standards® has organized the standards for accomplished Early Childhood/Generalist teachers into the following nine standards. The standards have been ordered to facilitate understanding, not to assign priorities. They each describe an important facet of accomplished teaching; they often occur concurrently because of the seamless quality of accomplished practice. These standards serve as the basis for National Board Certification® in this field.

I. Understanding Young Children

Accomplished early childhood teachers use their knowledge of child development and their relationships with children and families to understand children as individuals and to plan in response to their unique needs and potentials.

II. Equity, Fairness, and Diversity

Accomplished early childhood teachers model and teach behaviors appropriate in a diverse society by creating a safe, secure learning environment for all children; by showing appreciation of and respect for the individual differences and unique needs of each member of the learning community; and by empowering children to treat others with, and to expect from others, equity, fairness, and dignity.

III. Assessment

Accomplished early childhood teachers recognize the strengths and weaknesses of multiple assessment methodologies and know how to use them effectively. Employing a variety of methods, they systematically observe, monitor, and document children's activities and behavior, analyzing, communicating, and using the information they glean to improve their work with children, parents, and others.

IV. Promoting Child Development and Learning

Accomplished early childhood teachers promote children's cognitive, social, emotional, physical, and linguistic development by organizing and orchestrating the environment in ways that best facilitate the development and learning of young children.

V. Knowledge of Integrated Curriculum

On the basis of their knowledge of how young children learn, of academic subjects, and of assessment, accomplished early childhood teachers design and implement developmentally appropriate learning experiences that integrate within and across the disciplines.

VI. Multiple Teaching Strategies for Meaningful Learning

Accomplished early childhood teachers use a variety of practices and resources to promote individual development, meaningful learning, and social cooperation.

VII. Family and Community Partnerships

Accomplished early childhood teachers work with and through families and communities to support children's learning and development.

VIII. Professional Partnerships

Accomplished early childhood teachers work as leaders and collaborators in the professional community to improve programs and practices for young children and their families.

IX. Reflective Practice

Accomplished early childhood teachers regularly analyze, evaluate, and synthesize to strengthen the quality and effectiveness of their work.

Appendix A

Early Childhood/Generalist Standards Committee, 2d Ed.[2]

Ilna Rivera Colemere (Chair), Bilingual Kindergarten Teacher, Elma A. Neal Elementary School, San Antonio, Texas

Marlene E. Henriques, NBCT® (Vice Chair), Kindergarten Teacher, Kings Park Elementary School, Springfield, Virginia

Della P. Bacote, Second Grade Teacher, Gold Hill Elementary School, Fort Mill, South Carolina

Barbara J. Bushey, Kindergarten Teacher, Conant School, Bloomfield Hills, Michigan

Jerlean E. Daniel, Professor, Child Development and Child Care, University of Pittsburgh, Pittsburgh, Pennsylvania

Jacqualine Dedman, Associate Director, Region VI (Arkansas), DSQIC, Little Rock, Arkansas

Lois Distad, Reading/Writing Teacher, Crest Hill & Oregon Trail Elementary School, Casper, Wyoming

Antonio A. Fierro, Texas Reading Initiative Program Director, Region 19, Education Service Center, El Paso, Texas

Joyce W. Frazier, Clinical Assistant Professor/Supervisor of Student Teachers, College of Education, University of North Carolina at Charlotte, Charlotte, North Carolina

Mary Zapata Huerta, NBCT®, Kindergarten Teacher, Woodlawn Elementary School, San Antonio, Texas

Joyce Jech, Principal, Marrs Elementary School, Skiatook, Oklahoma

John M. Johnston, Professor, Early Childhood Teacher Education, University of Memphis, Memphis, Tennessee

Patricia A. McLaughlin, NBCT®, Consultant, Oakland Schools, Waterford, Michigan

Carol Midgett, NBCT®, Teacher-in-Residence, Donald R. Watson School of Education, University of North Carolina at Wilmington, Wilmington, North Carolina

Beverly C. Oglesby, Kindergarten Teacher, S. Bryan Jennings Elementary School, Orange Park, Florida

Barbara J. Renoux, NBCT®, First Grade Teacher, Baranof School, Sitka, Alaska

Nancy Smith, Associate Professor, Emporia State University, Emporia, Kansas

---

[2] All job titles reflect those held by committee members at the time this edition of the Early Childhood/Generalist Standards was adopted by the NBPTS Board of Directors.

Appendix B

Early Childhood/Generalist Standards Committee, 1st Ed.[3]

Baiba Woodall (Chair), First Grade Teacher, Trumansburg Central School, Trumansburg, New York

Mary Zapata Huerta (Vice Chair), Kindergarten Teacher, Woodlawn Elementary School, San Antonio, Texas

Leslee Bartlett, Second/Third Grade Teacher, Washington School, Salt Lake City, Utah

Barbara T. Bowman, President, Erikson Institute for Child Development, Chicago, Illinois

Barbara J. Bushey, Kindergarten Teacher, Conant School, Bloomfield Hills, Michigan

Margaret Eriacho, Second Grade Teacher, A:Shiwi Elementary School, Zuni, New Mexico

Barbara M. Flores, Associate Professor of Elementary and Bilingual Education, California State University, San Bernardino, San Bernardino, California

Donna B. Foglia, Assistant Principal, Norwood Creek School, Evergreen School District, San Jose, California

Joyce Jech, Principal, Marrs Elementary School, Skiatook, Oklahoma

John M. Johnston, Professor, Early Childhood Teacher Education, University of Memphis, Memphis, Tennessee

Sharon Lynn Kagan, Senior Associate, The Bush Center in Child Development and Social Policy, Yale University, New Haven, Connecticut

Juanita M. Robinson, Head Start Teacher, Bells Mills Elementary School, Potomac, Maryland

Yvonne Smith, Prekindergarten Teacher, Central Park East School, New York, New York

Mark R. Wolery, Senior Research Scientist, Child and Family Studies Program, Allegheny-Singer Research Institute, Pittsburgh, Pennsylvania

---

[3] All job titles reflect those held by committee members at the time this edition of the Early Childhood/Generalist Standards was adopted by the NBPTS Board of Directors.

Early years are learning years

Become a member of NAEYC, and help make them count!

Just as you help young children learn and grow, the National Association for the Education of Young Children—your professional organization—supports you in the work you love. NAEYC is the world's largest early childhood education organization, with a national network of local, state, and regional Affiliates. We are more than 100,000 members working together to bring high-quality early learning opportunities to all children from birth through age eight.

Since 1926, NAEYC has provided educational services and resources for people working with children, including:

• *Young Children*, the award-winning journal (six issues a year) for early childhood educators

• **Books, posters, brochures, and videos** to support your work with young children and families

• **The NAEYC Annual Conference**, which brings tens of thousands of people together from across the country and around the world to share their expertise and ideas on the education of young children

• **Insurance plans** for members and programs

• **A voluntary accreditation system** to help programs reach national standards for high-quality early childhood education

• **Young Children International** to promote global communication and information exchanges

• **www.naeyc.org**—a dynamic Website with up-to-date information on all of our services and resources

To join NAEYC

To find a complete list of membership benefits and options or to join NAEYC online, visit **www.naeyc.org/membership.** Or you can mail this form to us.

(Membership must be for an individual, not a center or school.)

Name _____

Address _____

City_____ State_____ ZIP_____

E-mail _____

Phone (H)_____ (W)_____

☐ New member

☐ Renewal ID # _____

Affiliate name/number _____

To determine your dues, you must visit **www.naeyc.org/membership** or call 800-424-2460, ext. 2002.

Indicate your payment option

☐ VISA   ☐ MasterCard

Card #_____

Exp. date _____

Cardholder's name _____

Signature _____

Note: By joining NAEYC you also become a member of your state and local Affiliates.

Send this form and payment to

NAEYC
PO Box 97156
Washington, DC 20090-7156